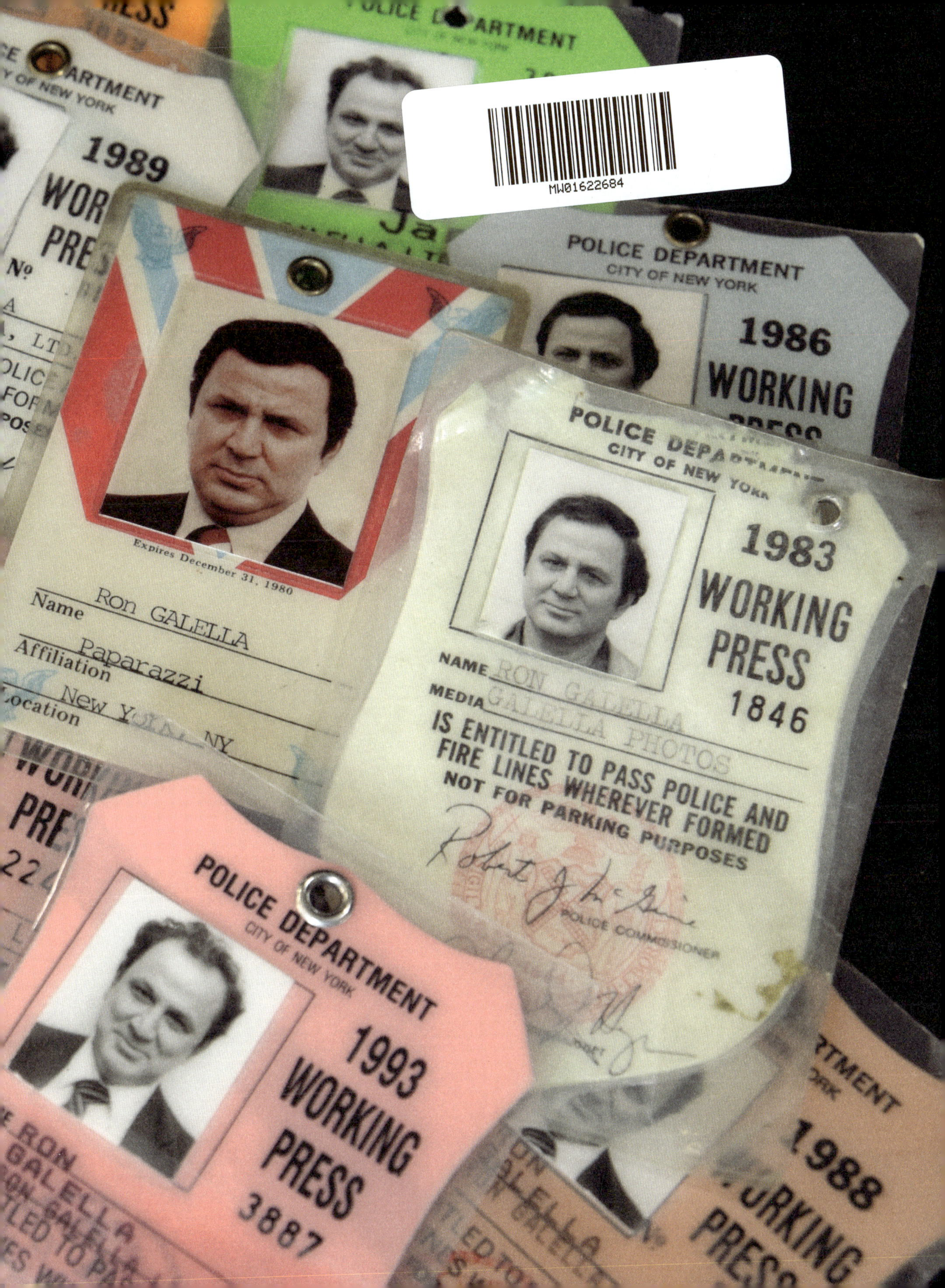
MW01622684
POLICE DEPARTMENT
CITY OF NEW YORK
1989
POLICE DEPARTMENT
CITY OF NEW YORK
1986
WORKING
Expires December 31, 1980
Ron GALELLA
Name
Paparazzi
Affiliation
Location
POLICE DEPARTMENT
CITY OF NEW YORK
1983
WORKING
PRESS
1846
NAME RON GALELLA
MEDIA GALELLA PHOTOS
IS ENTITLED TO PASS POLICE AND
FIRE LINES WHEREVER FORMED
NOT FOR PARKING PURPOSES
POLICE COMMISSIONER
POLICE DEPARTMENT
CITY OF NEW YORK
1993
WORKING
PRESS
3887
1988

100 **ICONIC** PHOTOGRAPHS

A Retrospective by

Ron Galella

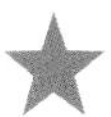

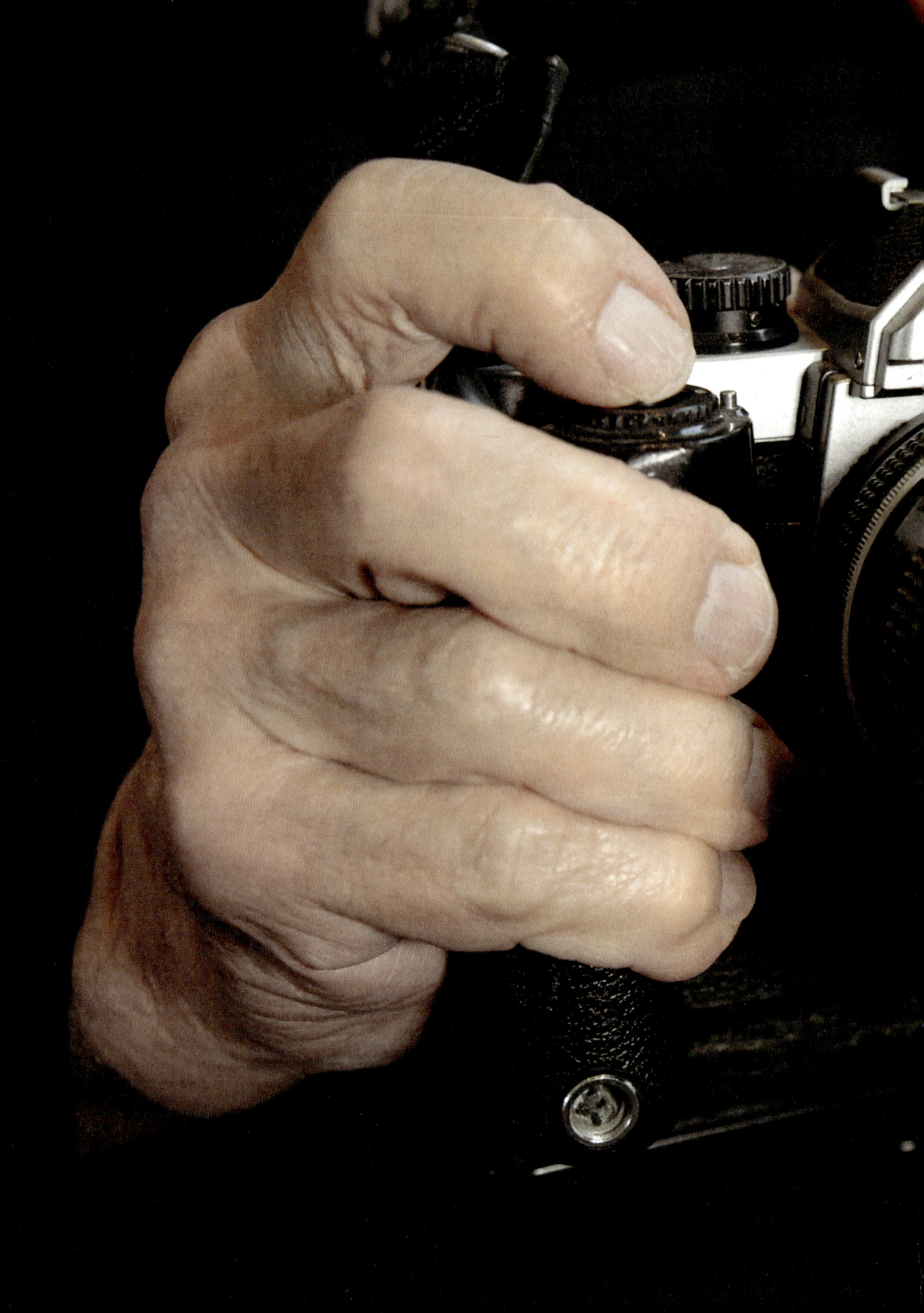

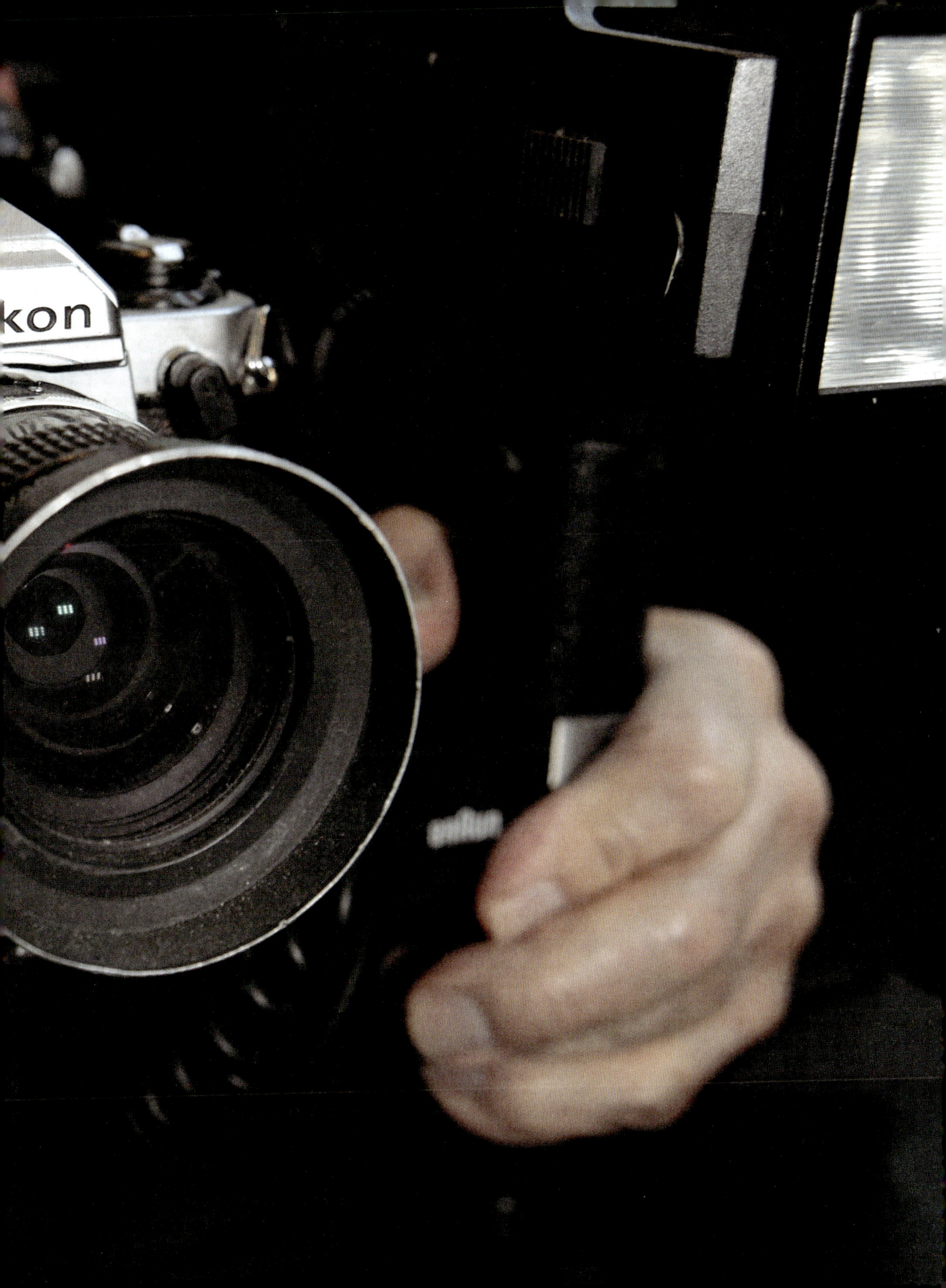
kon

INTRODUCTION

by Ron Galella

Over my five-plus-decades long career, I have taken millions of photographs of every conceivable type of celebrity – film, television and music stars, super models, athletes, politicians, business moguls, artists, socialites and innovators. Today these photos continue to be published and broadcast globally in news, film, entertainment magazines and books as well as collected at home and abroad. (Not bad for an Italian American kid from a working-class family raised in the Bronx!)

Recently, I set out on the daunting task of highlighting my most iconic photos. A truly iconic photograph is timeless – something that is valued, honored and treasured long after the photo was taken. It's also an image that represents a particular event from our past, a literal snapshot of a moment in time. I had to consider several points: the timeless nature of each image, including generations born after the moment, its cultural significance, historical and/or emotional connections. Does it represent a moment we will never see again, and can it be enjoyed forever by future generations? Are these photographs "unforgettable?"

This led me right away to my first and most obvious choice, "Windblown Jackie." My own Mona Lisa!

Luck, skill and quick thinking all played a role in capturing my most famous photograph! Taken in 1971, this image has withstood the test of time. It has been sold hundreds of times all over the world and is still purchased universally and collected by museums and fine-art photography lovers worldwide. In fact, in 2016 *Time Magazine* honored this photograph by proclaiming it as one of "The Most Influential Photos of all Time."

My second choice (this book's cover) is my photo of Mick Jagger and John Lennon (with May Pang) taken at the American Film Institute Salute to James Cagney, during Lennon's infamous eighteen-month "Lost Weekend" period without Yoko Ono.

Other photos include Andy Warhol at the Bronx Zoo, Elvis Presley leaving the Philadelphia Hilton surrounded by his bodyguards and the ever-cool actor, Steve McQueen, in Jamaica just off the set of his Oscar nominated 1973 film, "Papillon."

As time passed, I soon understood that being approachable and following my gut instinct was the key to my success. My journey led me to an unforeseen and unexpected conclusion: each personality's reaction to me produced an even more intimate and deeply thought-out final selection. Add in a little bit of chutzpah, hubris and humor and I realized that my interactions with my subjects paved a way beyond anything I could have ever imagined, creating a unique niche in the world of entertainment photojournalism.

I was fortunate to capture the following selection of photographs during my golden years, a time when film cameras were prominent, and photographers were not so ever-present. So many of my photographs are exclusive and come as a result of a combination of perseverance, hard work and love with a splash of good luck.

The choices were hard, at times painstaking and time-consuming and even surprising, but with a little help from my diligent staff and a few others I finally arrived at 100!

I thoroughly enjoyed this excursion down memory lane. Sometimes tearful, sometimes joyful, sometimes bittersweet; but as you leaf through this book I hope to pass along my passion for photography and the dedication it took to capture these decisive moments, which I hope, will endure for all time...snapped in my unique, spontaneous and off-guard style–the paparazzi approach!

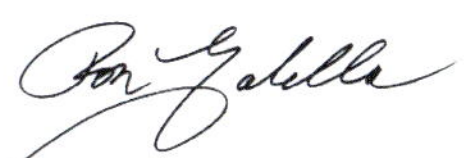

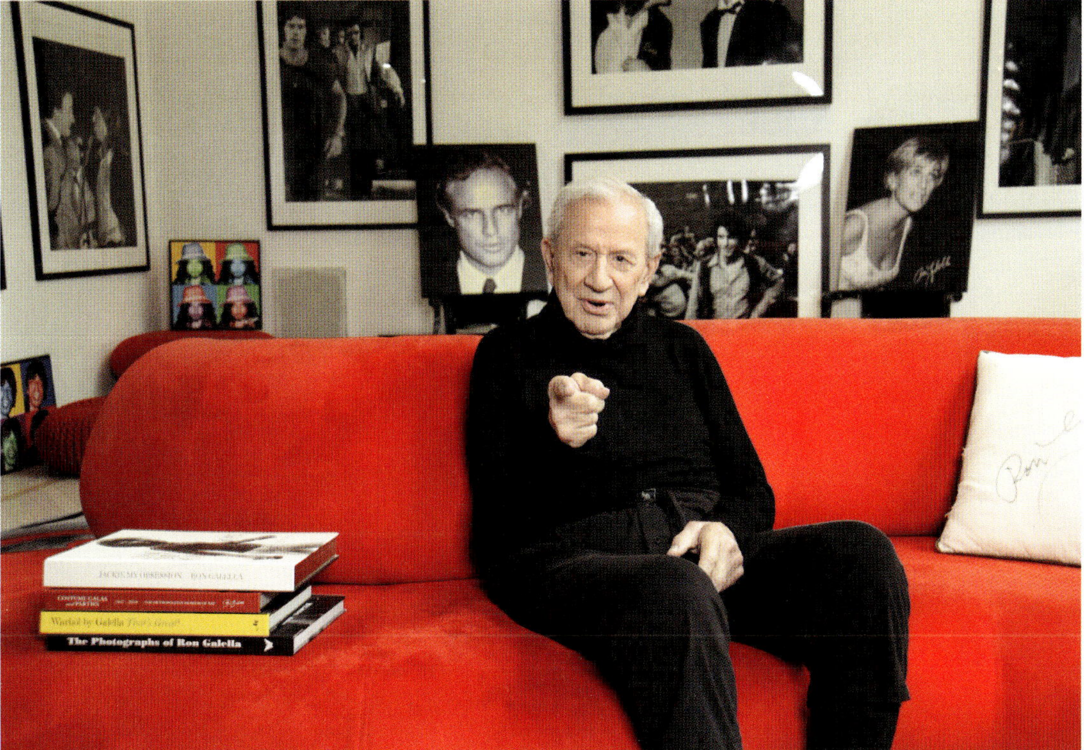

Ron Galella, age 90, at his New Jersey home, July 2021

FOREWORD

by Bob Ahern

In the early 20th century, it was through the hired lenses of the great portrait photographers such as George Hurrell, Ruth Harriet Louise, and Clarence Sinclair Bull that our love affair with "celebrity" was ignited. The luxuriant sculptured lighting and the elegant theatrics of the 10x8 Hollywood publicity still all conspired to say look, but do not touch. Through photography, the studio machine transformed stars into gods, and we have been mesmerized ever since.

By the late 1940's the Hollywood studio system had all but collapsed, and with it so did control of the talent. The monthly picture magazines were on the rise, and as scandals broke and the early gossip columns speculated, photography became our witness as well as our muse. I am often skeptical when photographers talk about a golden age of photography, but between the demise of the studio system and before contemporary PR pulled down shutters, there might have been just that.

I first met Ron Galella in the summer of 2011. Turning into the driveway of his house in New Jersey it was clear that five decades of rubbing shoulders, and elbows with the A-list had also rubbed off on Ron. No one it seems is immune from the fame game. From the handprints in the driveway to the hallway accented with the props and talismans from a career of notorious run-ins, it was clear that Ron had learned a thing or two about self-promotion along the way. Yet Galella himself was genial, charming and altogether way more modest than anyone could rightfully expect. I could also easily imagine his gentle, ironic laugh getting him in and out of trouble in equal measure.

Since Ron hung up his camera "celebrity" has become a very tweezered thing; accessible through a labyrinth of PR approval or through the believe-what-you-want-of social media, as talent finally turned the camera in on itself. The aesthetic of cynical show and tell. Yet by comparison Galella's photos feel as fresh, spontaneous and vibrant as the moment they were taken. His mantra of getting in quick, shooting wide and shooting fast made the once unobtainable, thrillingly present and real.

The genius of Ron Galella might lie somewhere between that great skill, irrepressible curiosity, and of course the nose for a good story and knowing the audience. If Jackie O was Ron's obsession, then it was also our obsession. So it is with good reason that Ron's work is exhibited in museums and art galleries across the world, providing a window not just on the stars themselves, but shining a light directly on our uneasy and unending fascination with getting up close. The budgets and exclusives of yesteryear may have long departed, but our love affair with celebrity is of course, far from done.

Bob Ahern

Director of Archive Photography – Getty Images, August 2021

"Ron Galella was a master of surprise. He was after the real emotions and genuine reactions. As a fashion designer, I have been influenced by Mr. Galella's photographs throughout my career."

Tom Ford
From "The Photographs of Ron Galella", Greybull Press, 2003

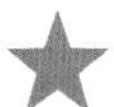

"Ron Galella's photographs are devoid of place, but enriched by the character of fame. Fame, that hollow calling to many, encountered by few. Ron Galella has given us the true landscape of celebrity in the faces of the eminently watchable, not so mysterious, victim of Narcissus' kiss."

Diane Keaton
From "The Photographs of Ron Galella", Greybull Press, 2003

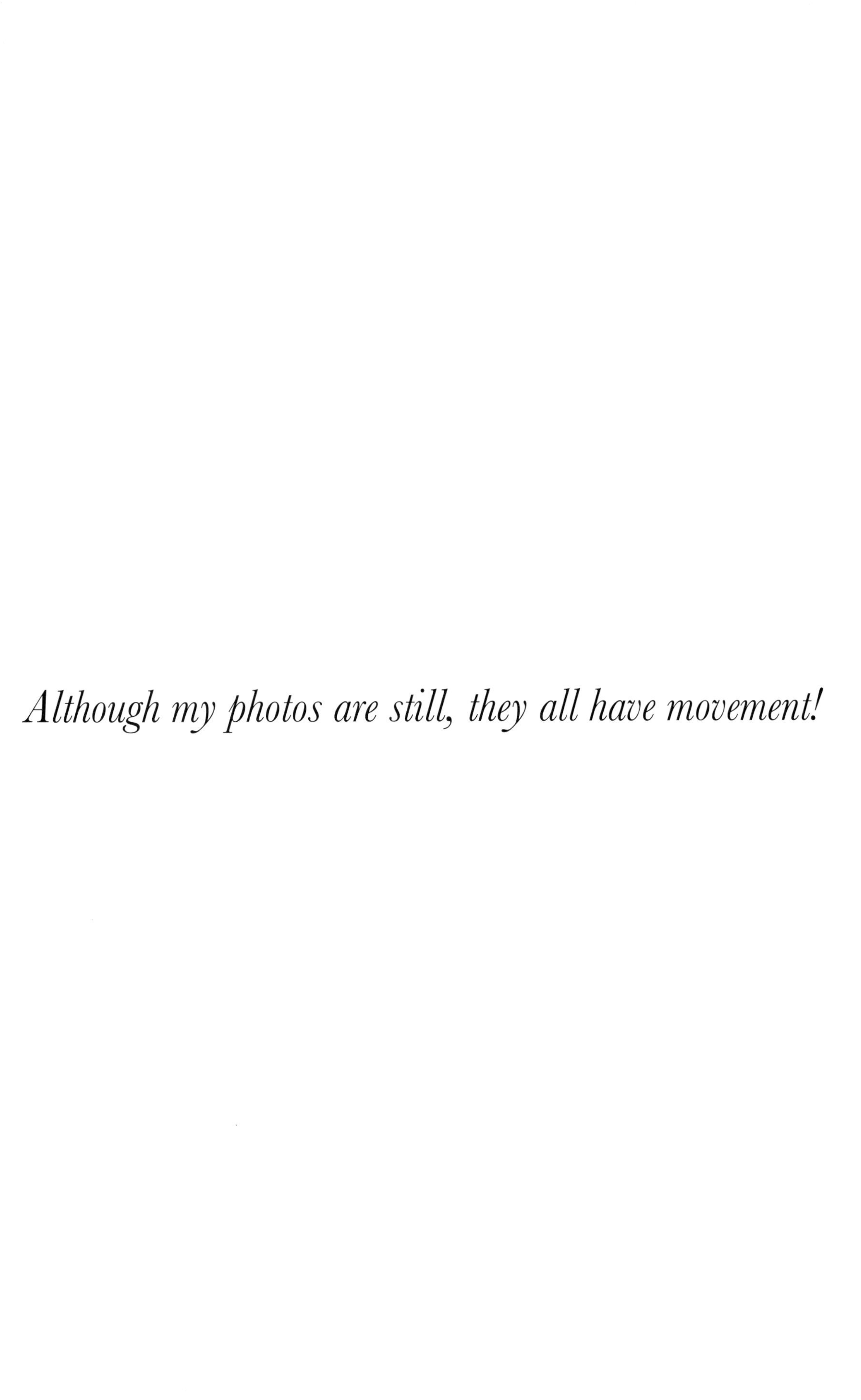

Although my photos are still, they all have movement!

SOPHIA LOREN

When Sophia Loren arrived at the after party for the "Dr. Zhivago" premiere at one in the morning, I photographed her at her table. Finishing up my take, I asked her what she found fascinating about the film's star, Omar Sharif. "His eyes!" she said making an expressive gesture. "I thought the Italians had the most beautiful eyes; now I think the Egyptians have!"

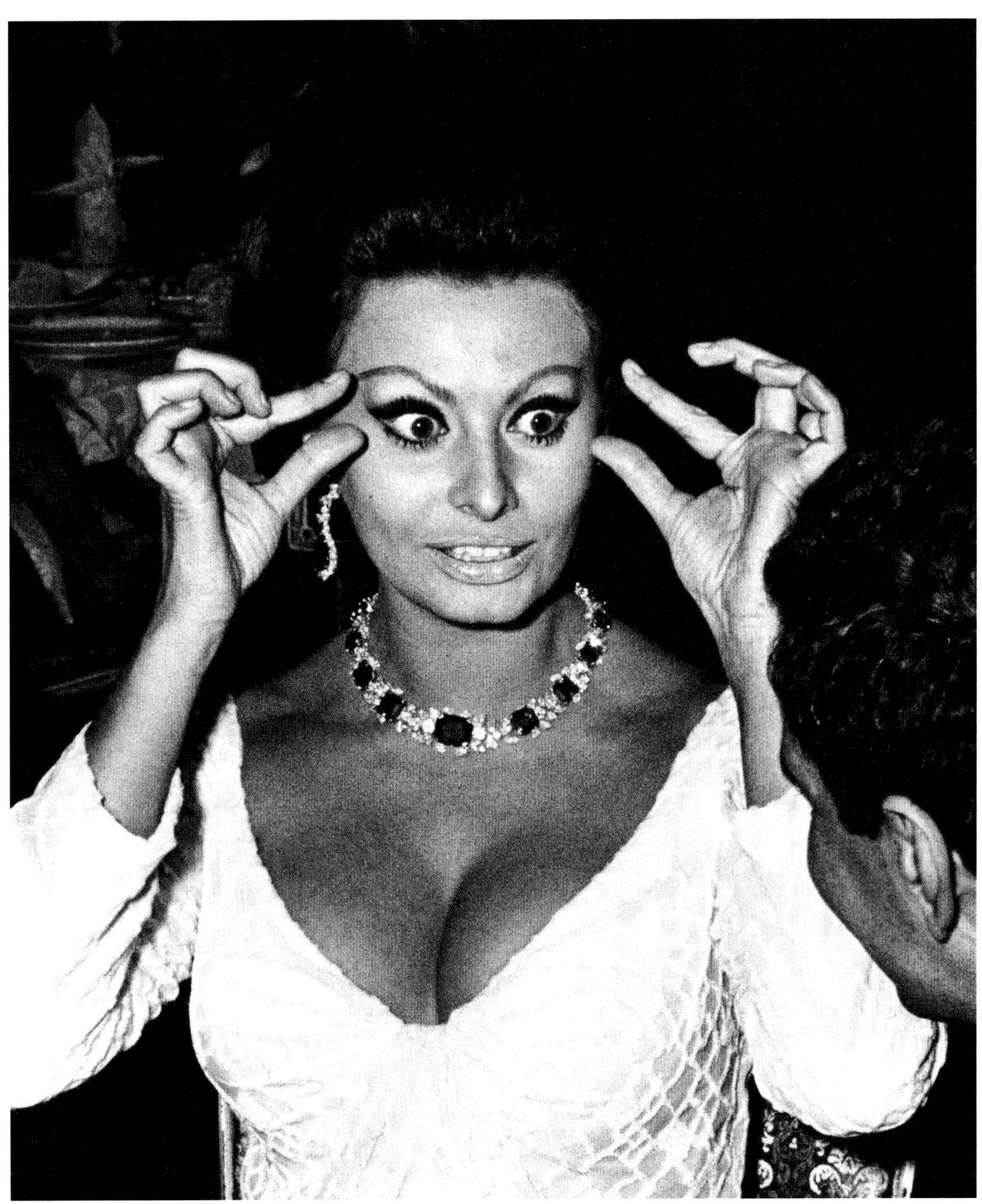

SOPHIA LOREN
December 22, 1965 – New York City
"Dr. Zhivago" Premiere Party at the Americana Hotel

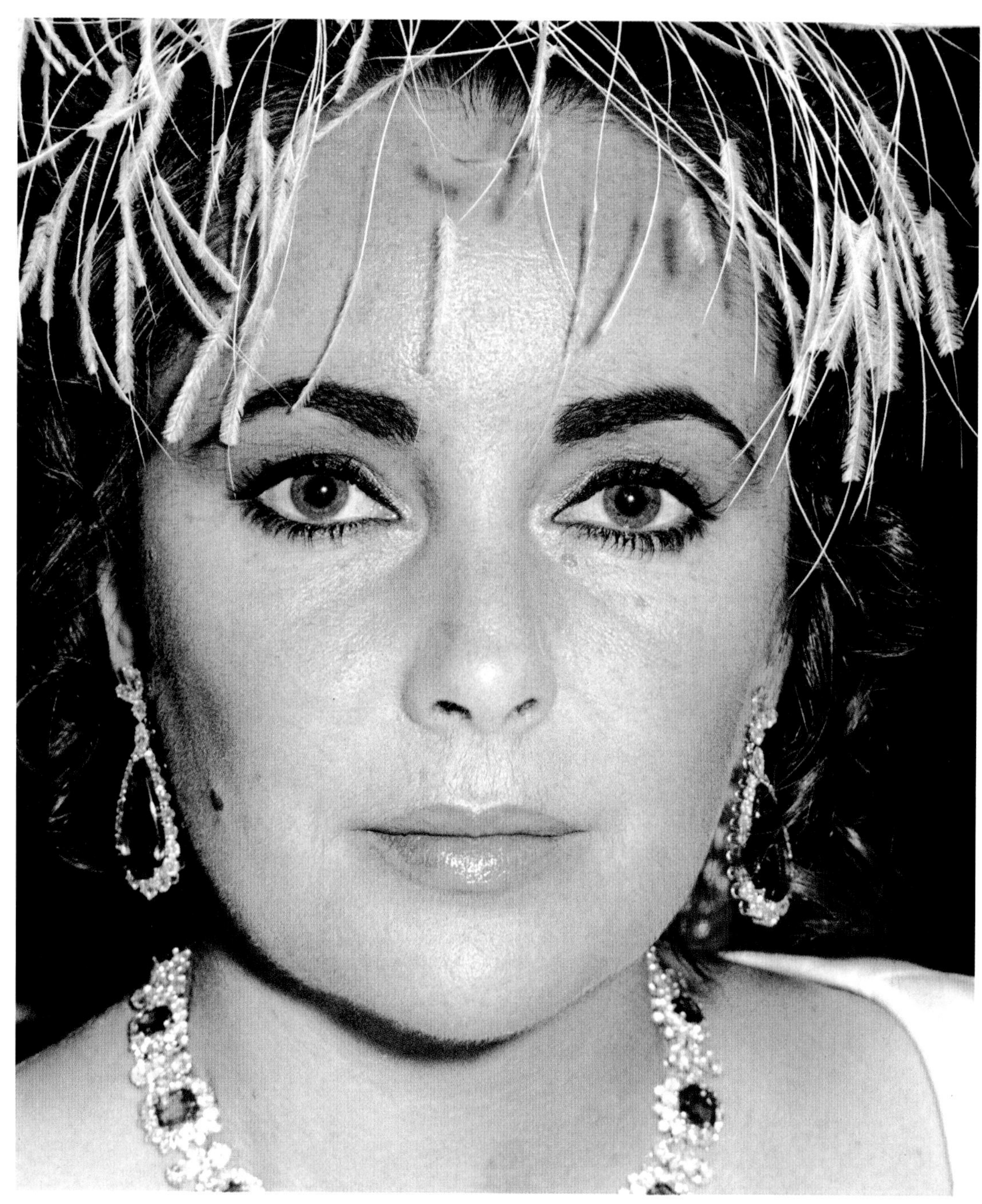

ELIZABETH TAYLOR
October 18, 1968 – Paris, France
"A Flea In Her Ear" Premiere

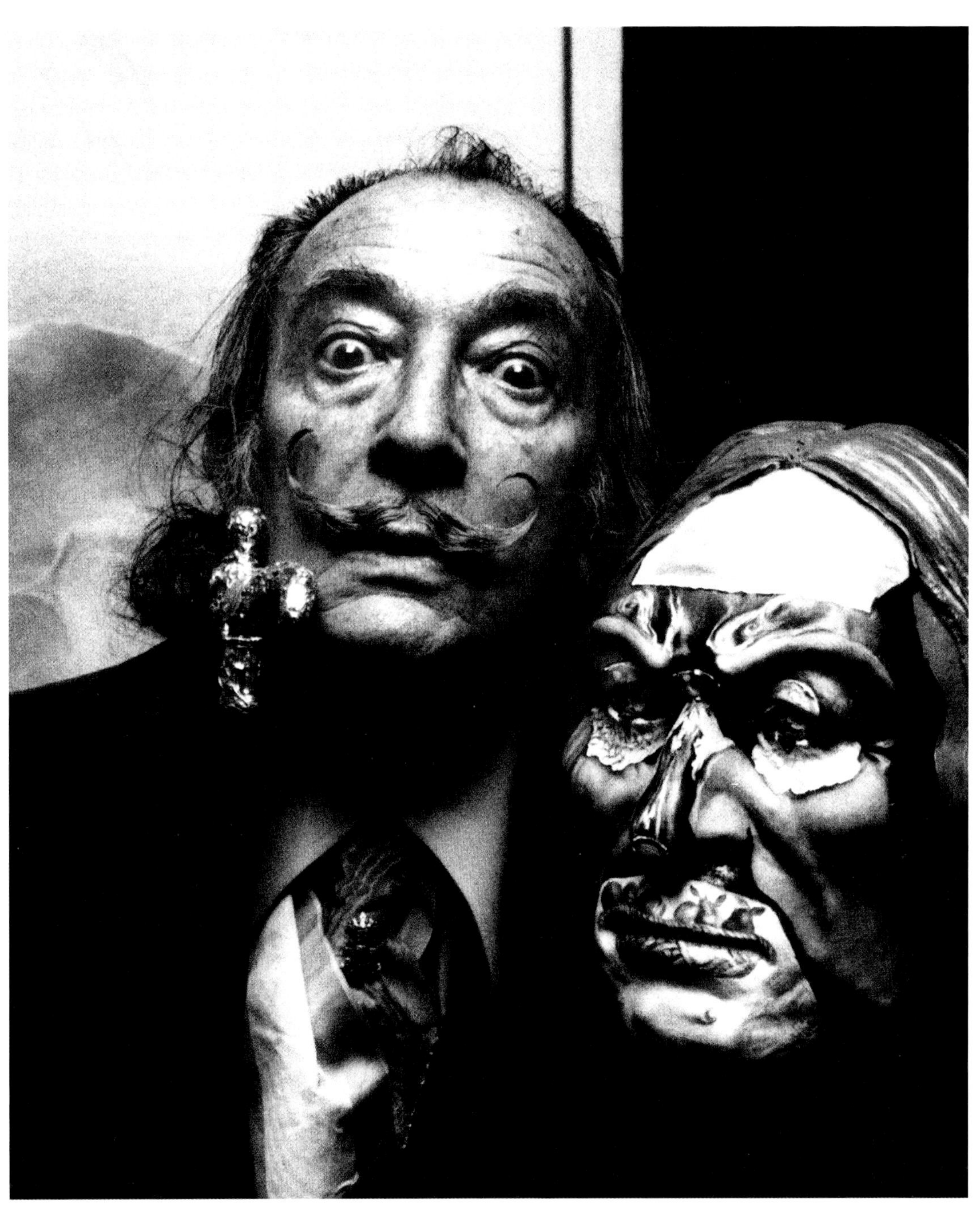

13

SALVADOR DALI
March 7, 1974 – New York City
Salvador Dali Art Exhibition

14 **LIZA MINNELLI**

February 13, 1972 – Beverly Hills, California
"Cabaret" Premiere Party
at the Beverly Hills Hotel

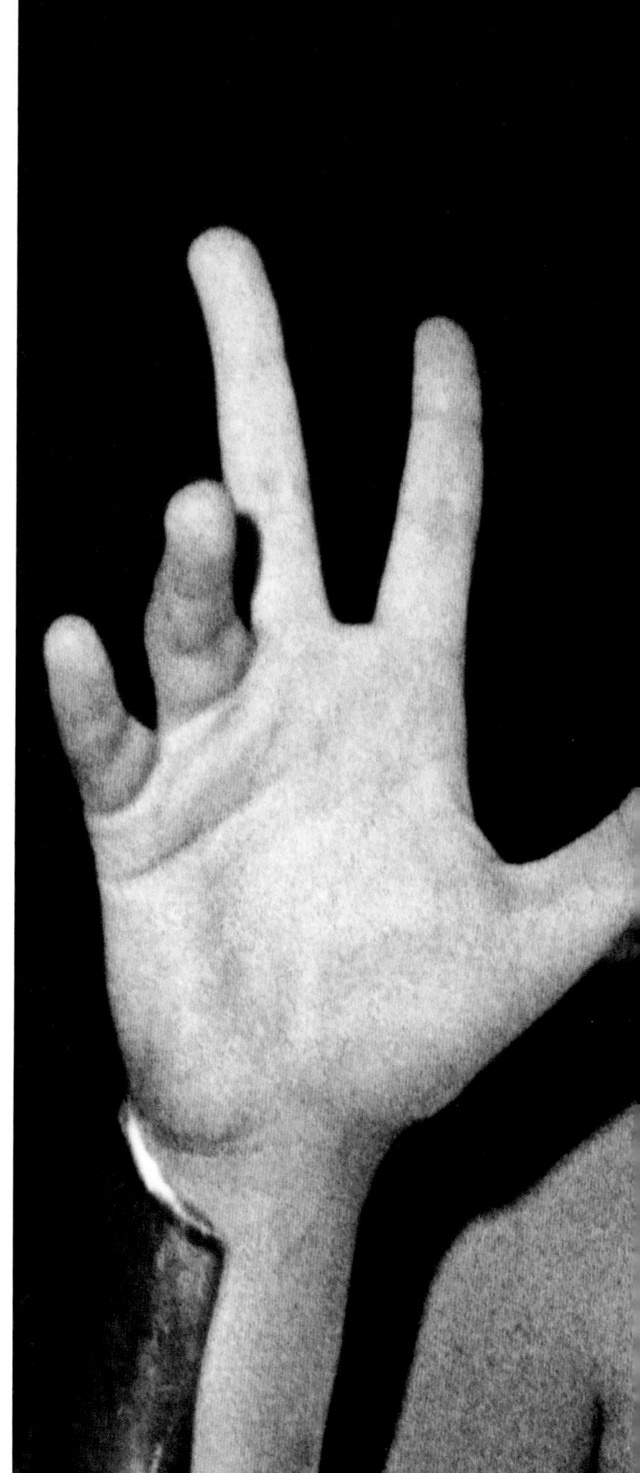

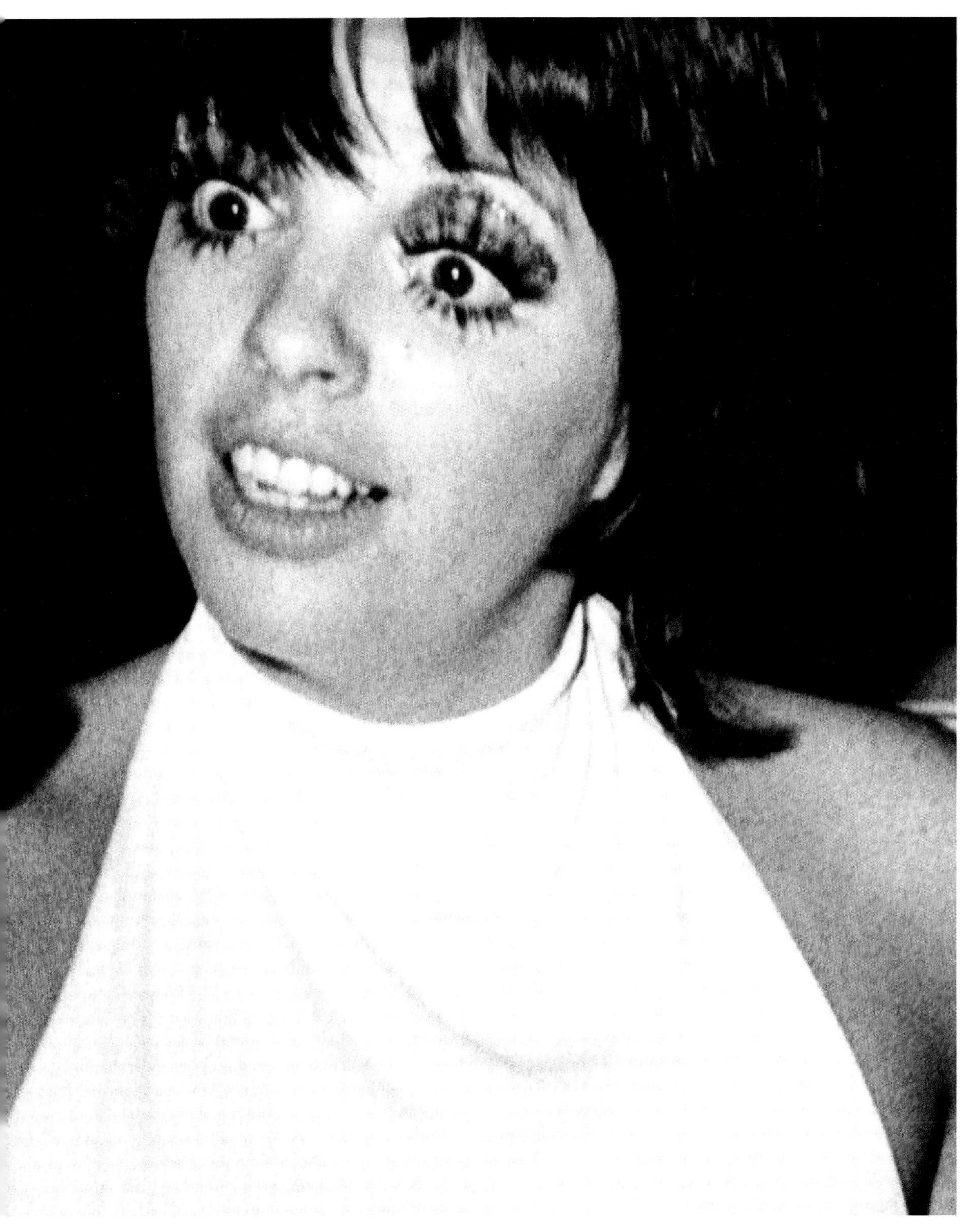

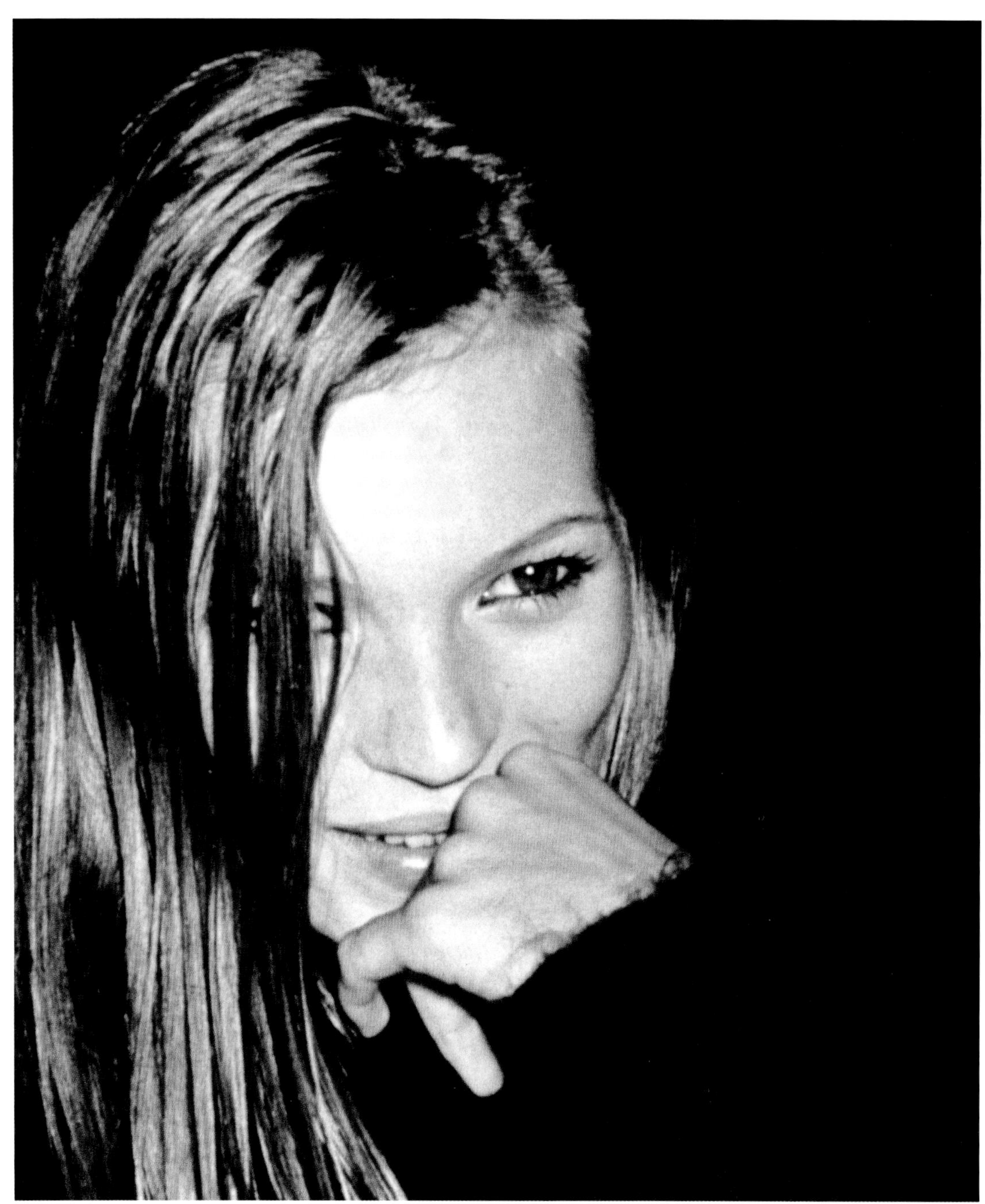

KATE MOSS
September 27, 1993 – New York City
The New Yorker Magazine Party for Richard Avedon at the New York Public Library

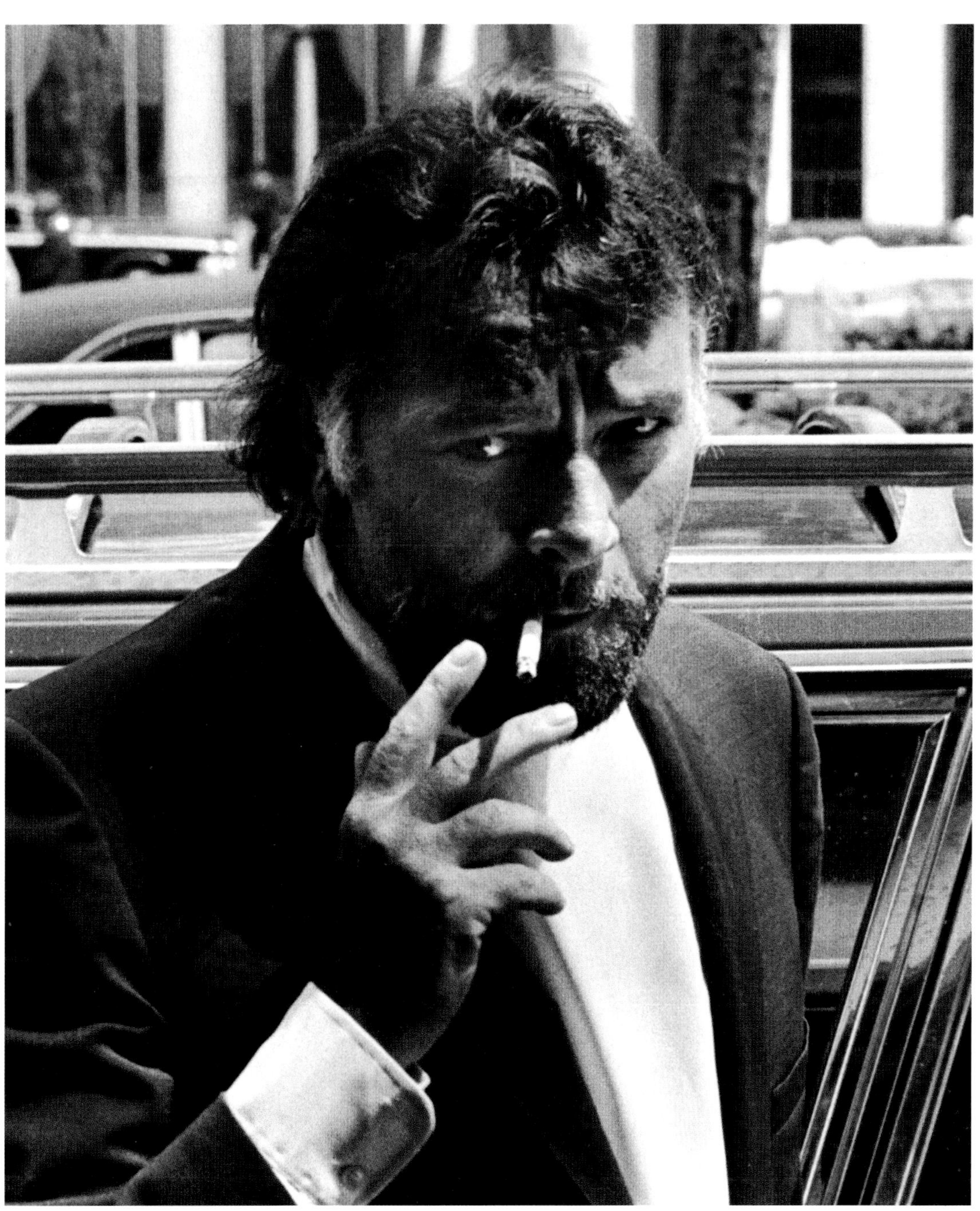

RICHARD BURTON
May 11, 1969 – New York City
Plaza Hotel

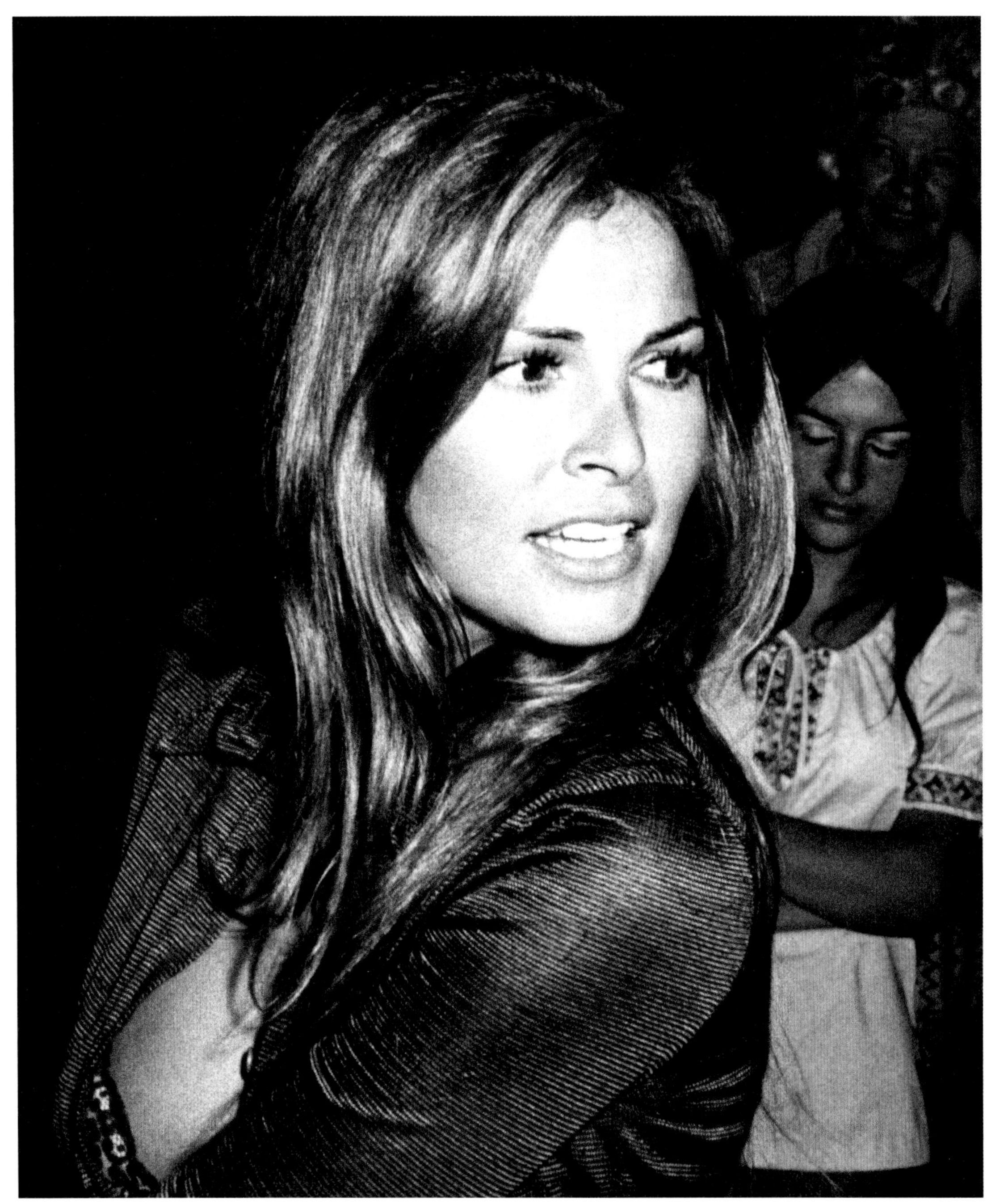

RAQUEL WELCH
June 12, 1971 – Beverly Hills, California
Polly Bergen House Party

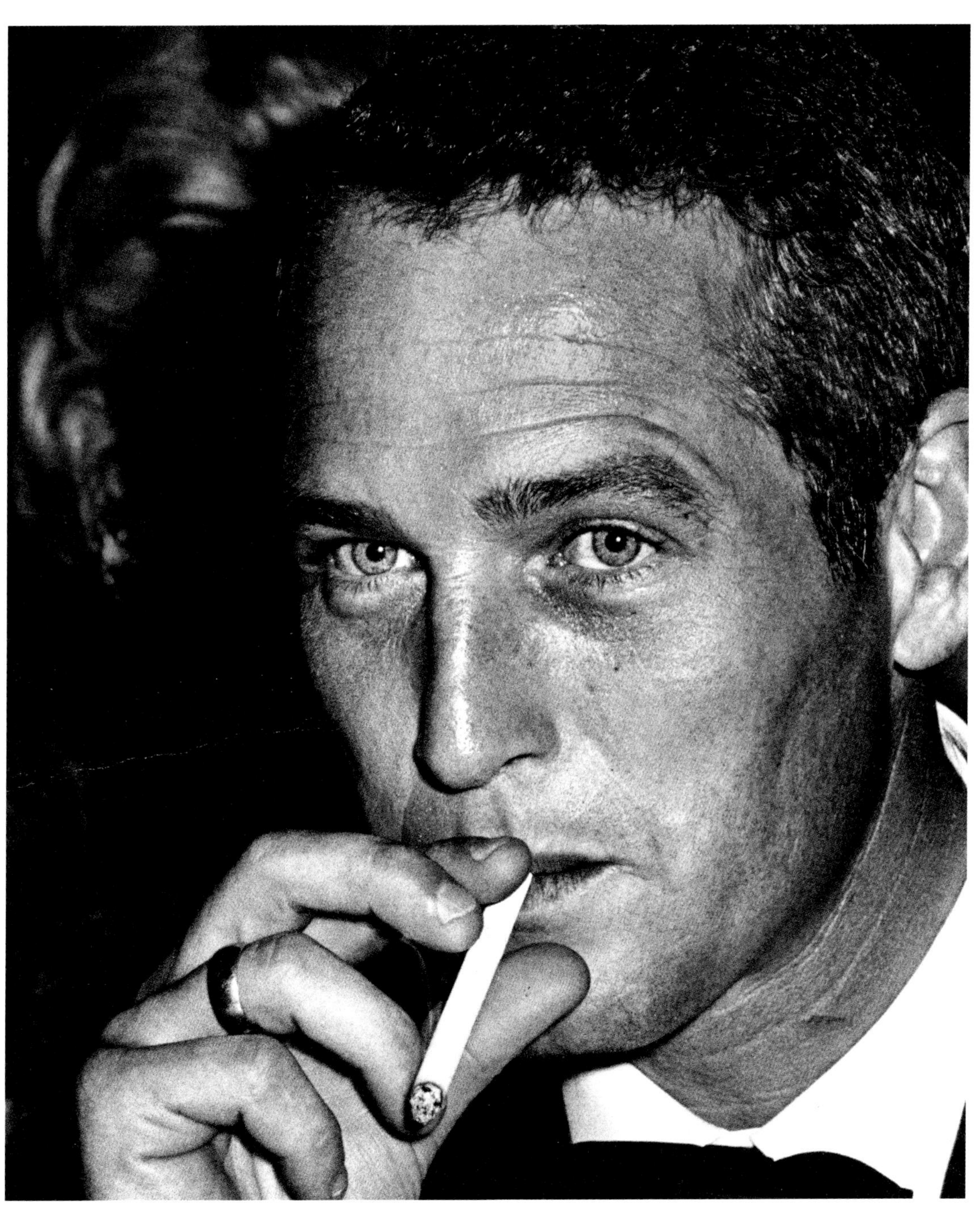

PAUL NEWMAN
November 1, 1967 – New York City
"Cool Hand Luke" Premiere Party at the Americana Hotel

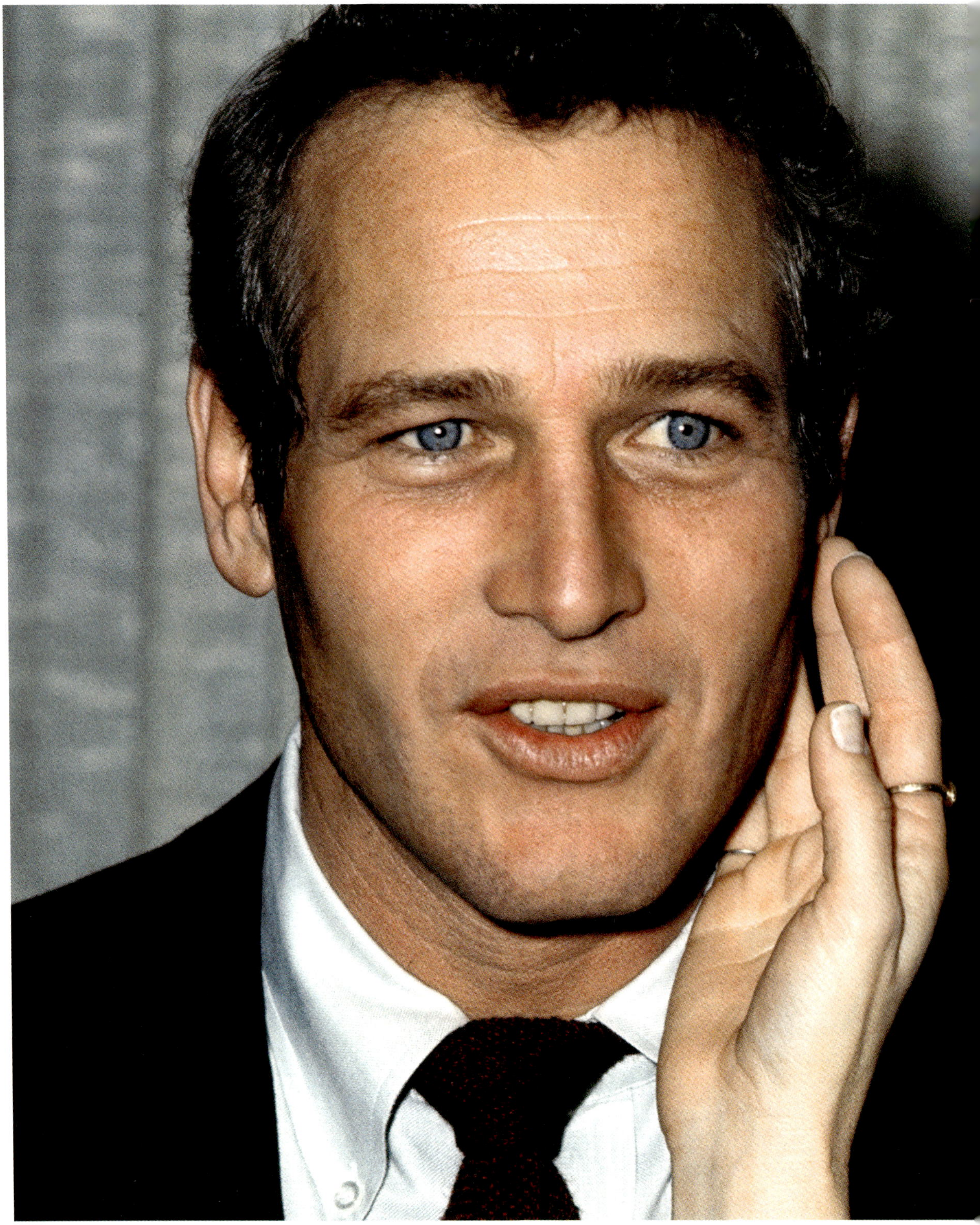

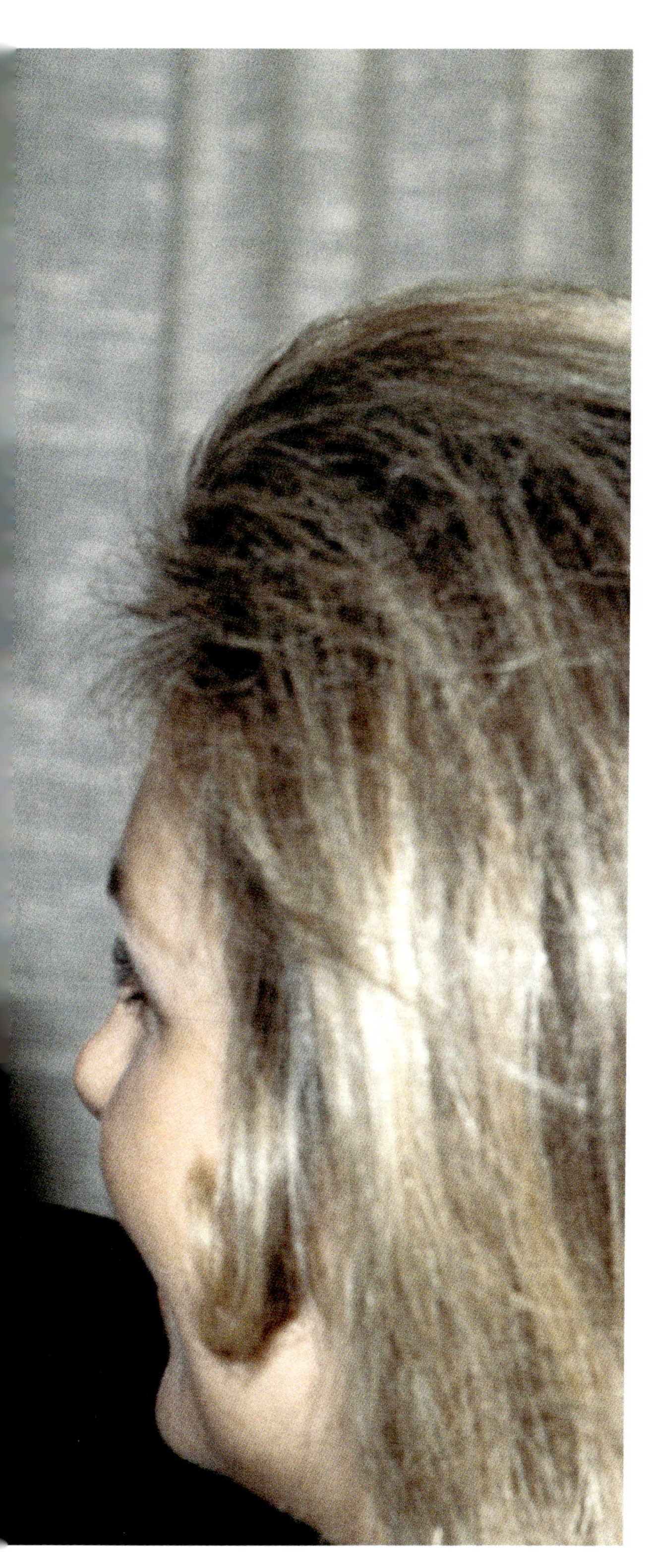

PAUL NEWMAN &
JOANNE WOODWARD
January 16, 1969 – New York City
New York Film Critics Circle Awards at the
Rainbow Room at Rockefeller Center

JOHN TRAVOLTA

August 1, 1976 – Westchester, New York
"Bus Stop" Opening
at John Burroughs Junior High School

A Sweathog Makes Good. John Travolta, 22, on the brink of superstardom.

The "Welcome Back, Kotter" star stirs up fans outside the John Burroughs Junior High School where he was starring in Westchester Playhouse's summer stock production of "Bus Stop." His portrayal of "Vinnie Barbarino" in the ABC Television series made him a fan favorite.

The play featured Brian Dennehy, as well as Travolta siblings Ellen and Ann. Travolta's parents attended the play's opening night as did "Kotter" co-creator and star Gabe Kaplan whom I photographed exclusively backstage.

The following year Travolta was on his way to becoming an international sensation with the release of back to back hits, "Saturday Night Fever", for which he received an Academy Award nomination for Best Actor, and "Grease", co-starring Olivia Newton-John.

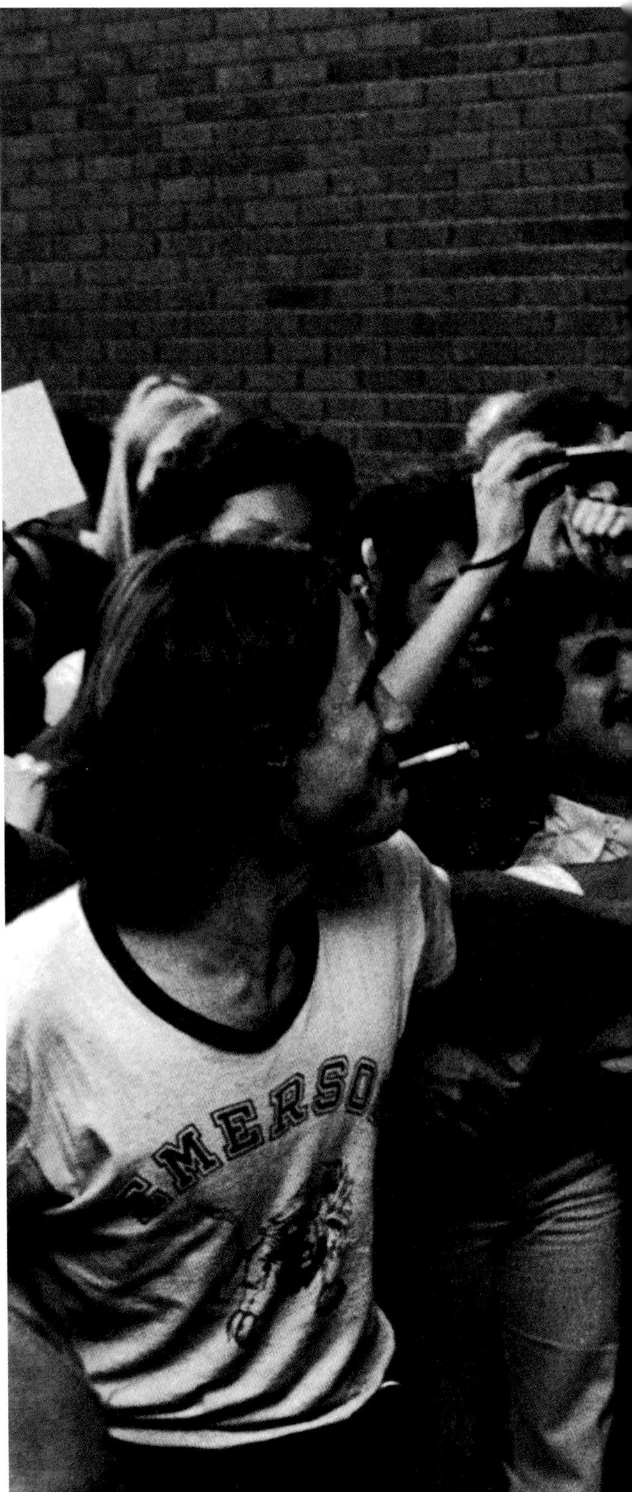

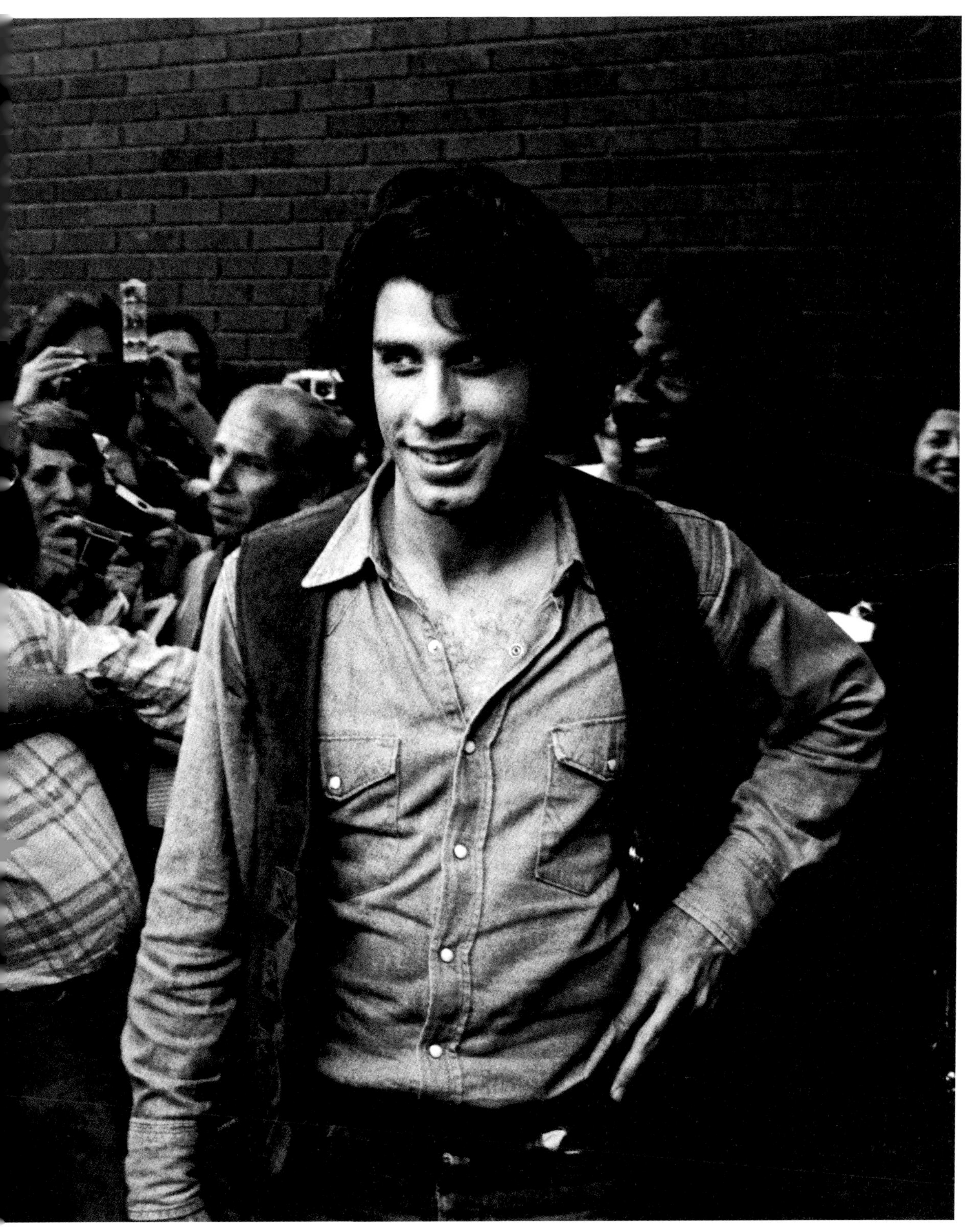

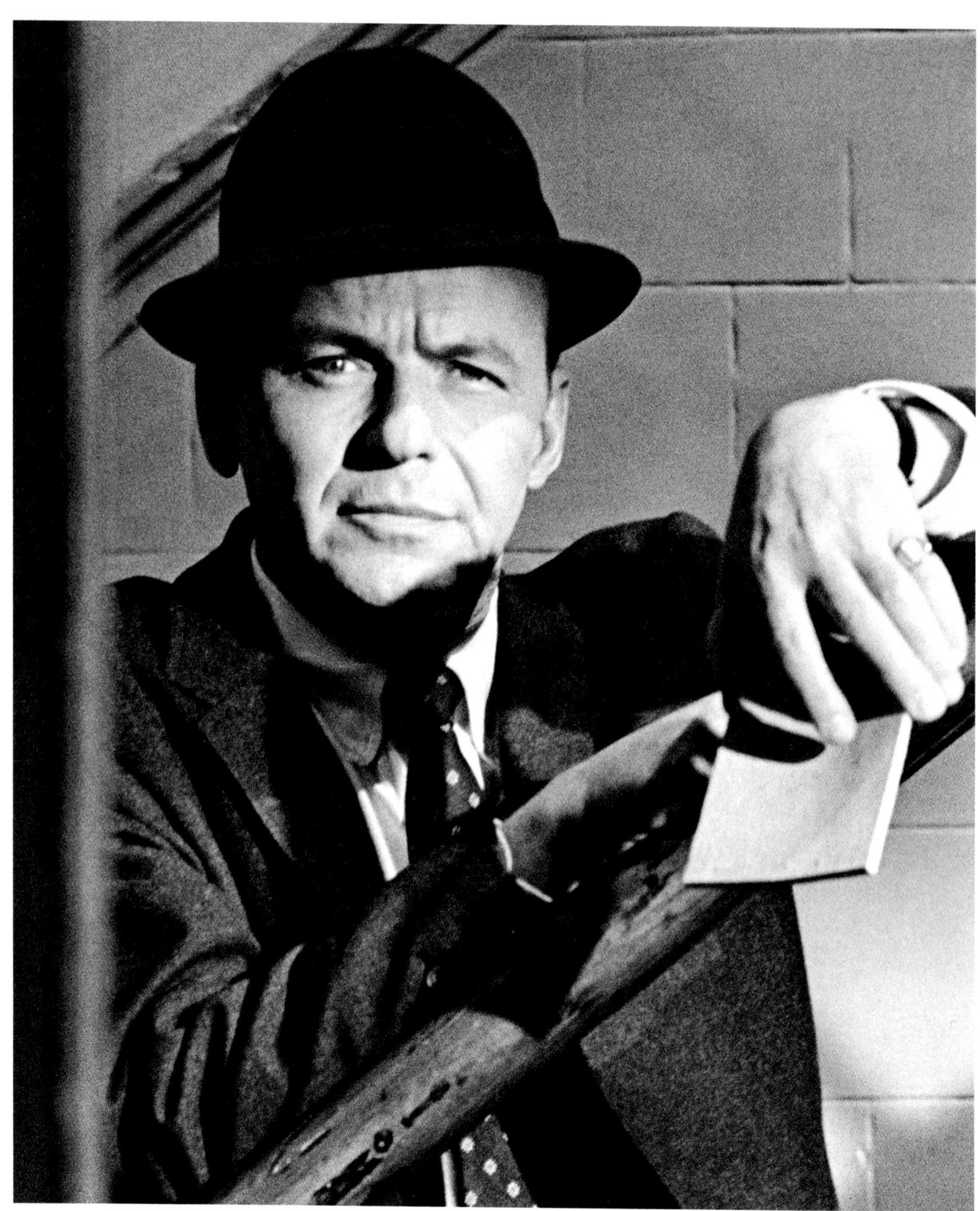

FRANK SINATRA
October 18, 1967 – New York City
On Location Filming "The Detective"

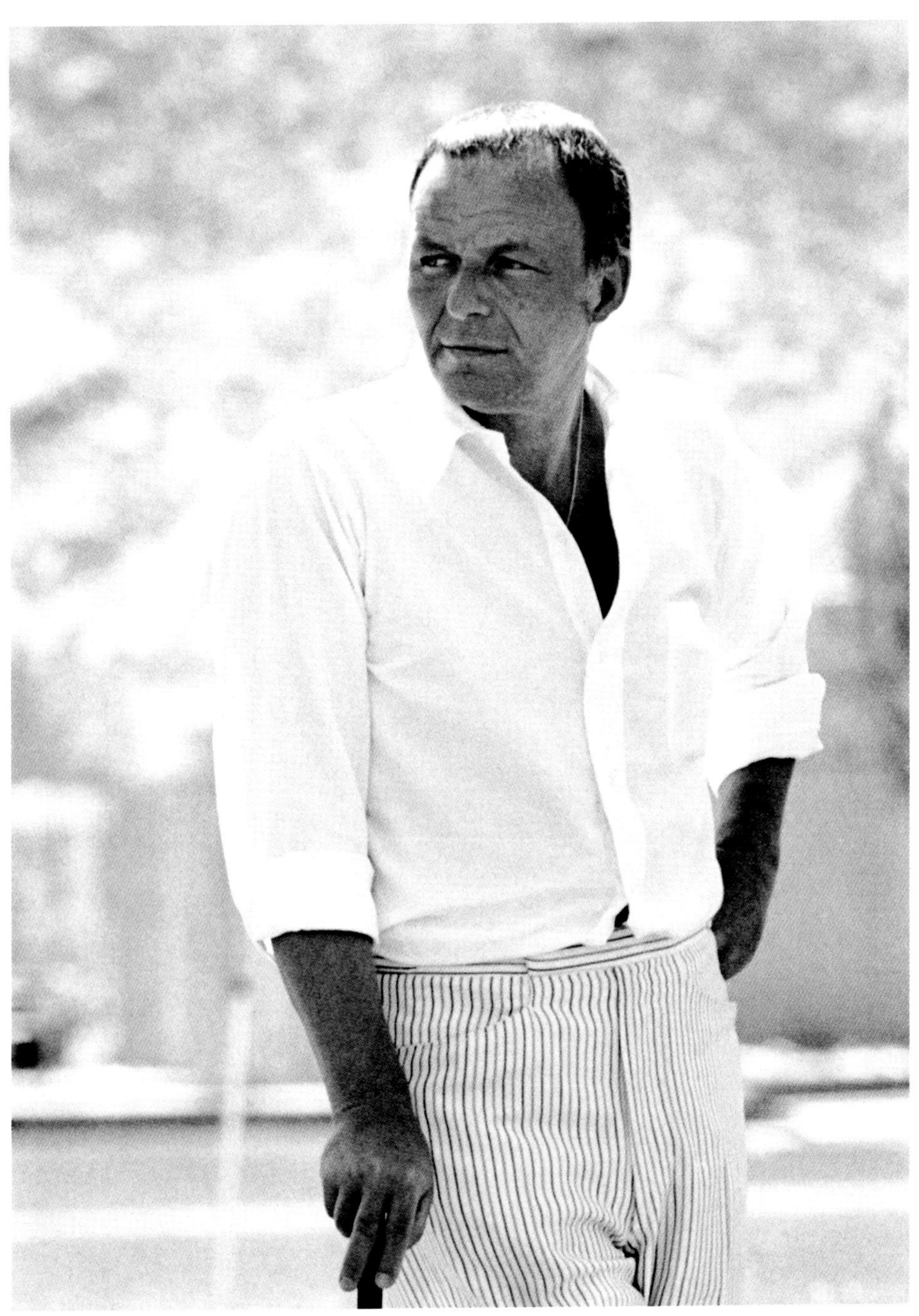

FRANK SINATRA
April 19, 1969 – Palm Springs, California
3rd Annual Chuck Connors Charity Invitational Golf Tournament
at the Palm Springs Racquet Club

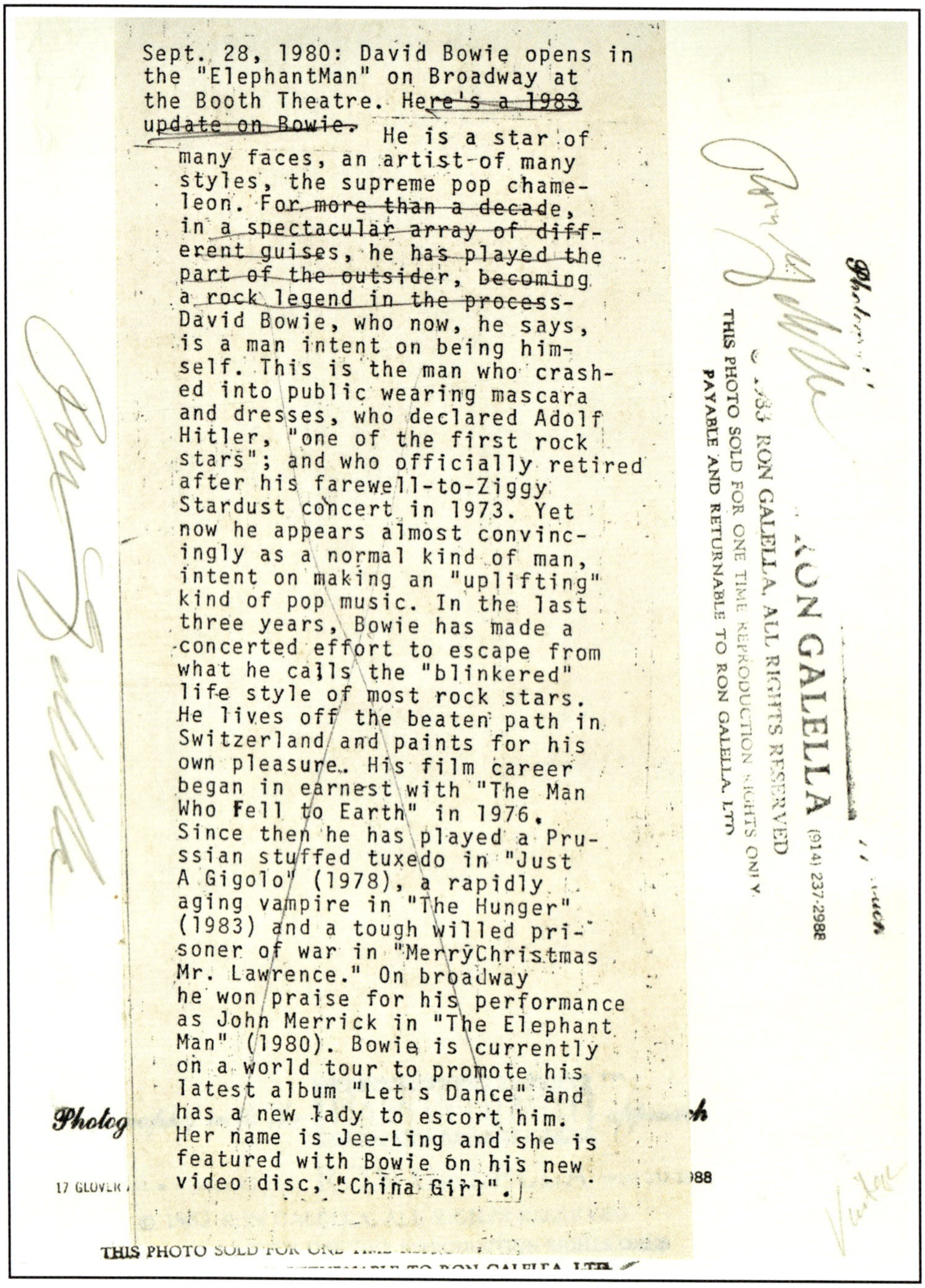

Sept. 28, 1980: David Bowie opens in the "ElephantMan" on Broadway at the Booth Theatre. He~~re's a 1983 update on Bowie.~~ He is a star of many faces, an artist of many styles, the supreme pop chameleon. Fo~~r more than a decade, in a spectacular array of different guises, he has played the part of the outsider, becoming a rock legend in the process~~- David Bowie, who now, he says, is a man intent on being himself. This is the man who crashed into public wearing mascara and dresses, who declared Adolf Hitler, "one of the first rock stars"; and who officially retired after his farewell-to-Ziggy Stardust concert in 1973. Yet now he appears almost convincingly as a normal kind of man, intent on making an "uplifting" kind of pop music. In the last three years, Bowie has made a concerted effort to escape from what he calls the "blinkered" life style of most rock stars. He lives off the beaten path in Switzerland and paints for his own pleasure. His film career began in earnest with "The Man Who Fell to Earth" in 1976. Since then he has played a Prussian stuffed tuxedo in "Just A Gigolo" (1978), a rapidly aging vampire in "The Hunger" (1983) and a tough willed prisoner of war in "MerryChristmas Mr. Lawrence." On broadway he won praise for his performance as John Merrick in "The Elephant Man" (1980). Bowie is currently on a world tour to promote his latest album "Let's Dance" and has a new lady to escort him. Her name is Jee-Ling and she is featured with Bowie on his new video disc, "China Girl".

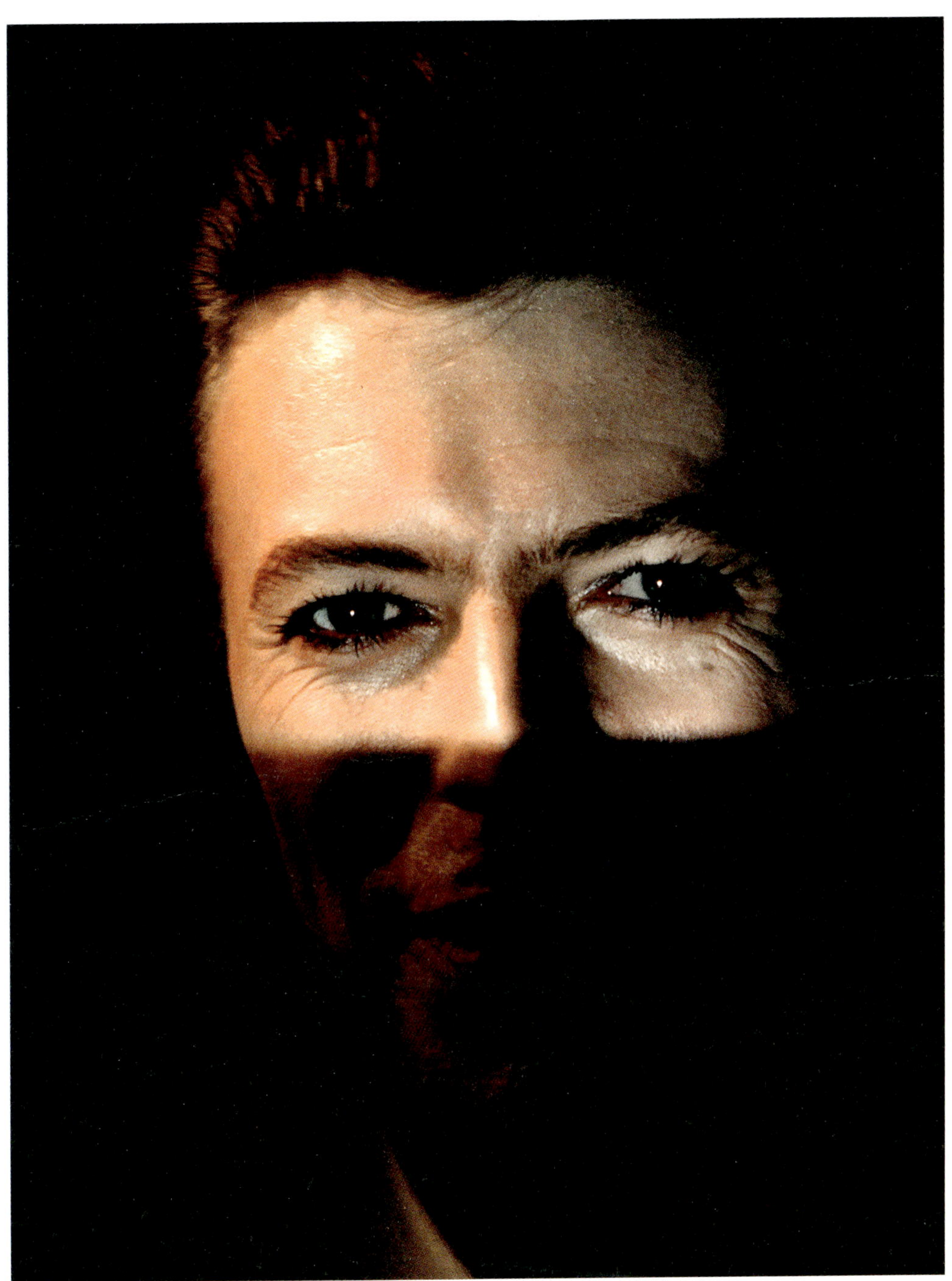

DAVID BOWIE
September 28, 1980 – New York City
David Bowie opens in "The Elephant Man" at the Booth Theatre

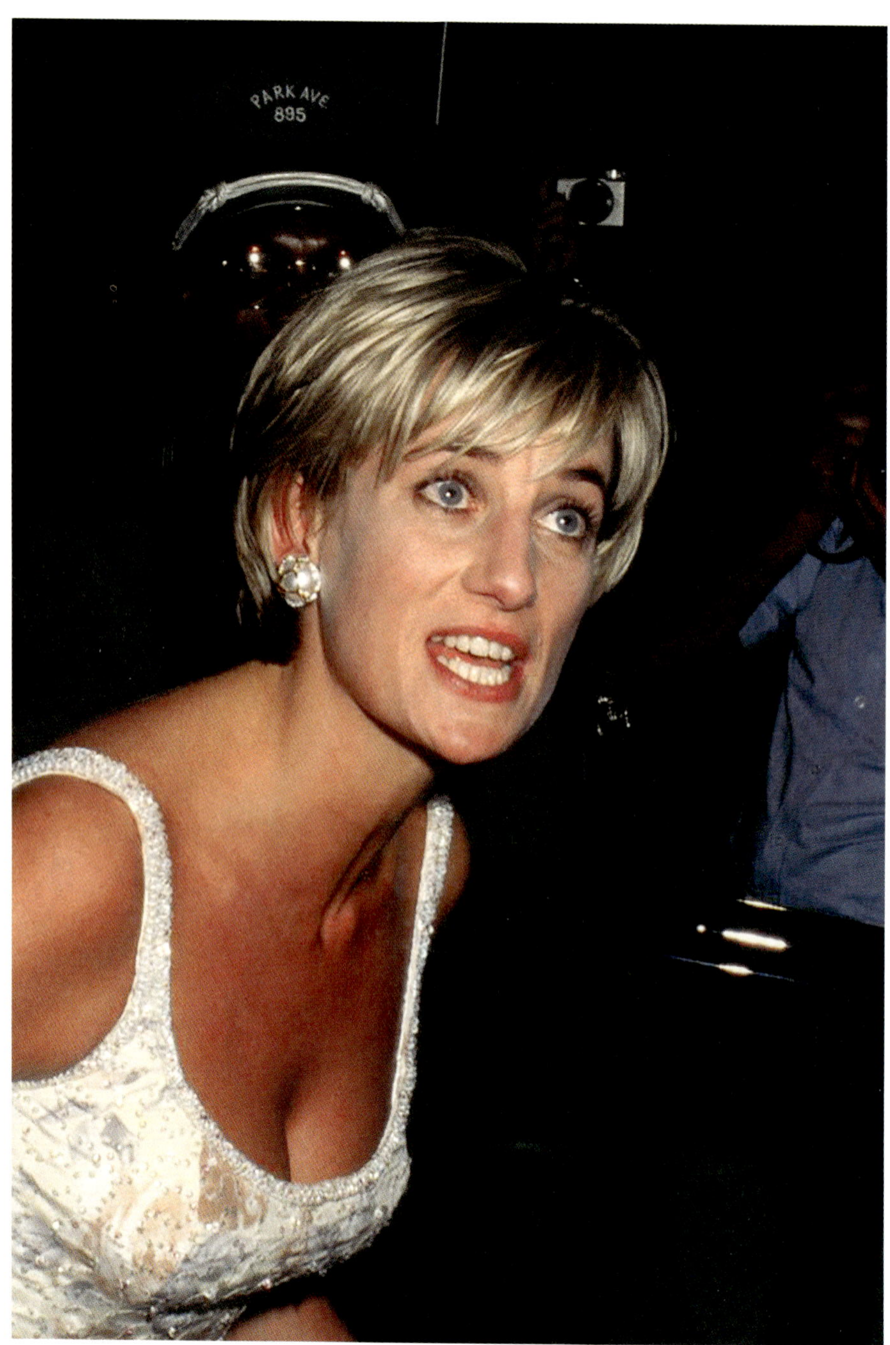

DIANA, PRINCESS OF WALES
June 23, 1997 – New York City
Dinner Party After Princess Diana's Christie's Auction
at Nan Kempner's Park Avenue Apartment

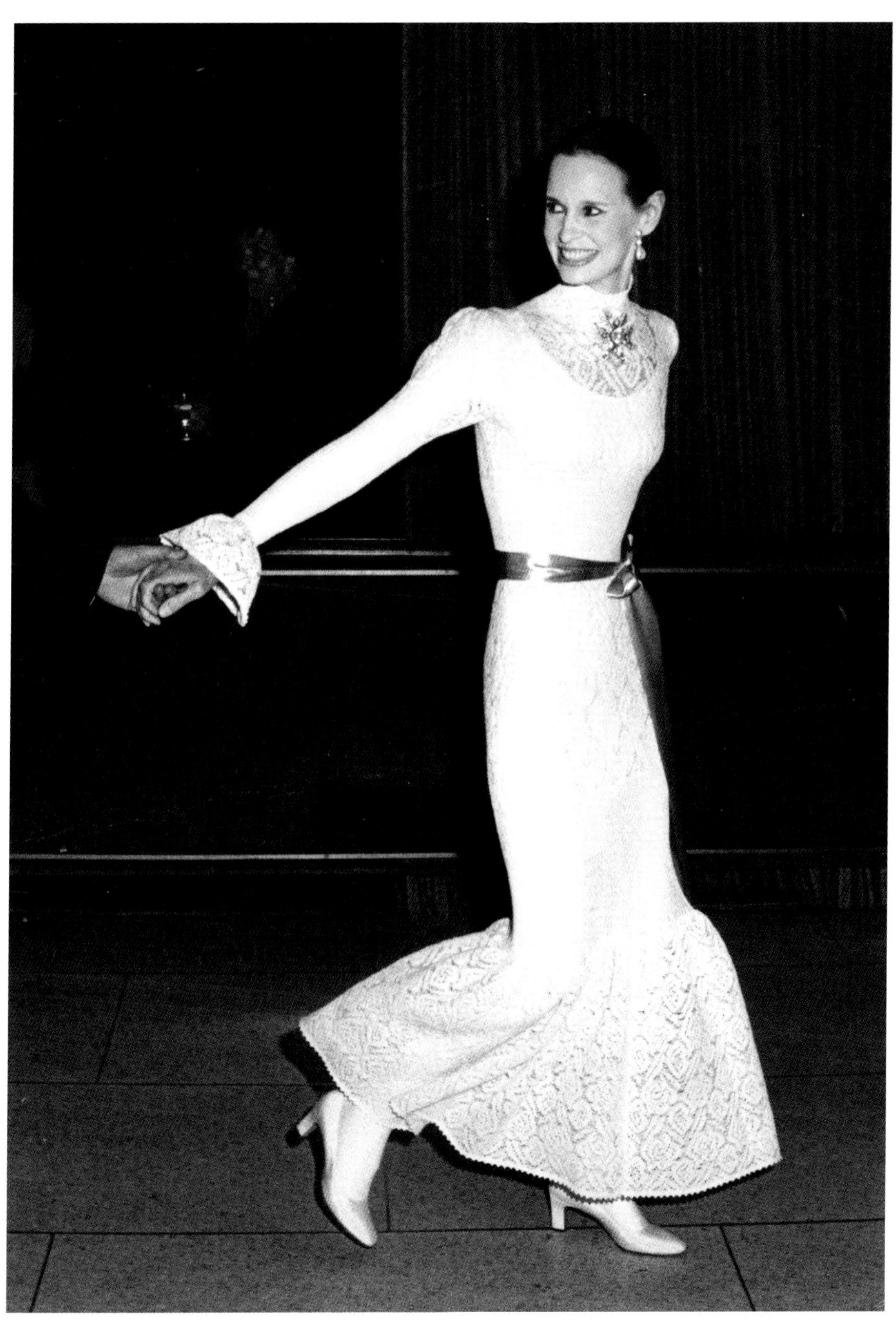

GLORIA VANDERBILT
April 8, 1972 – New York City
Tribute Gala Honoring Charlie Chaplin at Philharmonic Hall at Lincoln Center

TWIGGY & JUSTIN DE VILLENEUVE

Lesley Hornby, better known as Twiggy, arrived in the States in 1967 at the height of her appeal. My friend and colleague George Bernard and I received an assignment to interview and photograph Twiggy at renowned commercial photographer Bert Stern's studio. Stern is best known for his poignant photos of Marilyn Monroe. The day before Twiggy was to arrive, we spoke to Stern's secretary. She confirmed that on August 28th Twiggy had an appointment to be photographed by Stern, and would arrive around nine in the morning. Since I lived in the Bronx, twelve miles away, and Twiggy's arrival time was early the next morning, I planned to sleep at George's apartment on East 73rd Street. To my dismay, George knew that I snored and since he was a light sleeper, he gave me a blanket and pointed me in the direction of the roof where I found a lounge chair to sleep on.

Instead of shooting the stars, I slept under them on the rooftop of his fourteen-story apartment building. George woke me at seven. I showered and shaved and we got a bite to eat. We parked in front of the studio and waited. Sure enough, at nine a beige Rolls-Royce pulled up in front of us. We jumped out and shouted Twiggy's name. Twiggy and boyfriend Justin de Villeneuve were friendly, responded to George's questions and posed for pictures. Twiggy stated that the only good thing about being in the States was the music, and dropped a quarter in the studio's jukebox. With a hidden tape recorder in his pocket, George got his interview and I got the photos of this seventeen-year-old British-born beauty, who at the time was the fashion rage of the entire world.

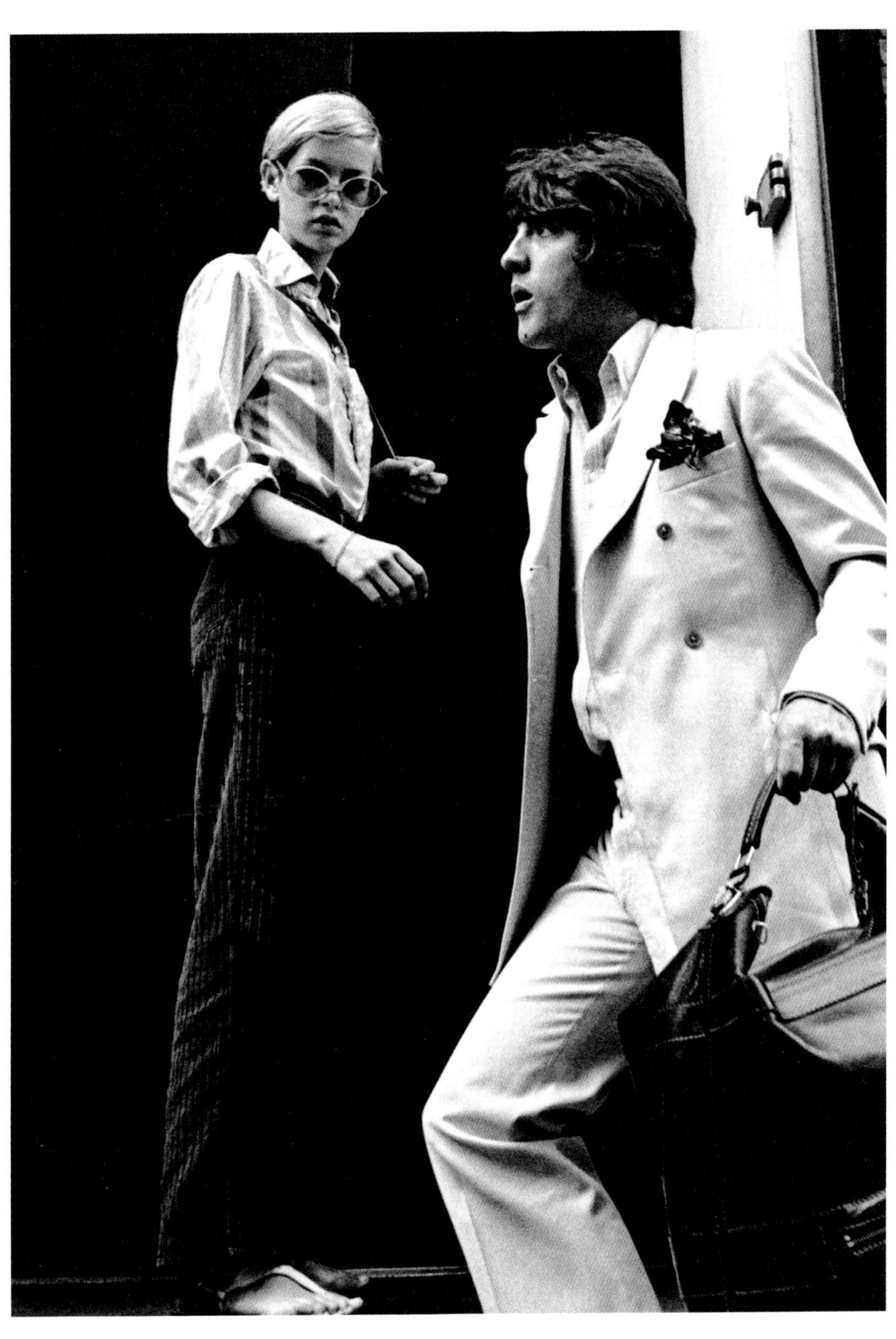

TWIGGY & JUSTIN DE VILLENEUVE
August 28, 1967 – New York City
Bert Stern's Studio

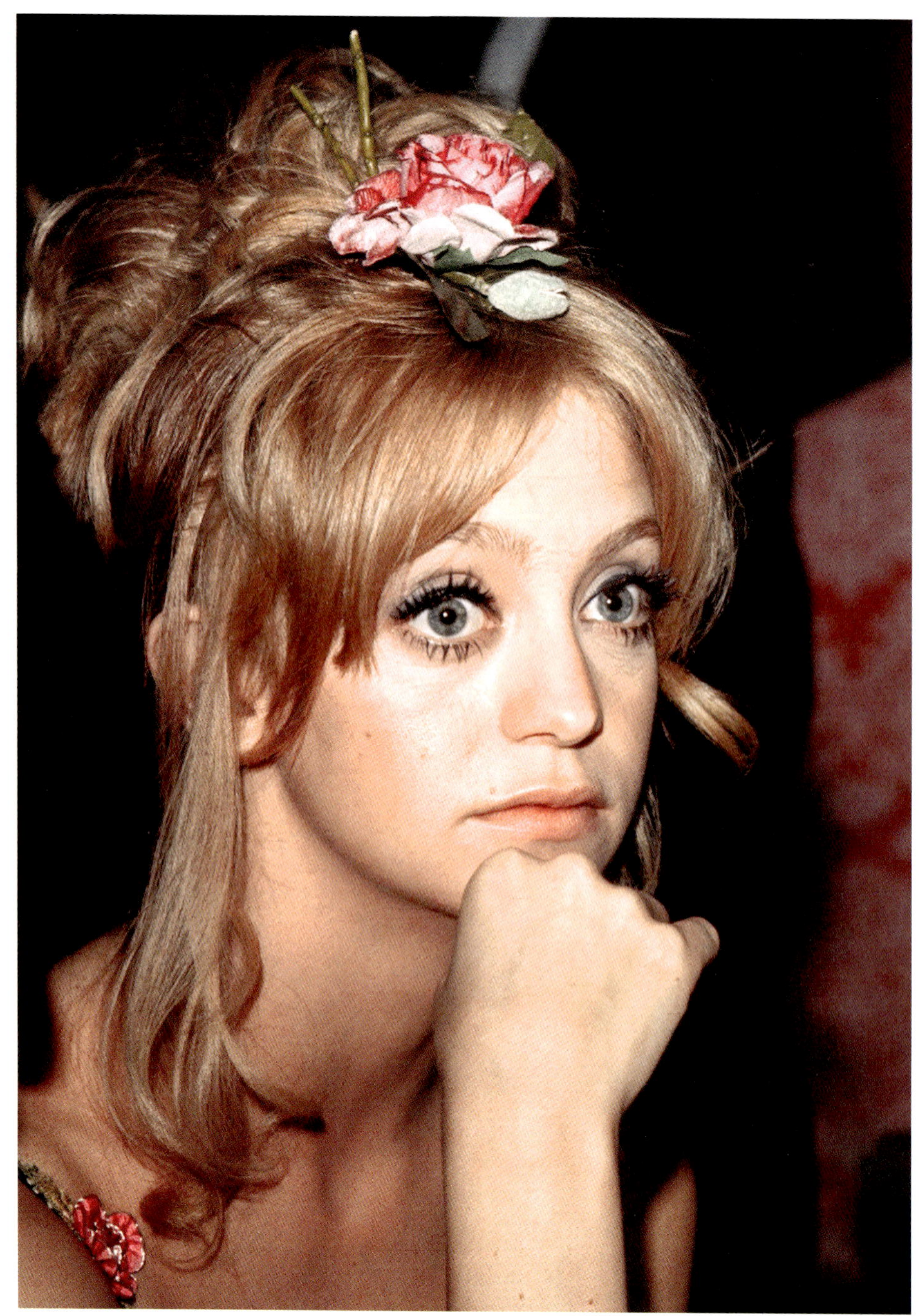

GOLDIE HAWN
April 15, 1971 – Los Angeles, California
43rd Annual Academy Awards at the Dorothy Chandler Pavillion

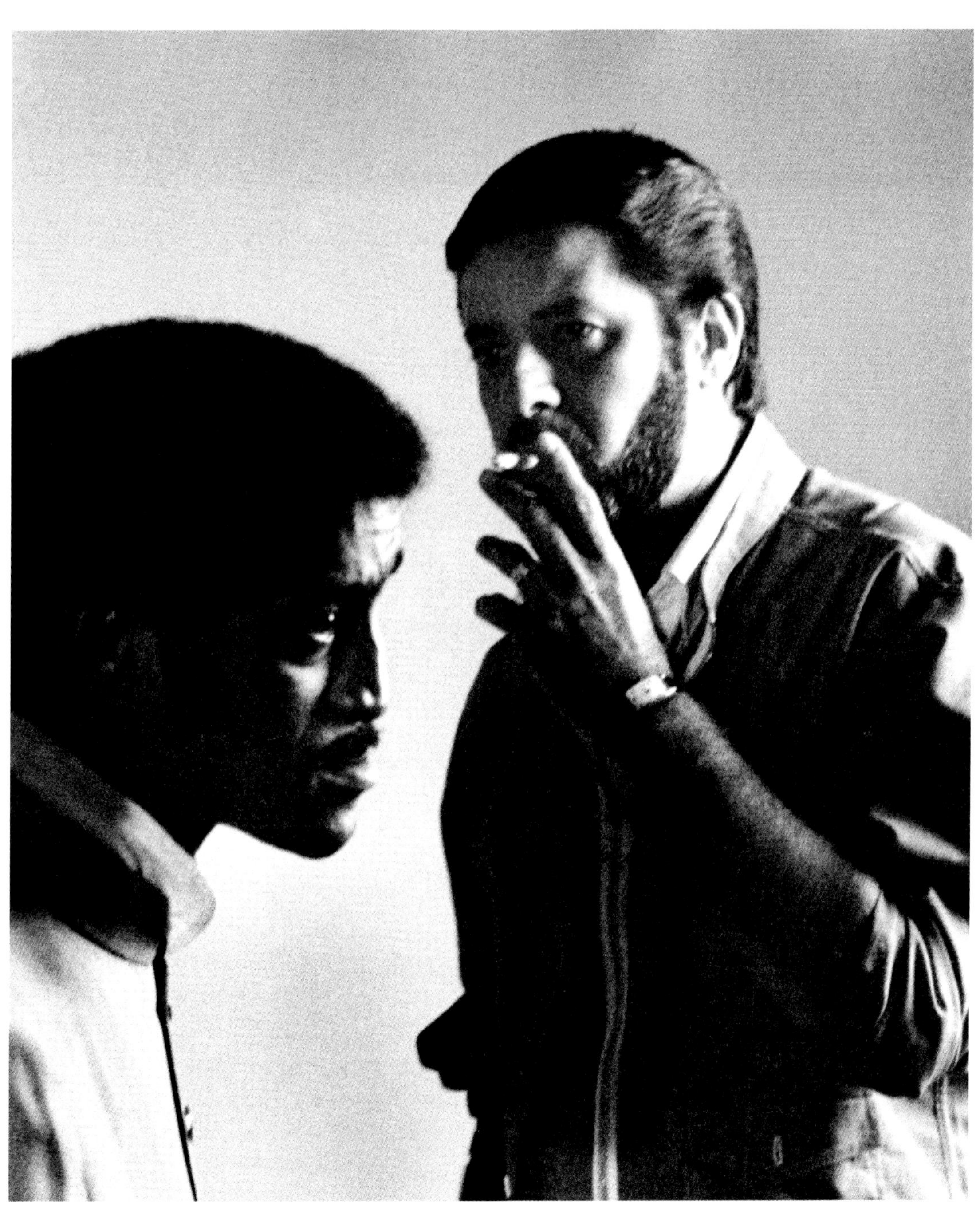

SAMMY DAVIS, JR. & JERRY LEWIS
September 9, 1969 – London, England
On Location Filming "One More Time"

NATALIE WOOD

I knocked on the door of Natalie Wood's Beverly Hills home and Natalie opened the door. She welcomed me with a warm hello, saying, "I'll be ready in five minutes." After taking a couple of shots of her at her front door, Natalie invited me along for an afternoon of shopping on Rodeo Drive in her convertible. Not fully matured as a paparazzo, and without a developed technique, my shyness got the best of me and I turned Natalie down.

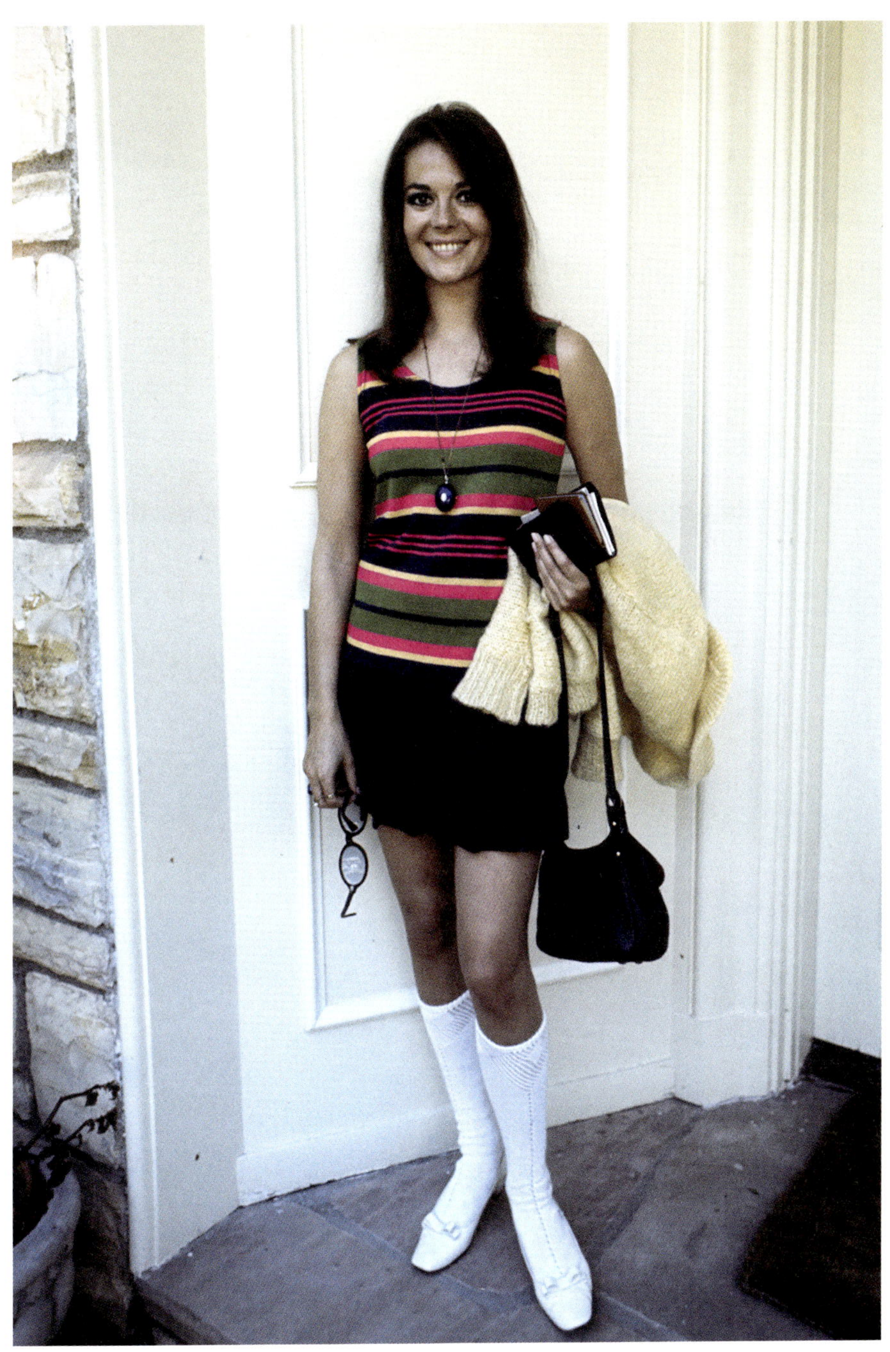

NATALIE WOOD
April 4, 1968 – Beverly Hills, California

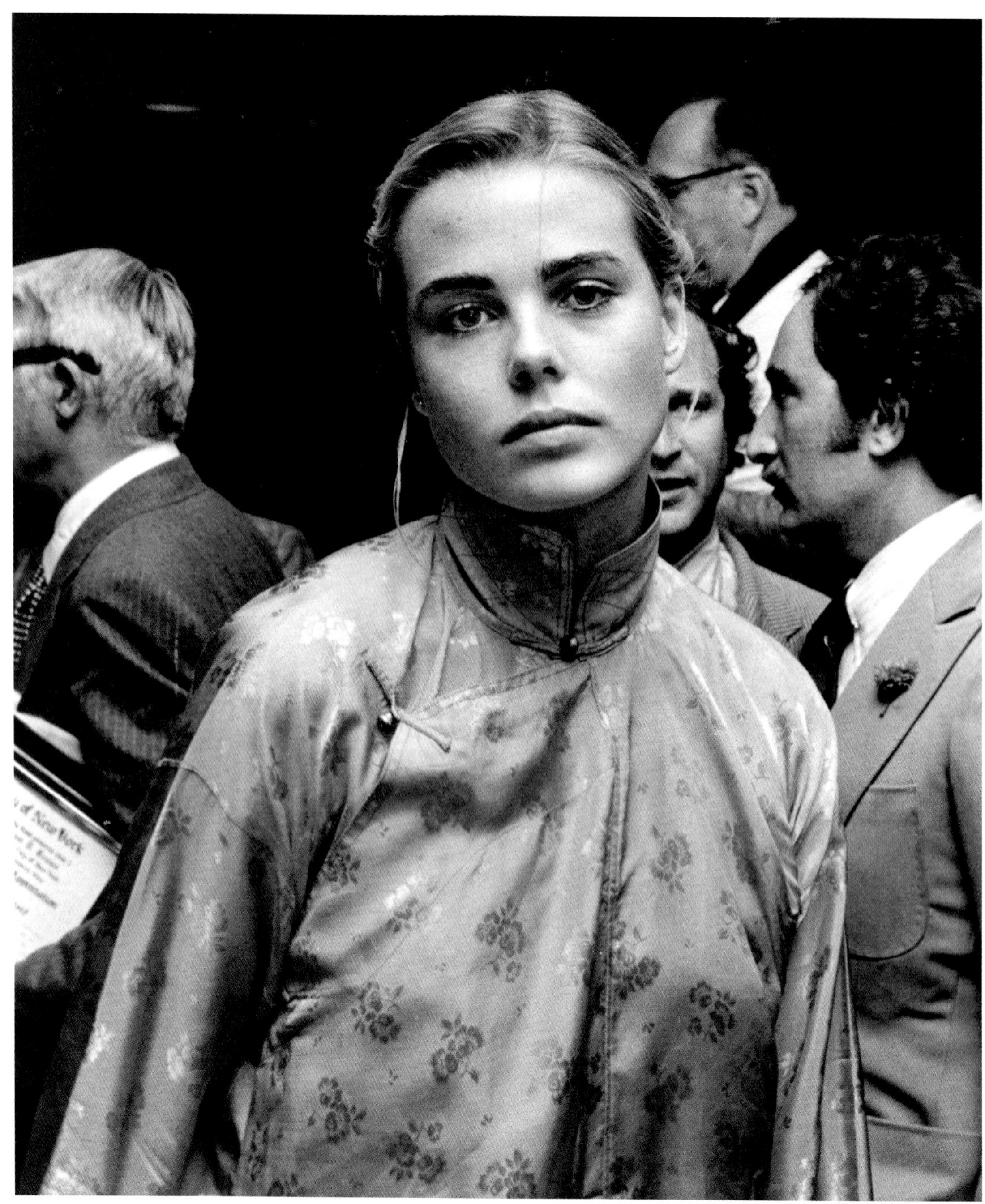

MARGAUX HEMINGWAY
May 29, 1975 – New York City
6th Annual Straw Hat Awards at Jimmy's Restaurant

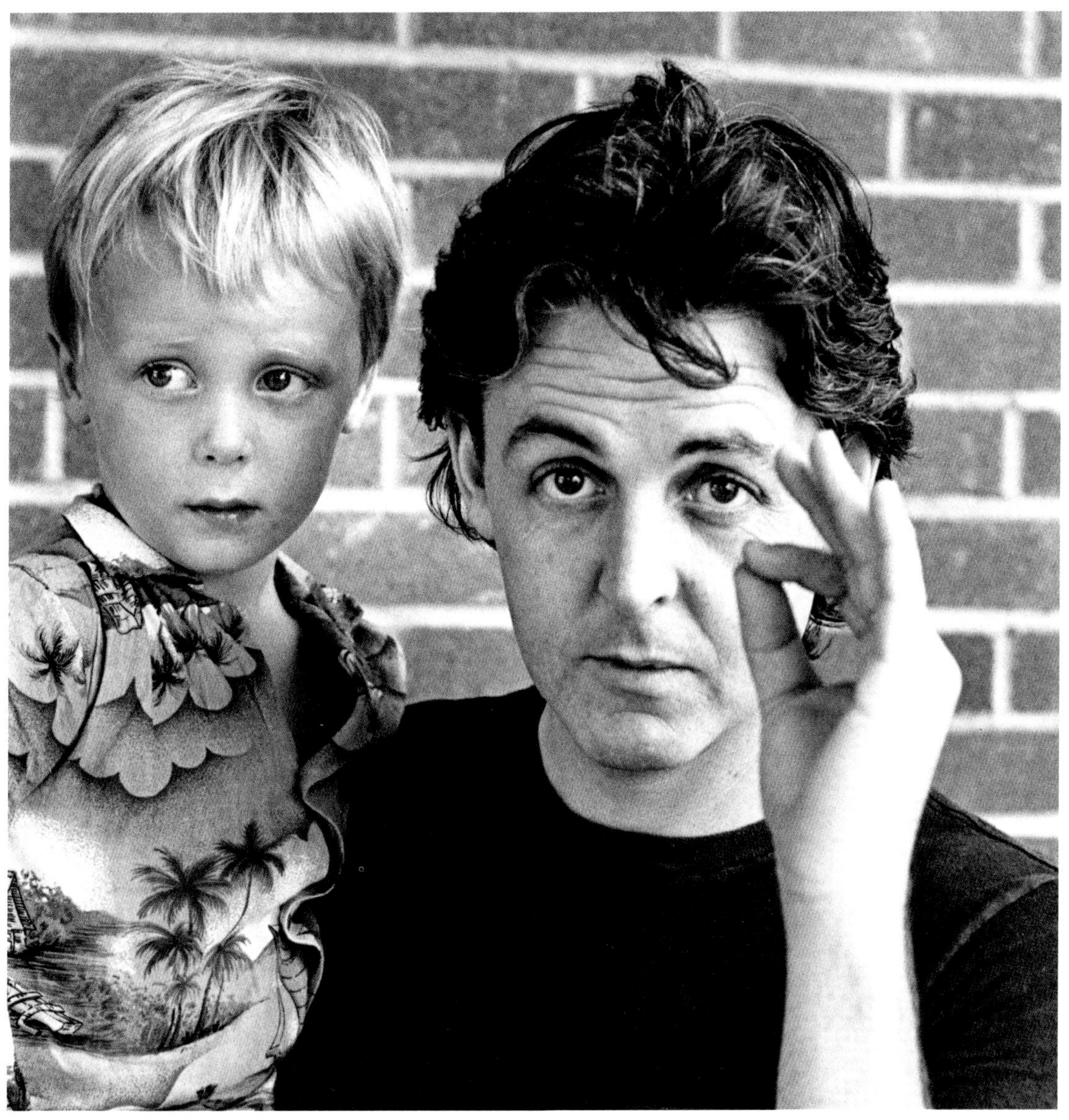

PAUL McCARTNEY & SON JAMES (AGE 4)
August 16, 1981 – East Hampton, New York
The East Hampton Supermarket

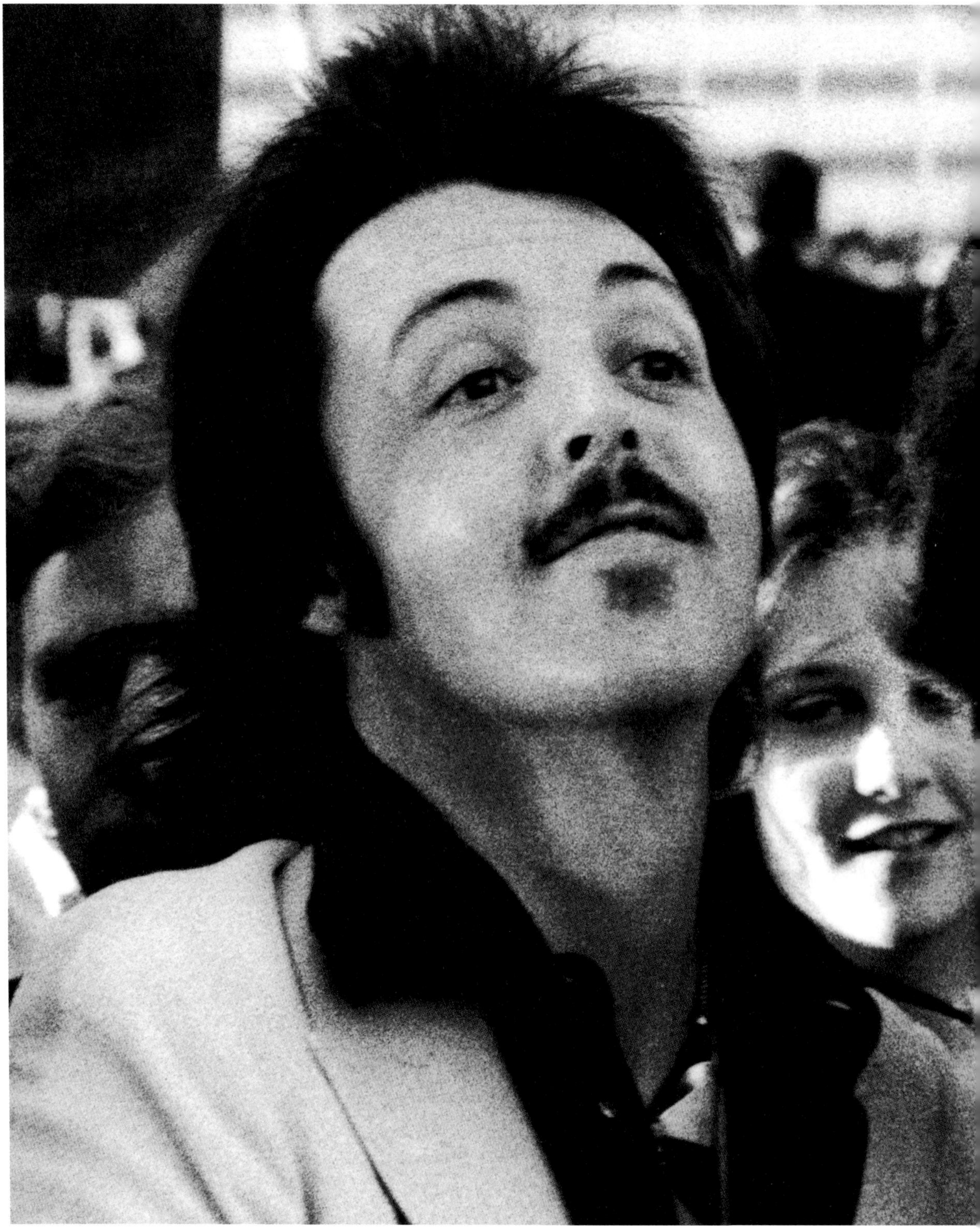

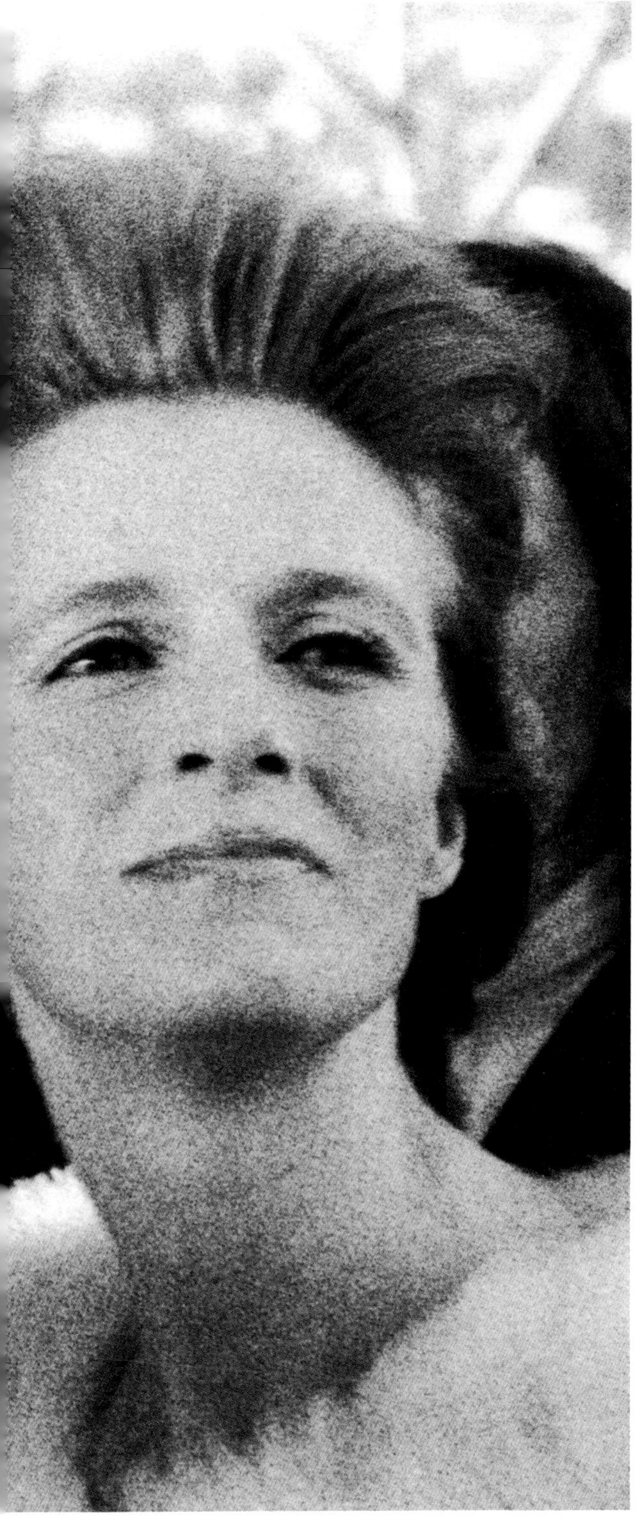

PAUL & LINDA McCARTNEY 39

April 2, 1974 – Los Angeles, California
46th Annual Academy Awards
at the Dorothy Chandler Pavilion

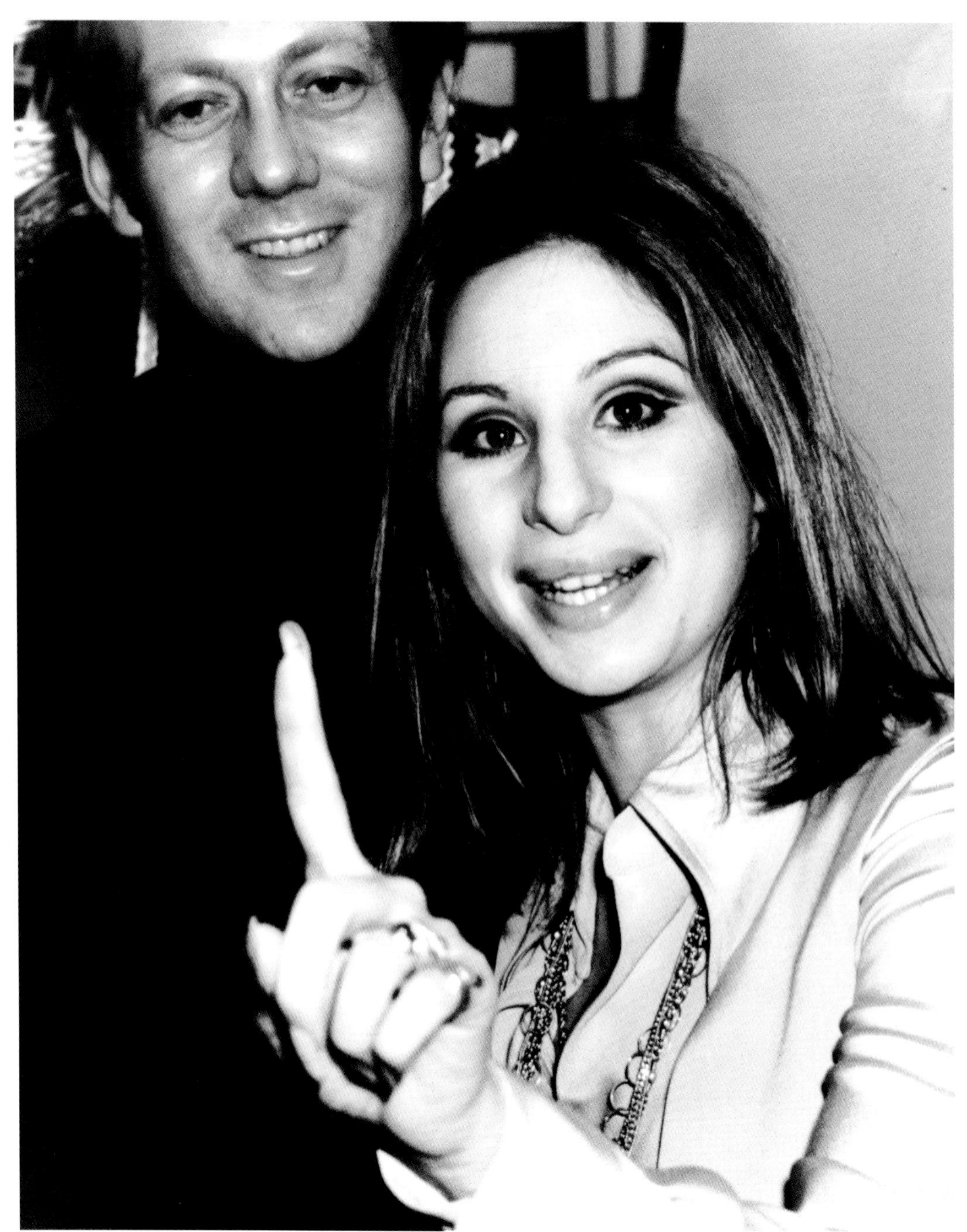

BARBRA STREISAND
June 1, 1969 – New York City
At Boutique Shop on 61st Street

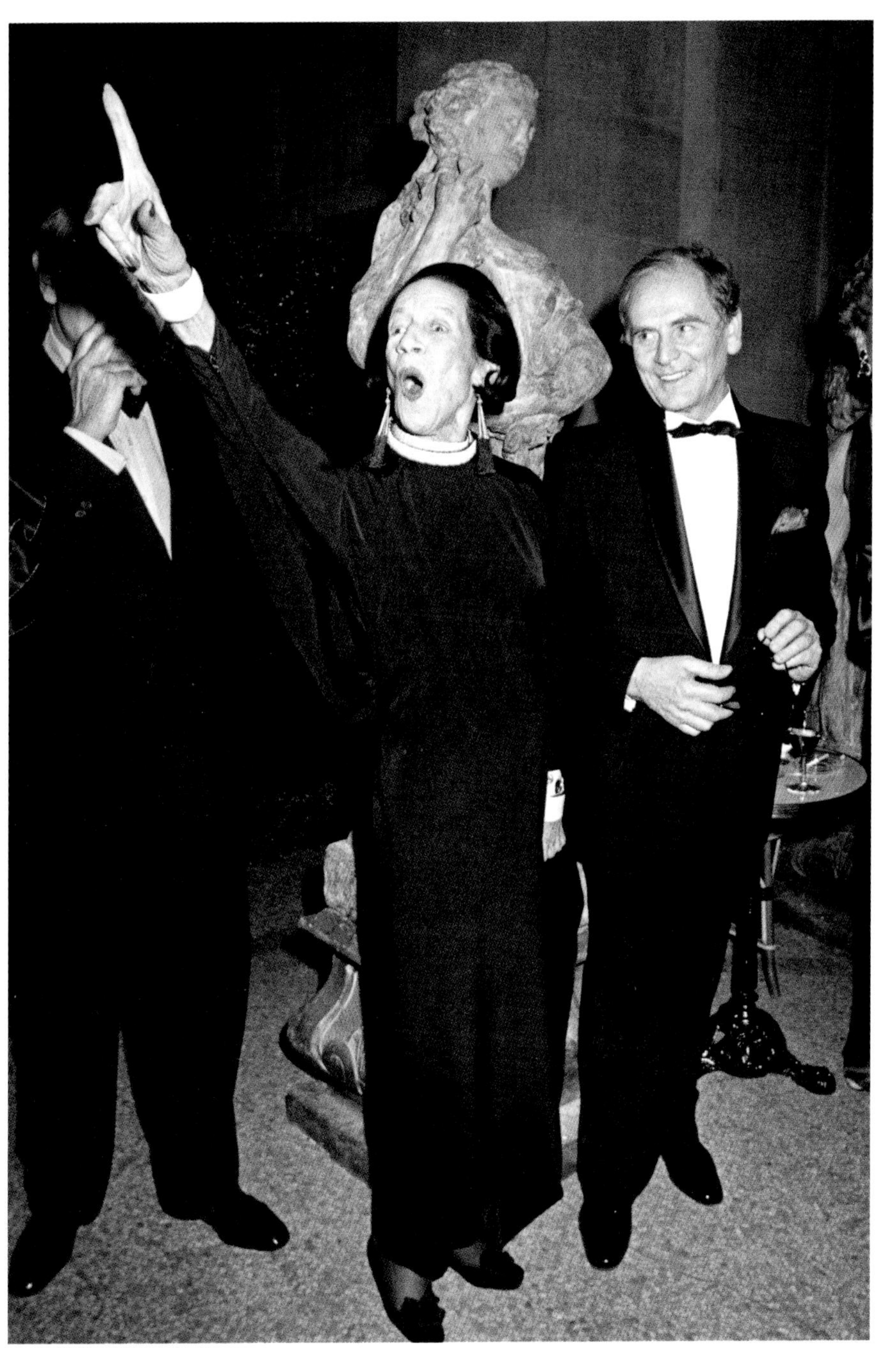

DIANA VREELAND & PIERRE CARDIN
December 6, 1982 – New York City
The Metropolitan Museum of Art Costume Institute Exhibition "La Belle Epoque"
at The Metropolitan Museum of Art

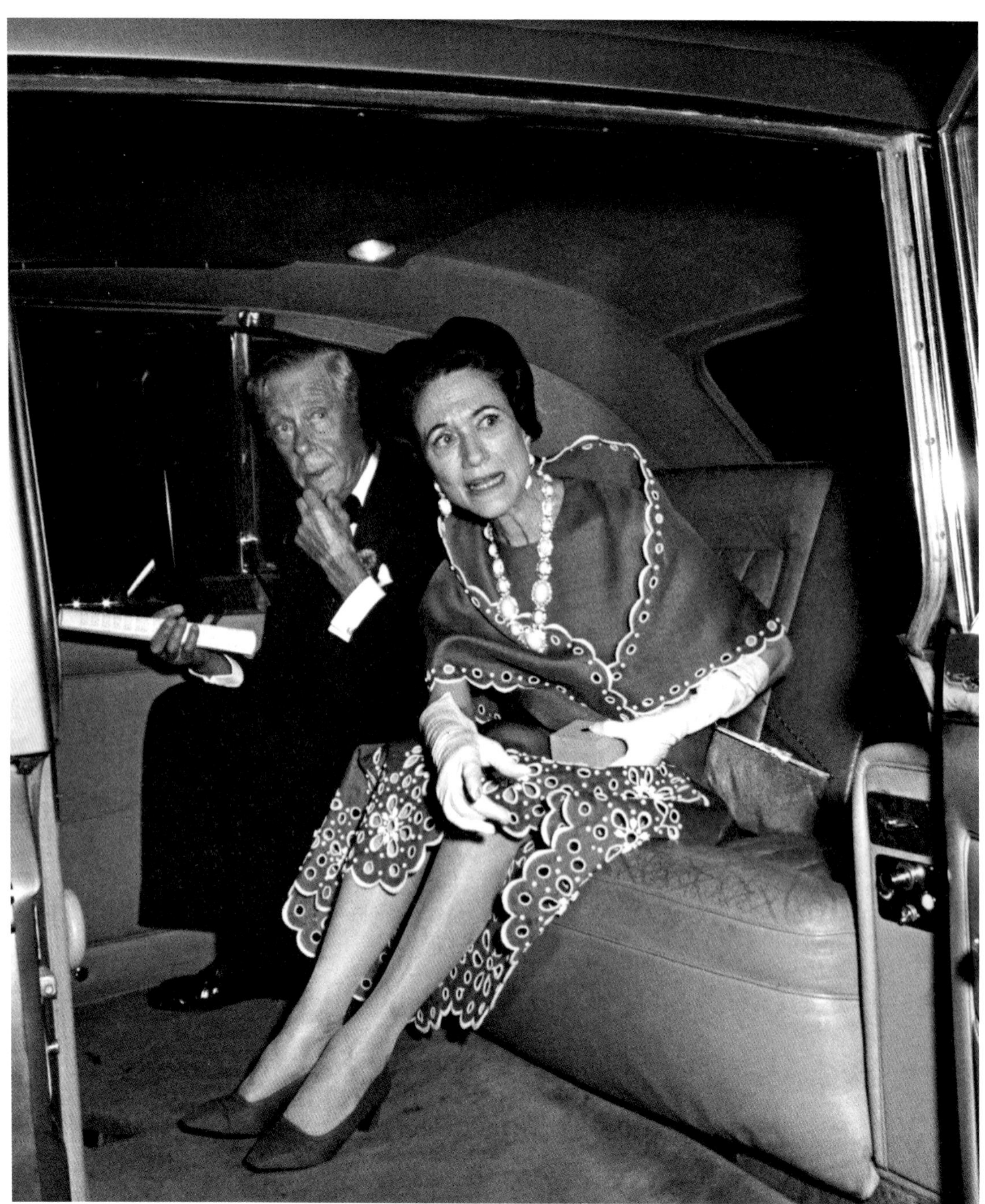

EDWARD VIII & WALLIS SIMPSON
DUKE & DUCHESS OF WINDSOR
May 21, 1968 – New York City
Wildenstein Gallery Opening

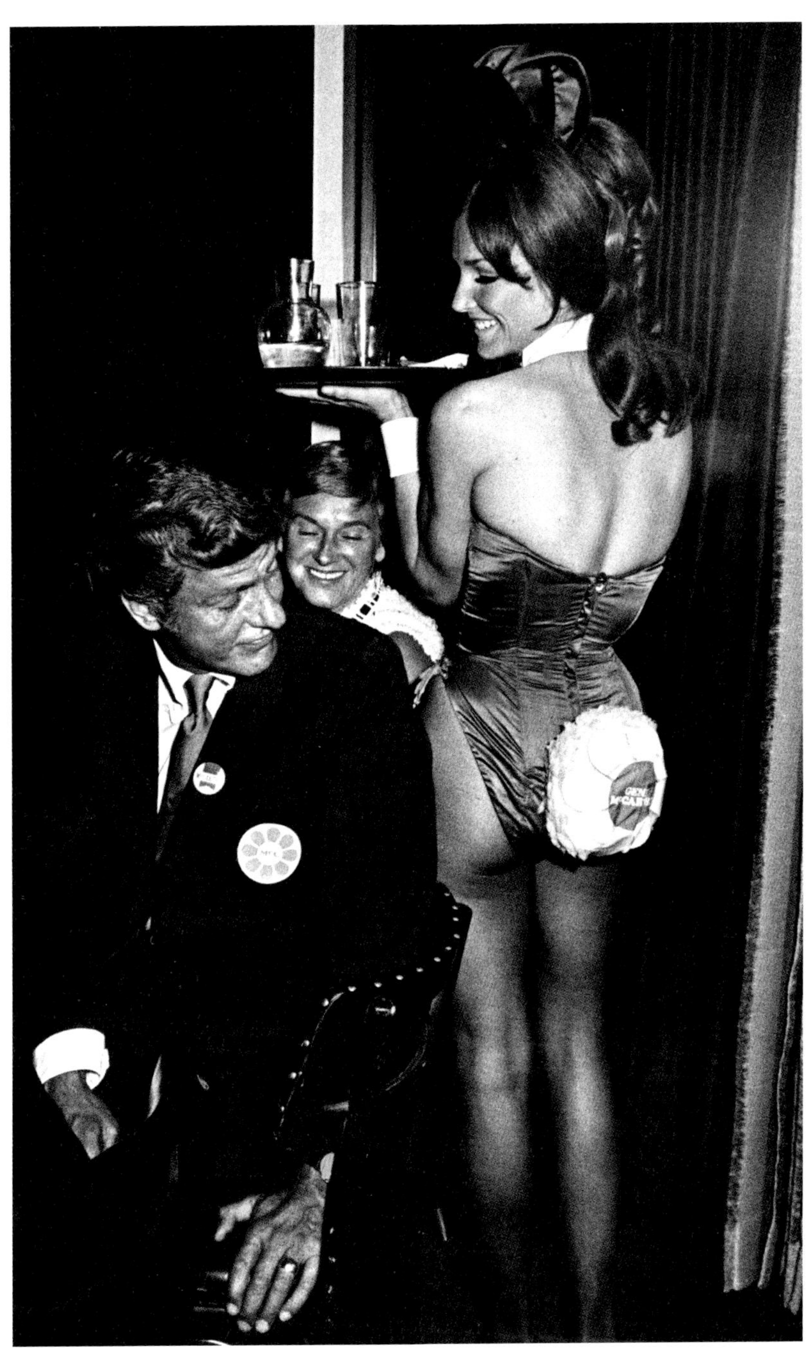

DICK VAN DYKE

June 2, 1968 – Beverly Hills, California

Eugene McCarthy Political Fundraising Party at the Playboy Club

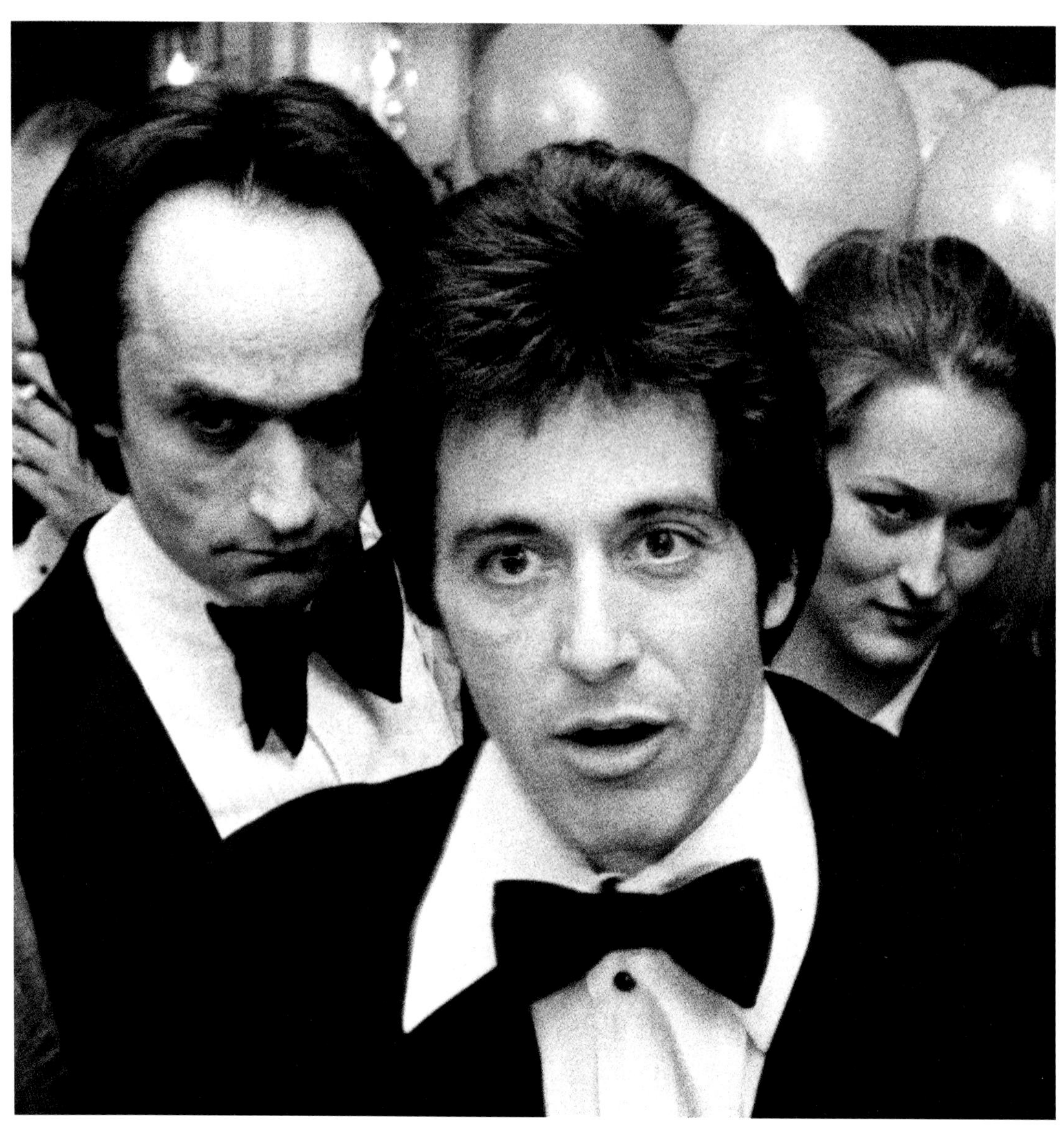

(L-R) JOHN CAZALE, AL PACINO & MERYL STREEP
November 19, 1976 – New York City
75th Birthday Party for Lee Strasberg at the Pierre Hotel

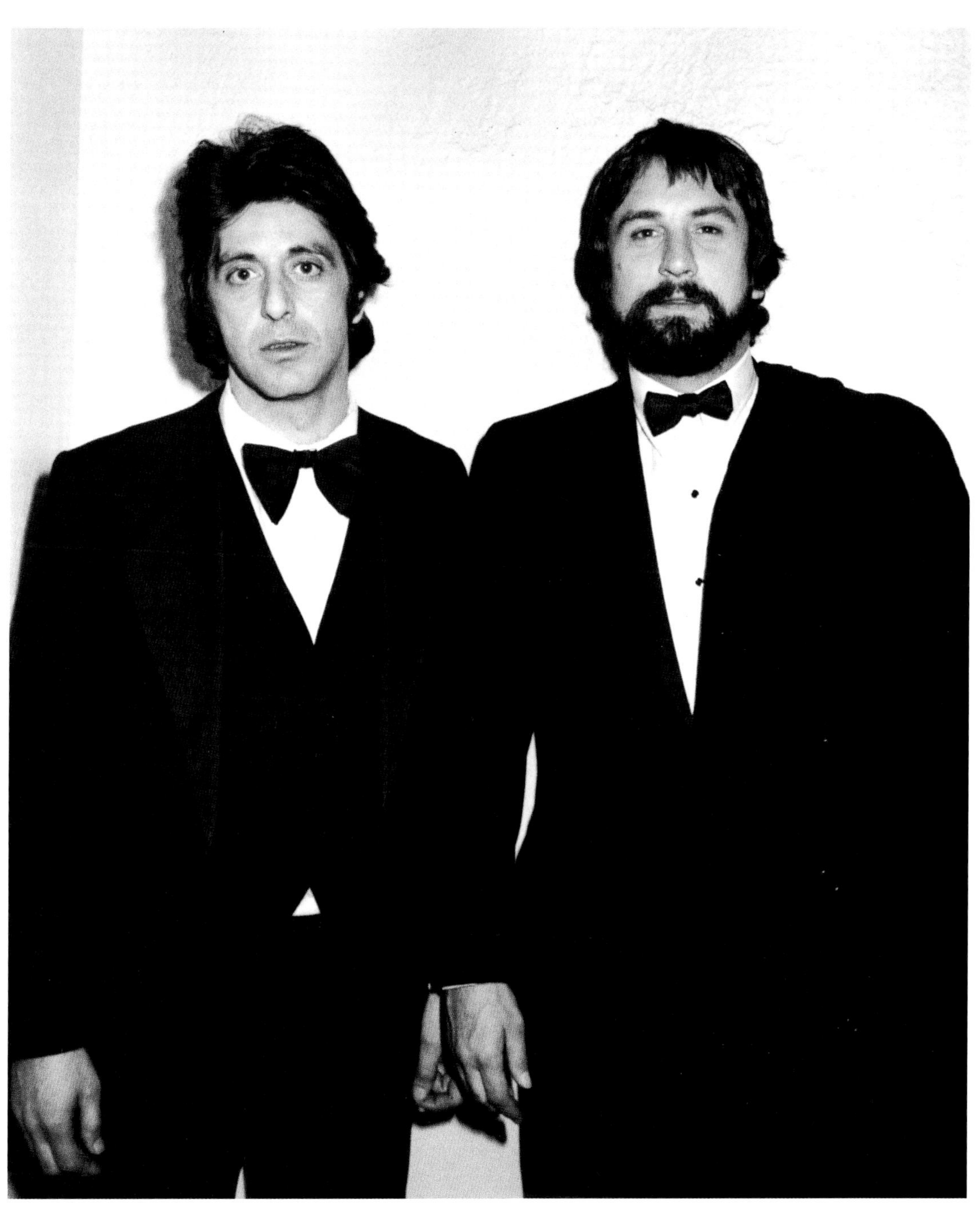

AL PACINO & ROBERT DE NIRO
February 14, 1982 – New York City
Night of 100 Stars Gala at Radio City Music Hall

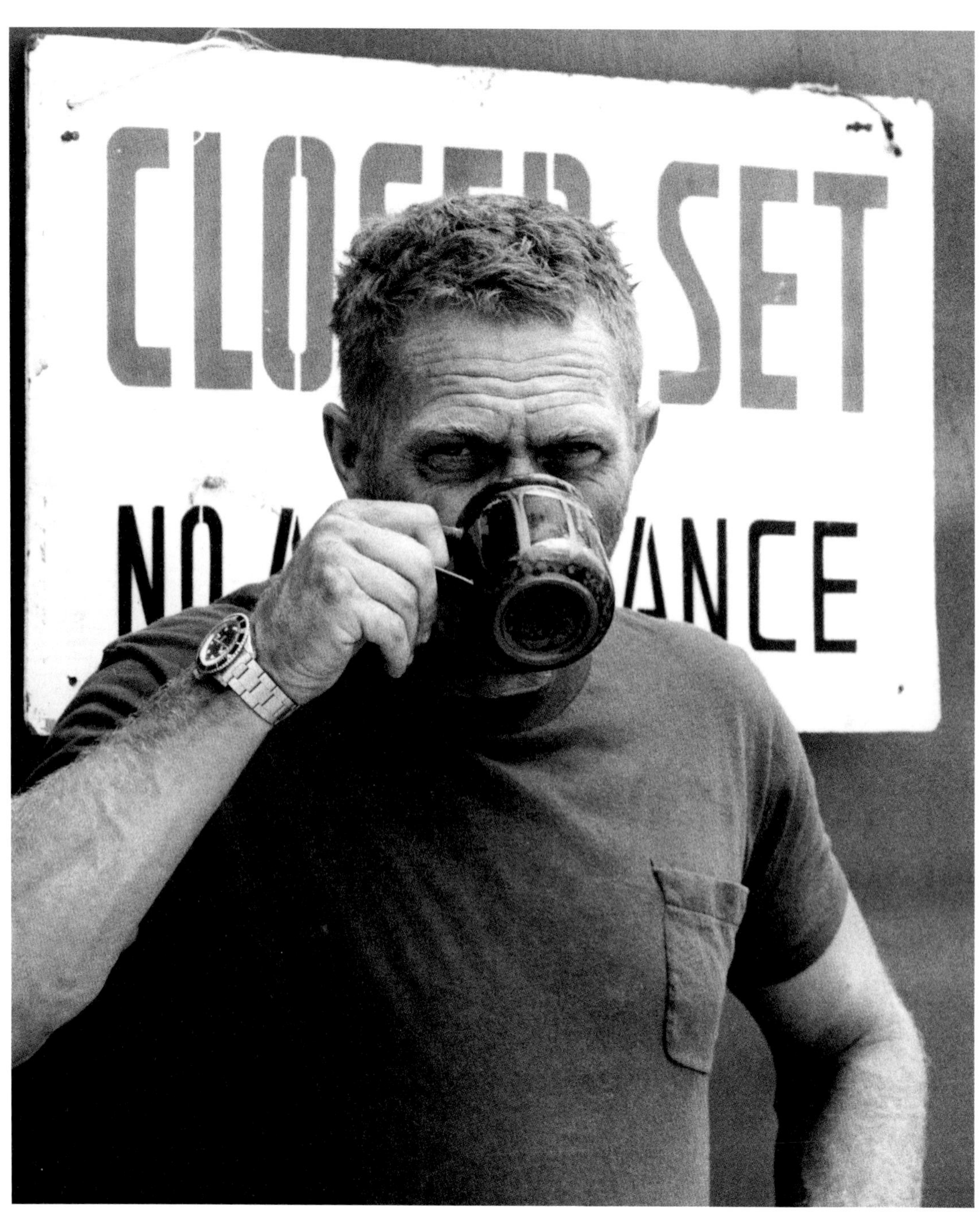

STEVE McQUEEN
April 15, 1973 – Montego Bay, Jamaica
On Location Filming "Papillon"

STEVE McQUEEN

Whenever I photographed Ali MacGraw, she was always friendly. So in 1971 I decided to drop off a package of photographs to her at her home in Malibu Beach, California. In July of that same year, I received a handwritten response from Ali thanking me for the "marvelous photographs." In my note attached to the photographs, I asked for a sitting and Ali responded that she would not be available until her next film. During this time she was married to producer Bob Evans and they had a newborn son, Joshua.

In 1972, Ali accepted a co-starring role in the film "The Getaway" alongside "the king of cool," actor Steve McQueen. This role proved to be a pivotal move for her. While filming the movie, and even though she was still married to Bob Evans, she and McQueen fell madly in love.

In April 1973, John Durniak, the photo editor of *Time Magazine*, invited me to lecture at the Wilson Hicks International Conference on Visual Communication in Miami, Florida. My topic was "Photography with the Paparazzi Approach," which included a slideshow. I was in good company as Eddie Adams, Arthur Rothstein, Larry Schiller, and other notable photographers agreed to host lectures.

To promote the lectures, writer Patricia Burstein interviewed me for a piece in the *Miami Herald* and coined the phrase that was also the article's title, "Paparazzo Superstar!". Patricia asked me, "What's next?" and recorded my response thusly: "His next stop is Jamaica. Galella read in *Show Magazine* that MacGraw and McQueen, currently romantically linked, are making a movie there. 'It's a gamble,' he says, 'even though Ali knows and likes me. I've got to watch out for McQueen, he's kind of touchy.' But first Ron will give his lecture at Wilson Hicks."

Due to the complexity of Ali's situation, a photo of her and Steve together was considered "hot" by newspapers and magazines worldwide and I planned on getting the exclusive shots! As soon as I arrived in Jamaica and knowing all the location filming was complete, I found my way to the Papillon studio gates. I addressed a handwritten note on my "Photography with the Paparazzi Approach" letterhead and sent it with a copy of the *Miami Herald* article to Ali, requesting a picture of her with Steve at the gate of the studio. Steve, not Ali, came to the gate and declared there would be no interviews and no visitors.

Being streetwise, he threatened to send his posse of friends after me if I did not leave. "I want you out on the next plane!" Steve shouted. I did not want to go home without any photos, so I asked for a fifteen-minute photo-op of him ALONE and then I would leave. He agreed only after I signed an agreement, and stated, "I'll give you 15 minutes of me provided you leave on the next plane out of Jamaica." I signed and had him pose in front of a Closed Set – No Admittance sign.

During the shoot, McQueen spoke quite candidly: "You got a tough job. To be quite frank, I don't like your job." McQueen then added, "You must play it straight, get 'Paparazzi' off your letterhead and business card – it's a bad word." I said, "I do not agree." For me, the word "paparazzi" demands respect for truth and realism. (Although in 1992, when I moved to Montville, NJ, I took McQueen's advice and removed the word "Paparazzi" from my letterhead and replaced it with "superstar.")

Then, to my surprise, McQueen mentioned Jackie: "You f*cked up with Jackie. Do you know why children of stars should not be photographed?" I replied, "Because of crackpots." McQueen came back with, "Because of blackmail, or kidnappers can force children into a life of prostitution." He also spoke of Ali as his fiancée. In August of the same year, they were married, and the union ended five years later.

Even though I did not get the pictures I sought, I did not give up and did not leave empty-handed. The photos I shot that day have become some of my most popular, iconic shots. To this day, this take is sold repeatedly through my fine art gallery representation worldwide.

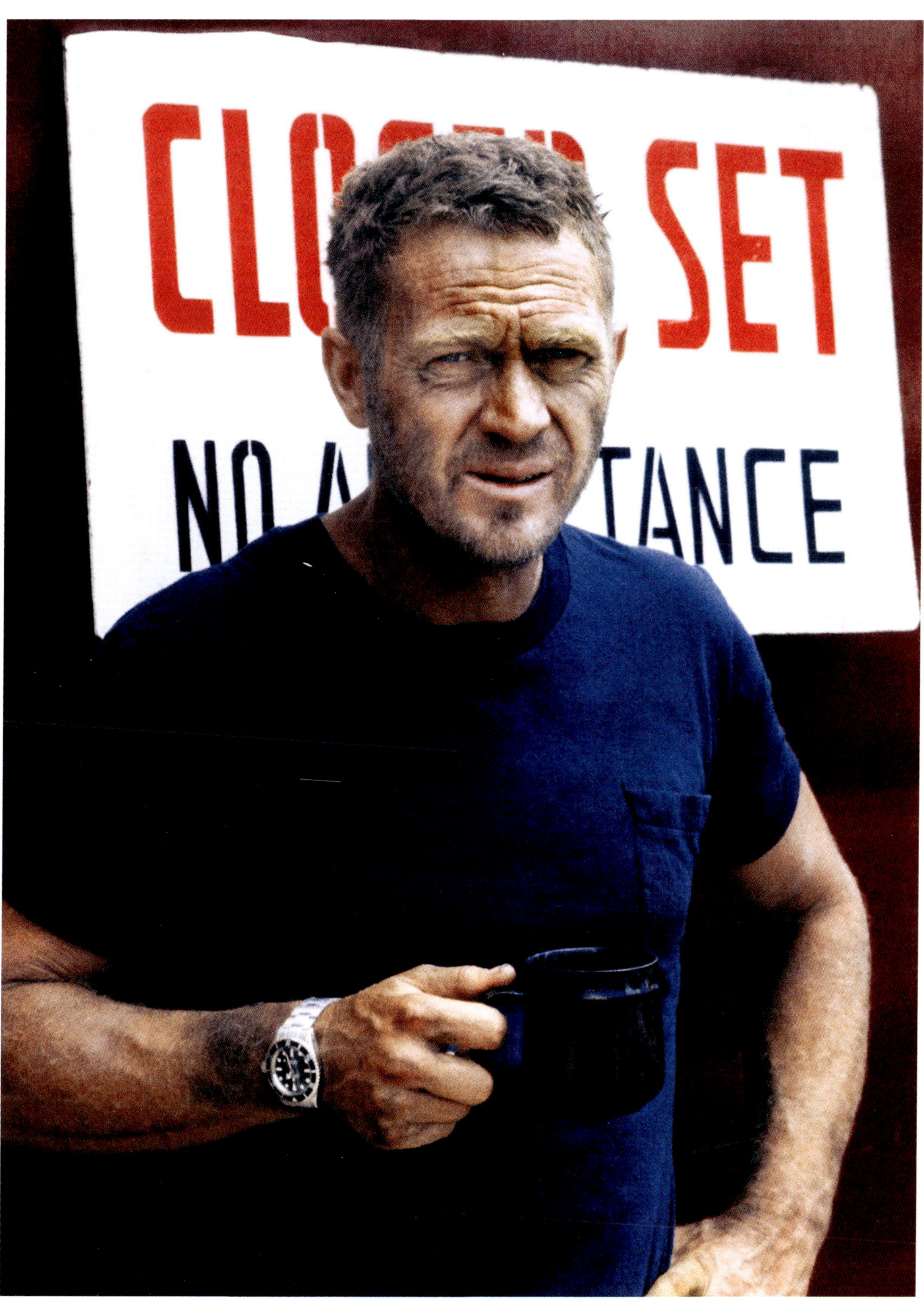
CLO SET
NO A TANCE

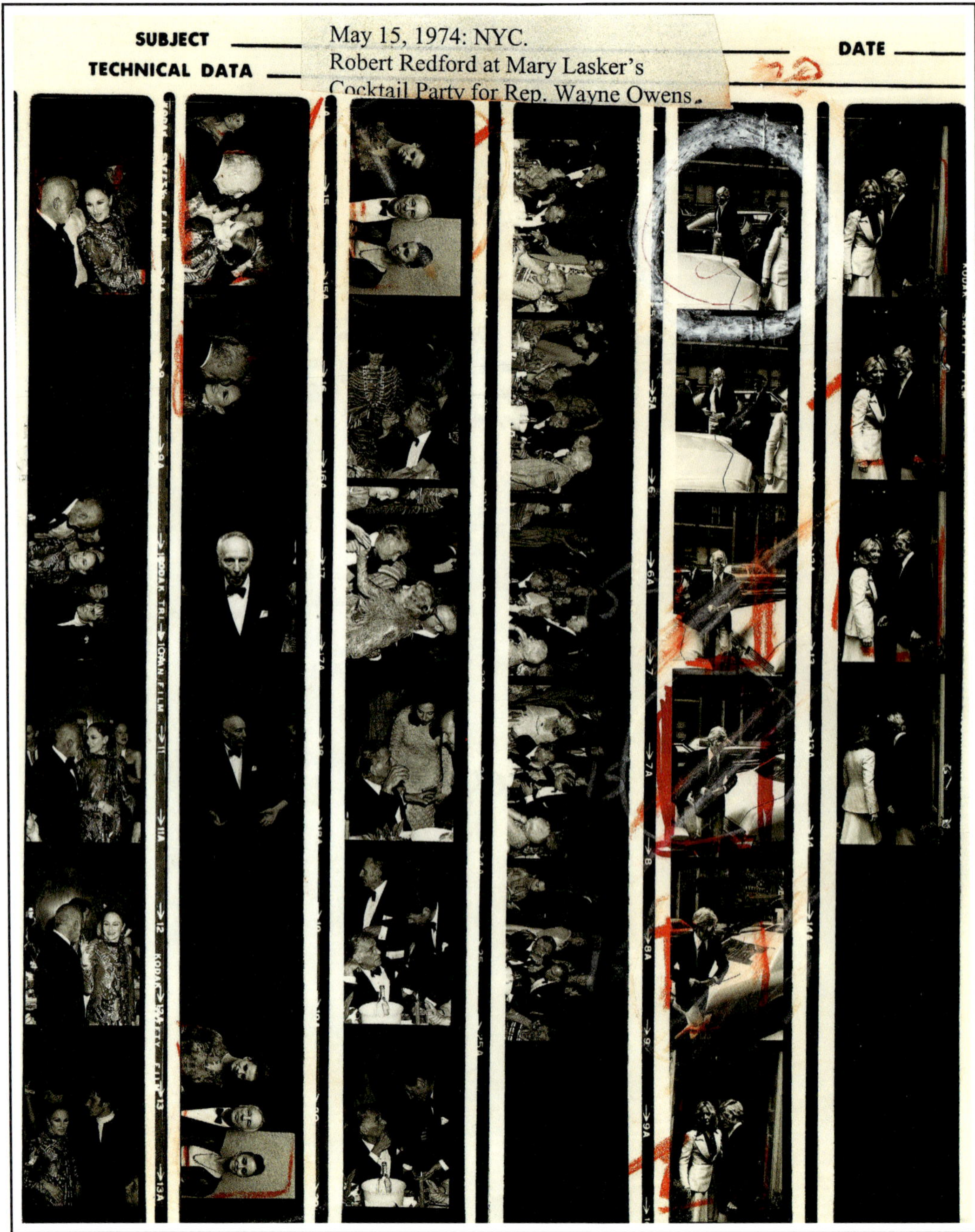
SUBJECT
TECHNICAL DATA
DATE
May 15, 1974: NYC.
Robert Redford at Mary Lasker's
Cocktail Party for Rep. Wayne Owens.

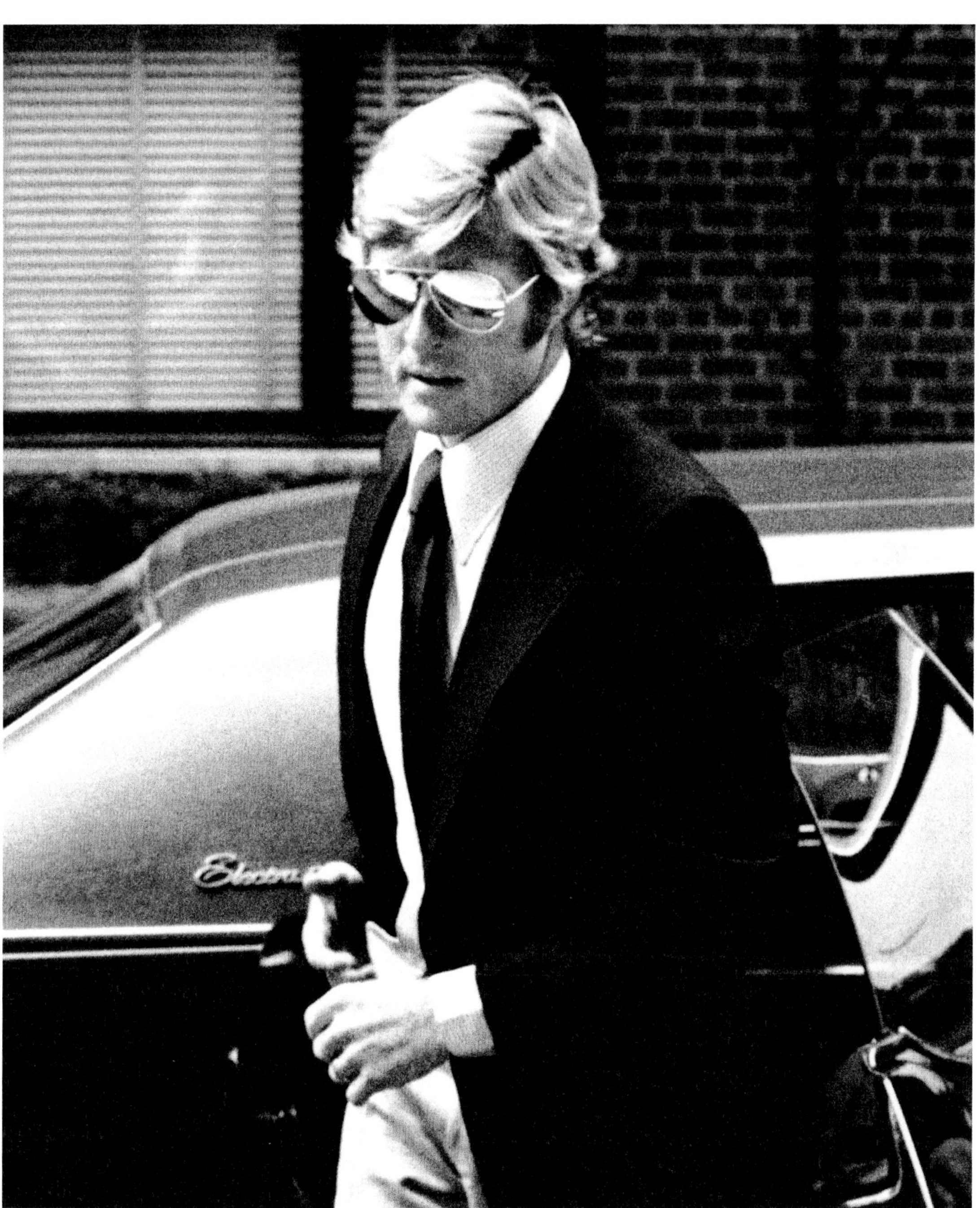

ROBERT REDFORD
May 15, 1974 – New York City
Mary Lasker's Party For Wayne Owens at her home

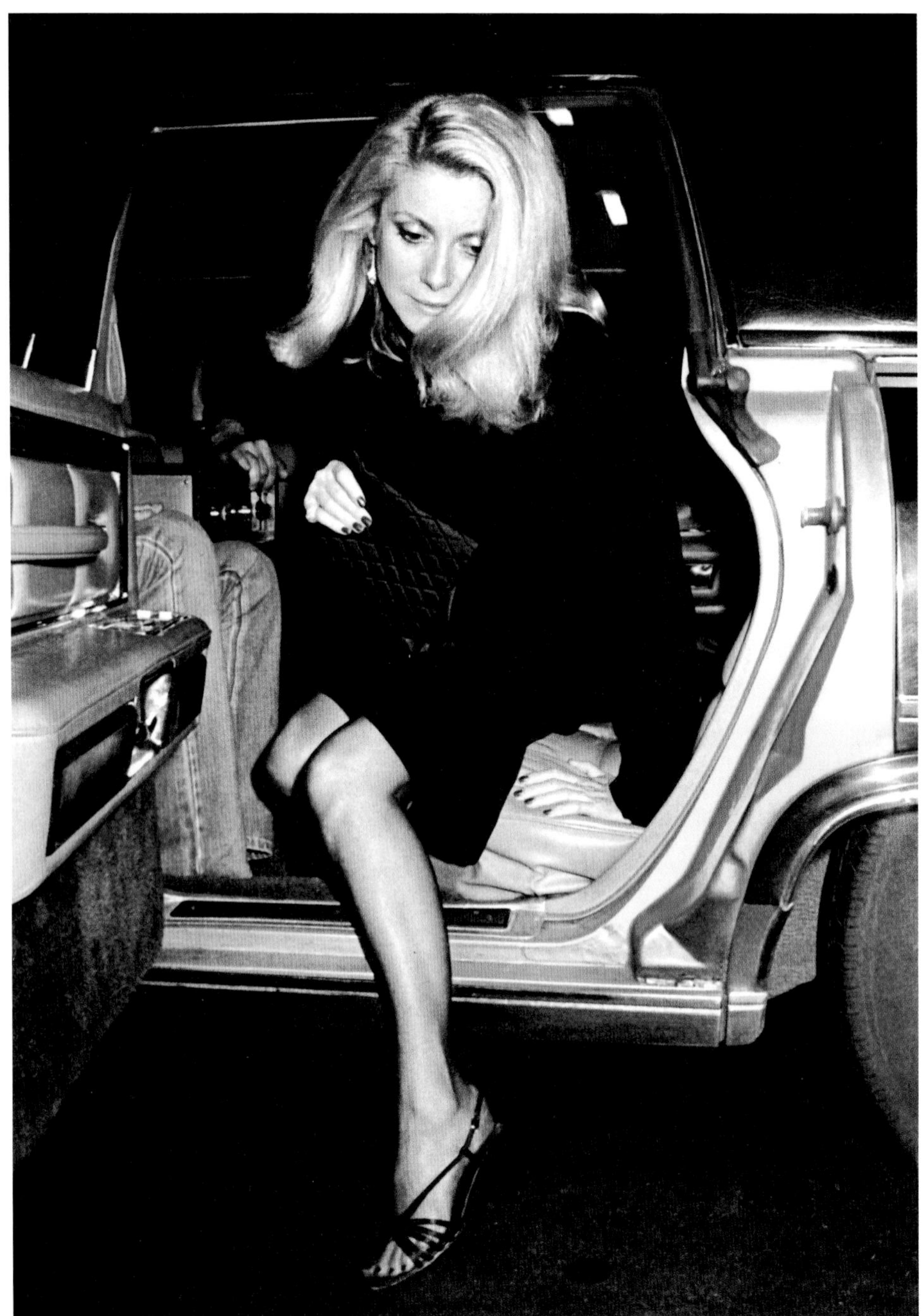

CATHERINE DENEUVE
October 12, 1980 – New York City
"The Last Metro" Premiere Party at the Rock Lounge

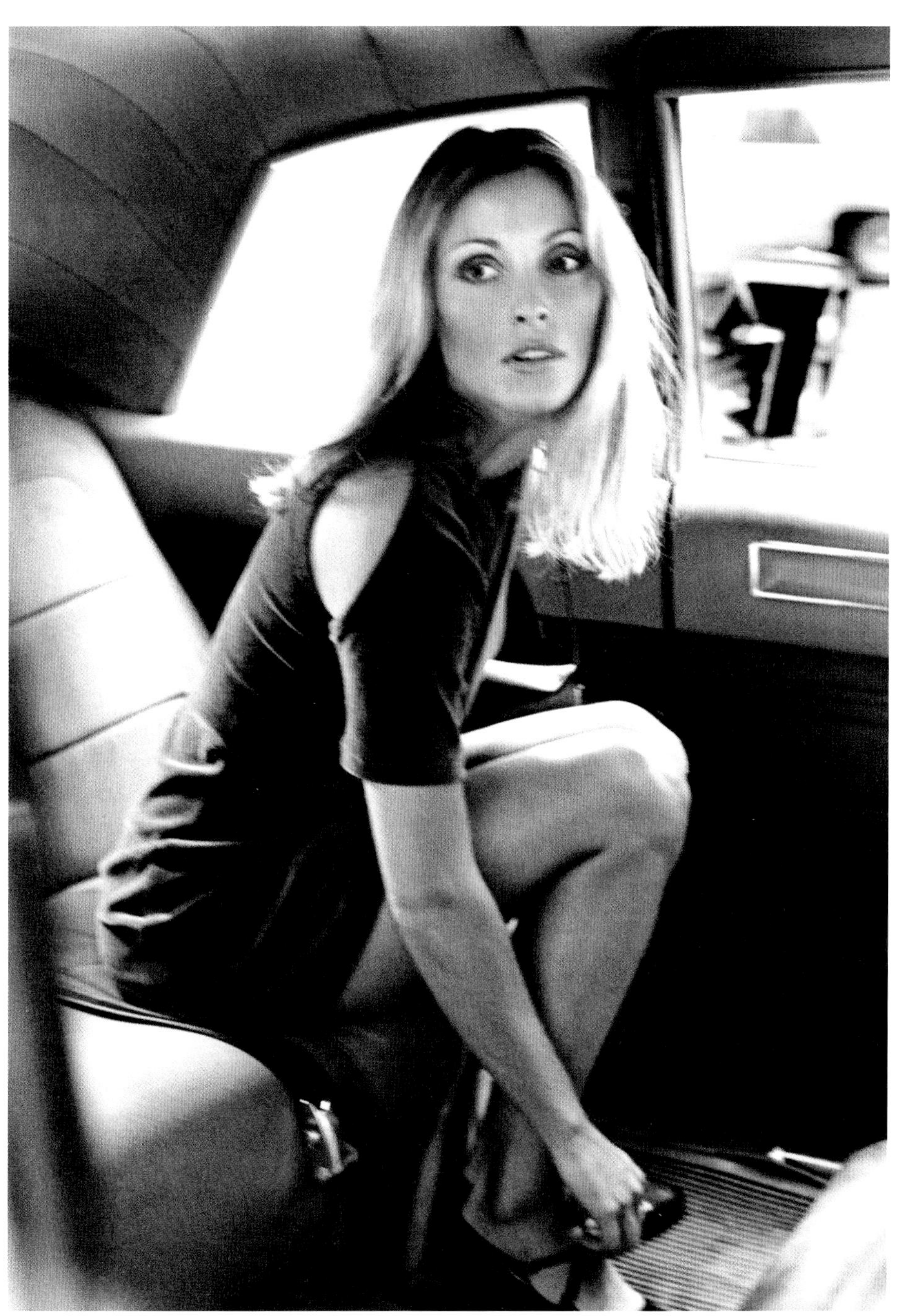

SHARON TATE
August 27, 1967 – New York City
On Location Filming "Rosemary's Baby"

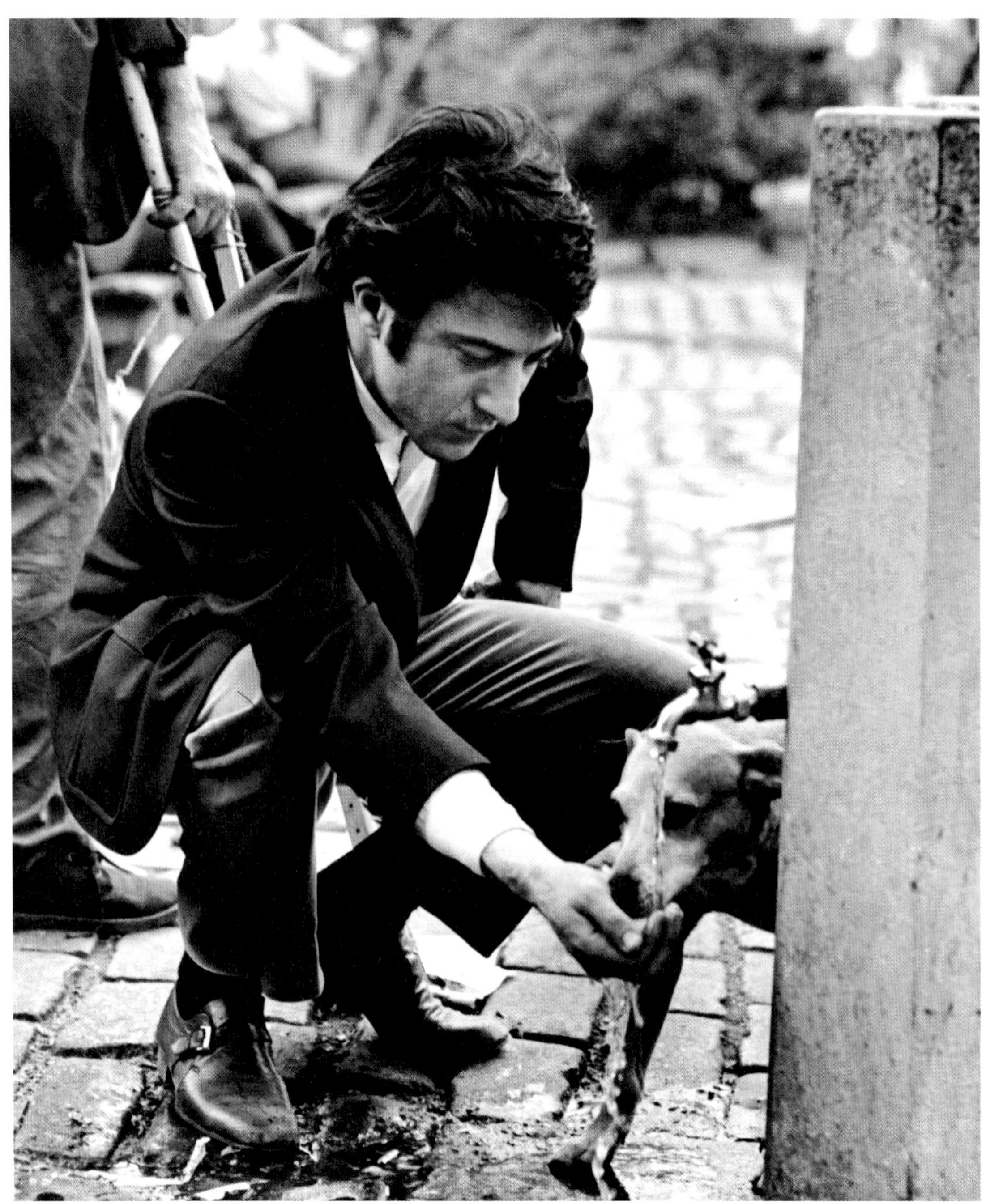

DUSTIN HOFFMAN
June 1, 1969 – New York City
Central Park

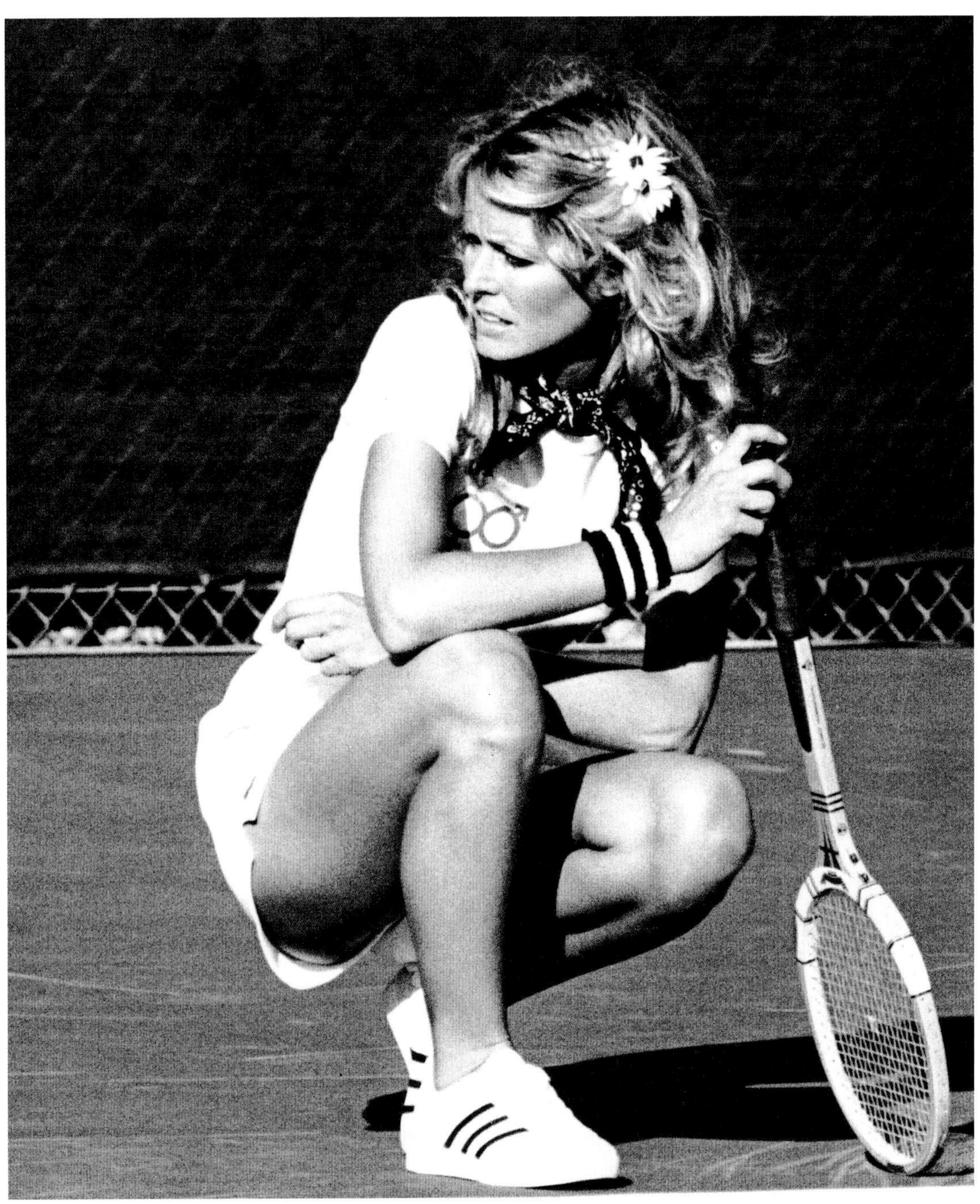

FARRAH FAWCETT
August 3, 1977 – Mission Viejo, California
Celebrity Battle Of The Sexes at Marguerite Park

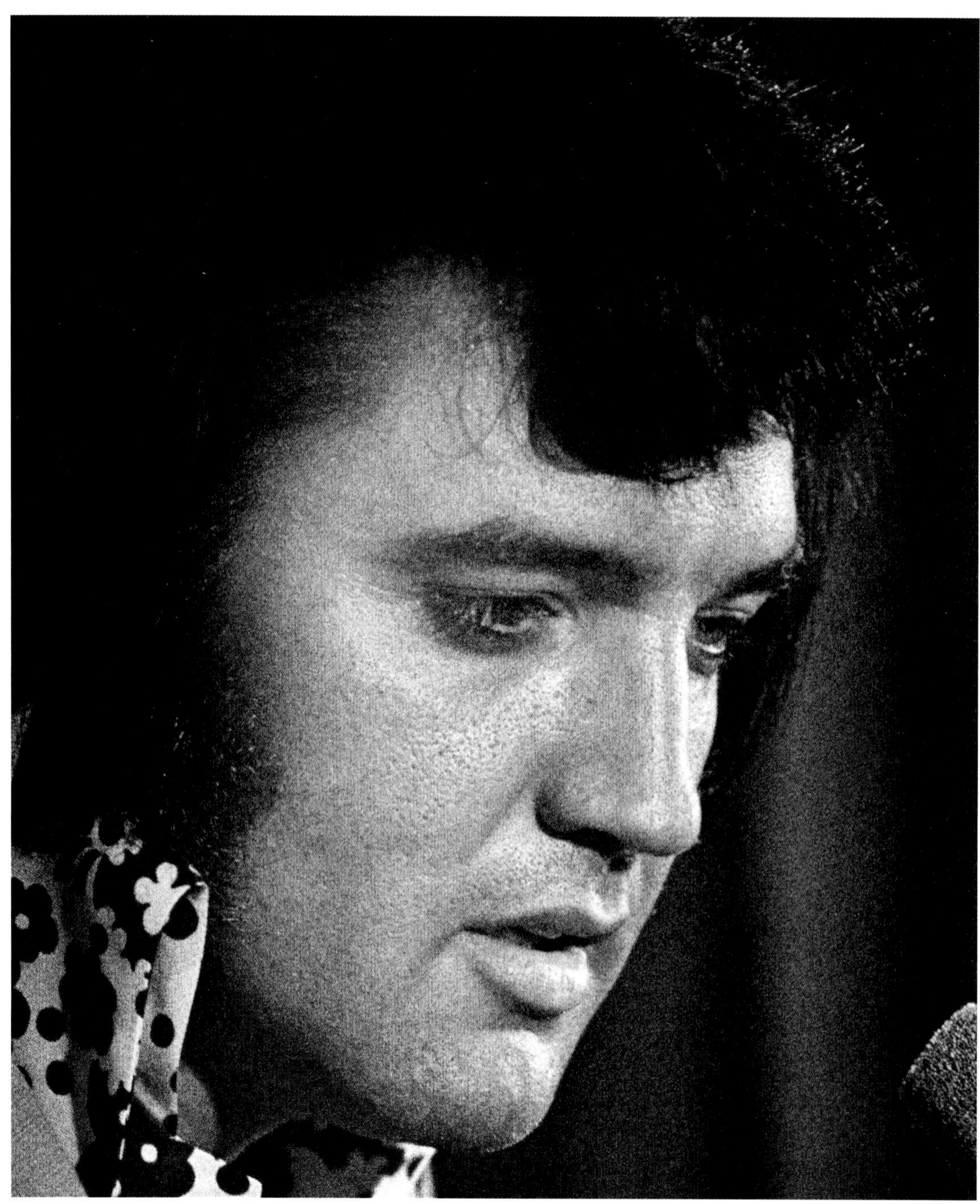

ELVIS PRESLEY
June 9, 1972 – New York City
Elvis Presley Press Conference at the New York Hilton Hotel

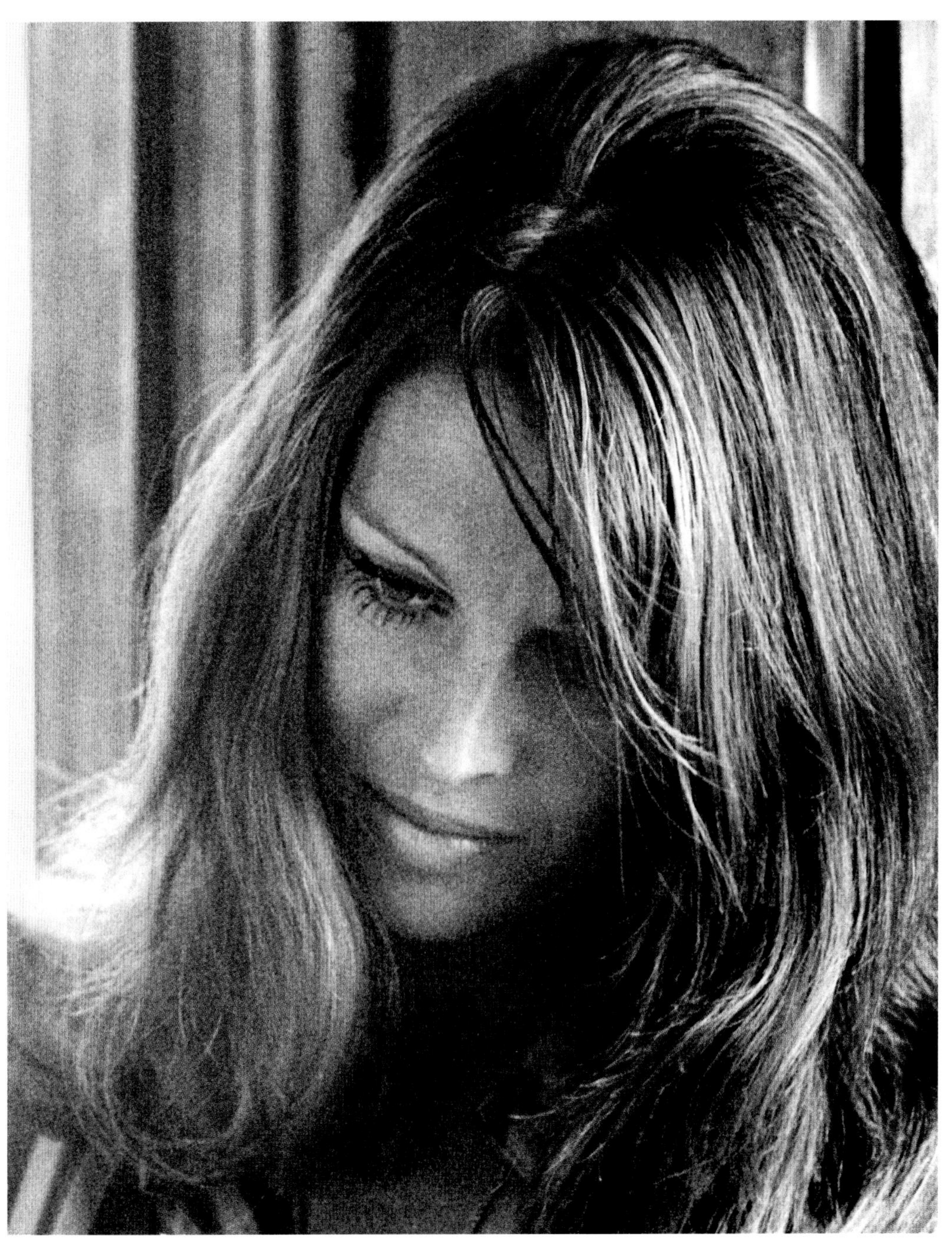

JULIE CHRISTIE
September 13, 1968 – Lake Geneva, Switzerland
On Location Filming "In Search of Gregory"

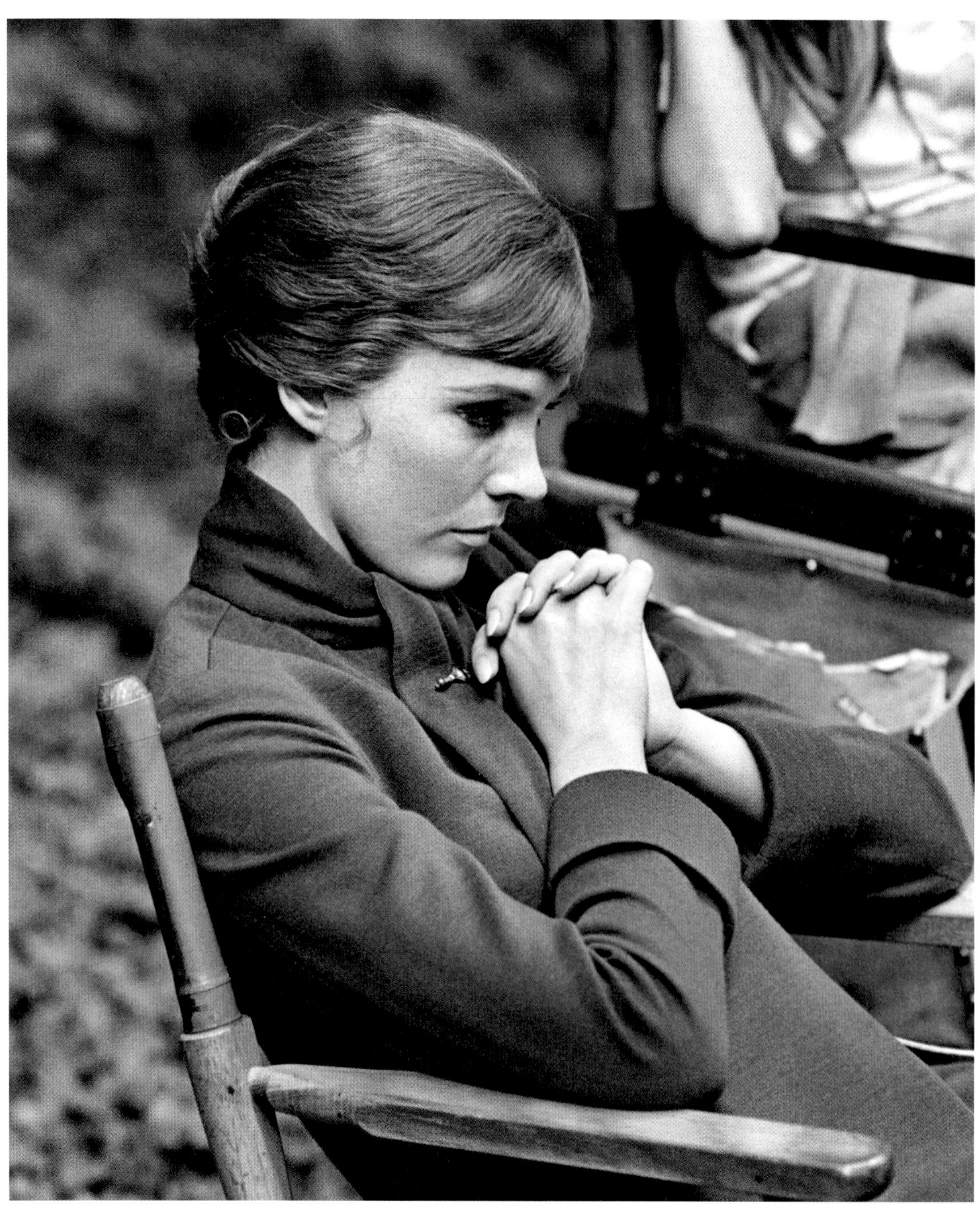

JULIE ANDREWS
September 27, 1968 – Paris, France
On Location Filming "Darling Lili"

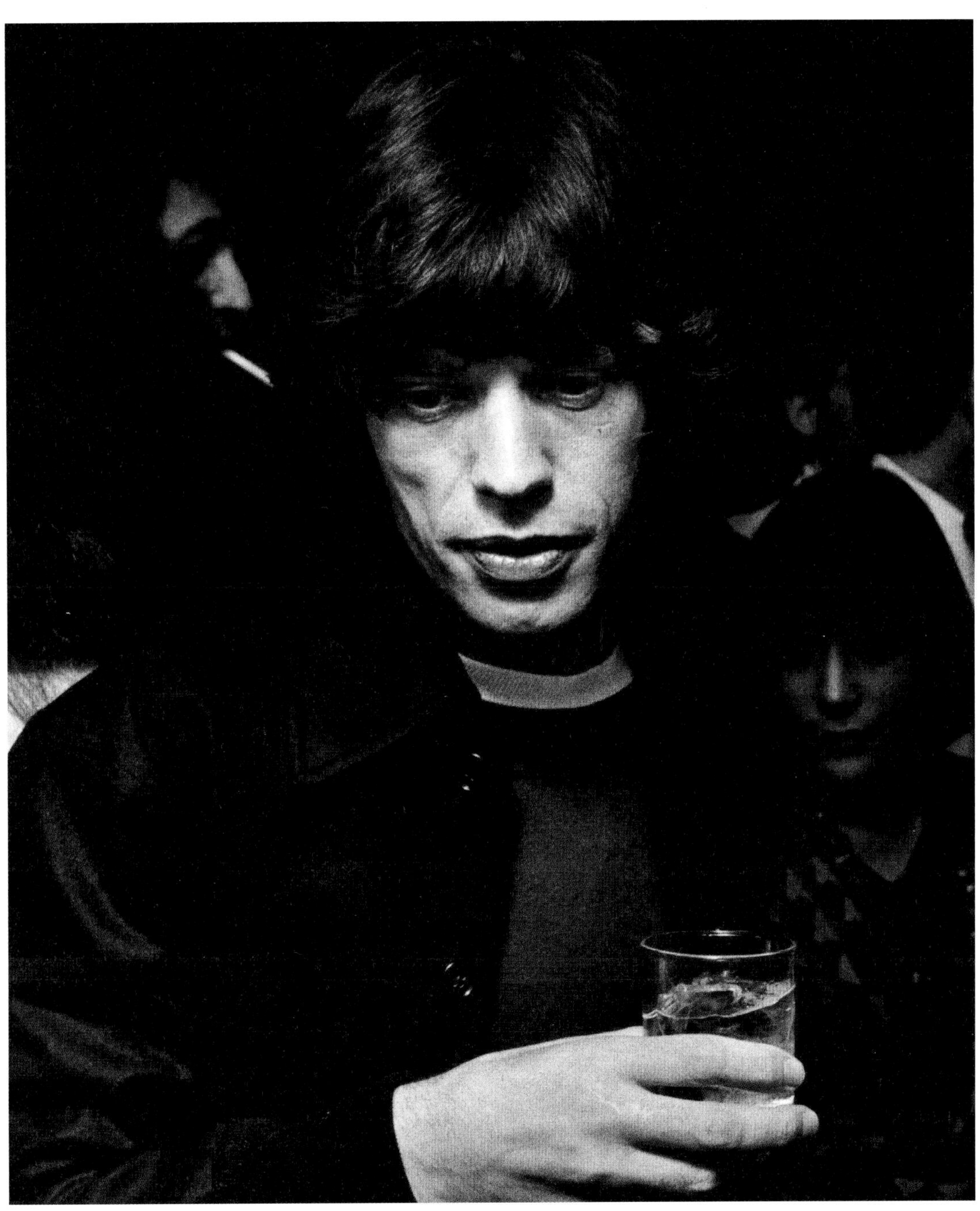

MICK JAGGER
April 23, 1973 – New York City
After Dark Annual Ruby Awards at Casino Russe - Delmonico Hotel

60 **JOHN LENNON & MICK JAGGER (with MAY PANG)**

March 13, 1974 – Los Angeles, California
2nd Annual American Film Institute Lifetime Achievement Awards Honoring James Cagney at the Century Plaza Hotel

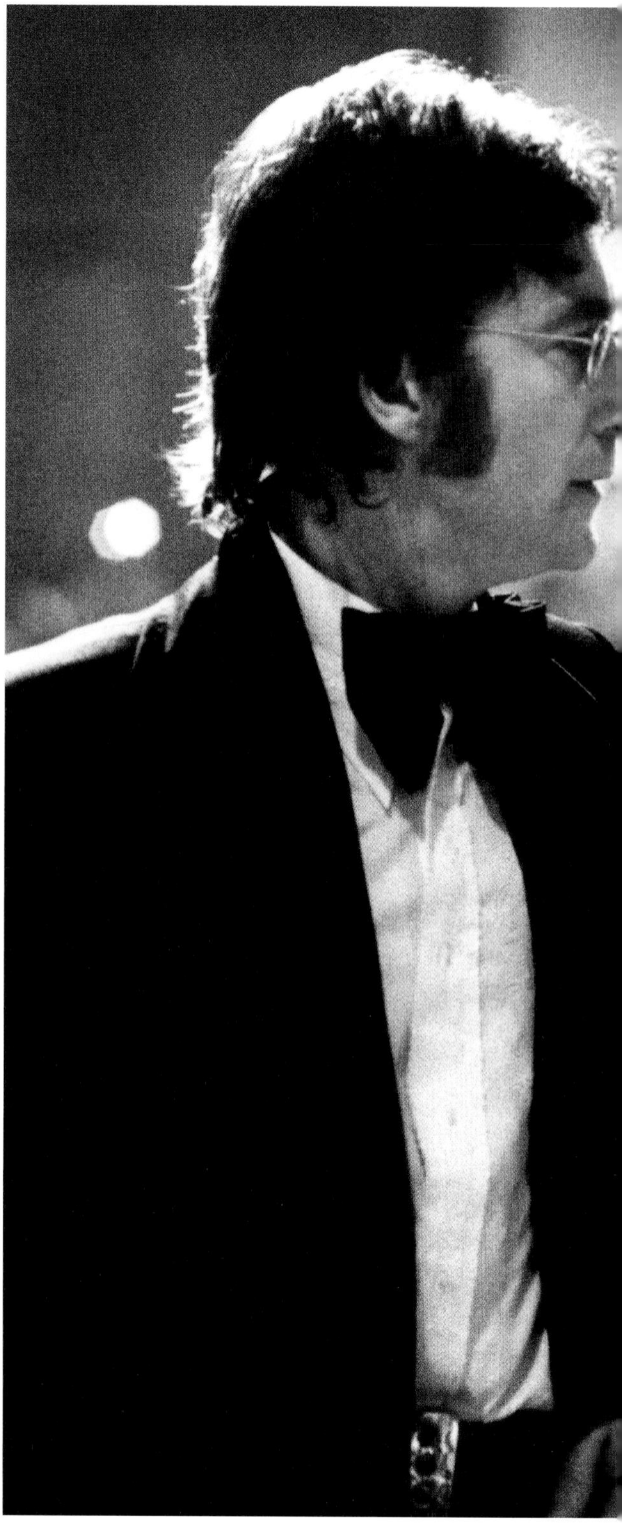

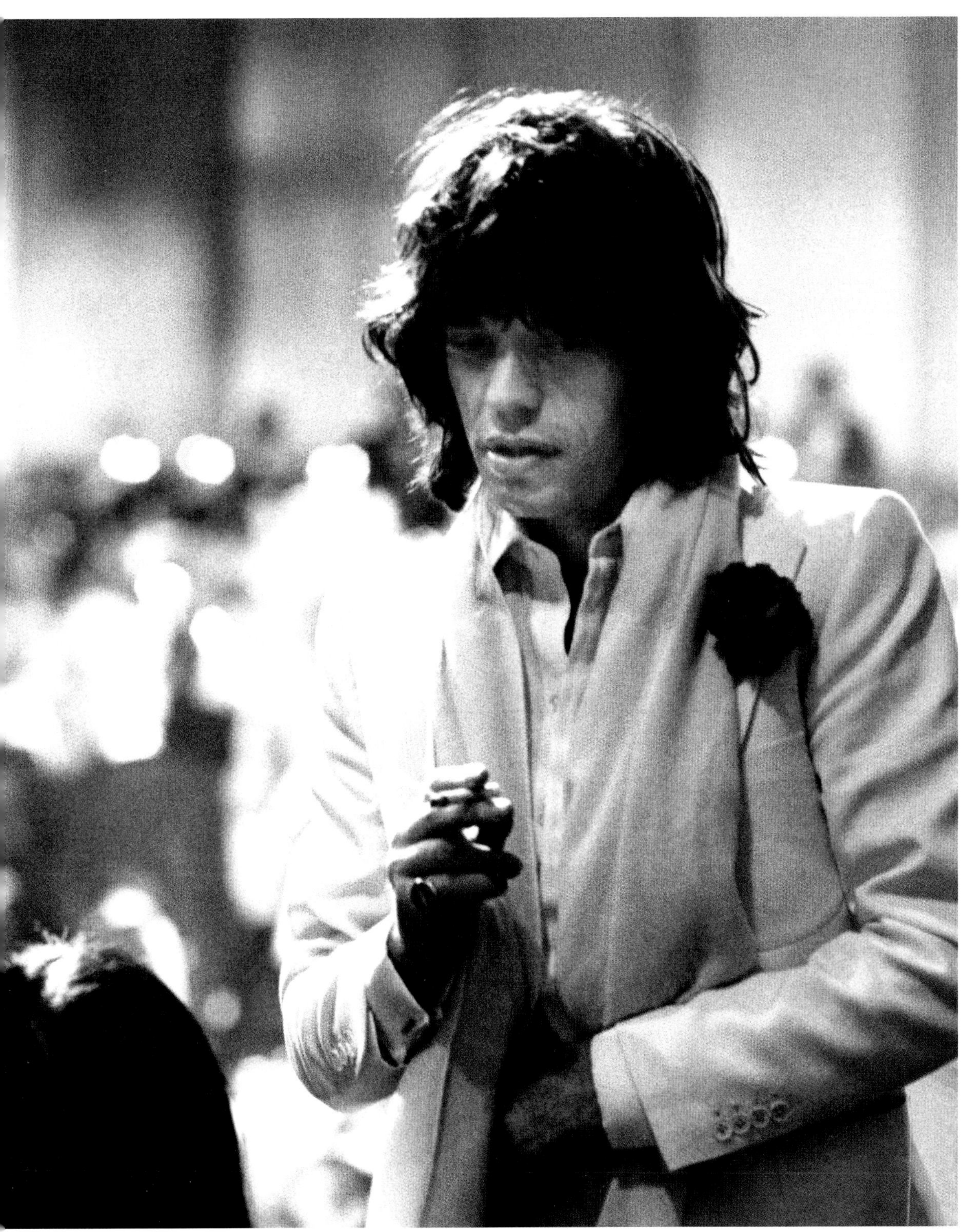

LAST FRAME

My top two selling photographs - John Lennon & Mick Jagger, (previous pages) and Windblown Jackie - have one thing in common, none of the subjects knew they were being photographed.

The unguarded moment between two popular music icons caught in conversation, bathed in soft, diffused light was captured using a 300mm lens. Mick, wearing a white tuxedo jacket, white scarf and a boutonnière in his lapel pocket; (he had shed his black and white tie and unbuttoned his top shirt button earlier) looking slightly down, and John, in a black tuxedo, looking at him in profile. John's date, May Pang, is obscured with her back to the camera.

It's a great photo because our eyes prefer to go to one subject. In this case John looks at Mick who is the focal point, it's a bull's-eye effect. Mick is the hero. John looking at Mick makes Mick more important.

It was a big night. Cagney drew the biggest amount of celebrities; there were so many stars. I covered that event for many years and I never saw so many big names come out for one star. Guests included John Wayne, Charlton Heston, Paul Newman, Kirk Douglas, Doris Day, Clint Eastwood, Bob Hope, Governor Ronald Reagan, Jimmy Stewart, Billy Wilder, Sam Peckinpah, Loretta Young, Gene Kelly, Natalie Wood with Robert Wagner, Barbara Stanwyck, and Shirley MacLaine.

Dressed in a tuxedo, I crashed the event after shooting arrivals and gained access to the ballroom through the kitchen. After dinner, Jagger, who had been sitting with Ali MacGraw and Steve McQueen, came over to Lennon's table to greet him. That's how they were talking and that's how I got the picture using my 300mm lens. I was also lucky because CBS TV network lit the ballroom for the prime-time TV special, which aired five days later. The back lighting was tremendous and that added to the picture. I didn't have to use a strobe because the lighting was great. I later shot with the strobe and a 85mm lens with color film but it's the diffused, backlit image of two old friends caught in that particular moment in time that is so iconic and meaningful.

Later I found out that a jealous photographer told security that I crashed the event, but AFI founder, and the event producer, George Stevens, Jr., intervened on my behalf and told them it was OK for me to stay to cover the event. I believe George allowed me to stay because I had gotten photos of other AFI events published in many publications including *Time* and *Newsweek.*

Nostalgia is one way to explain the popularity of the image.

Everybody likes the past when there were great stars. Today you don't have those great stars. Also the public reacts to the image because of the tragic way John Lennon died.

John and May Pang later split up and the former Beatle went back to Yoko Ono. Their son Sean was born the following year, in October 1975.

This iconic image was shot on the final frame of Tri-X film roll. It may also be the last professional photograph taken of the two music legends together.

That night I was lucky, thanks to George Stevens, Jr.!

THE NIGHT I SAW STARS

by May Pang

I remember that night like the back of my hand! John and I were both big fans of Hollywood; he actually grew up on Americana. We jumped at the chance to dress to the nines and attend the AFI Dinner to honor James Cagney. We soon found ourselves surrounded by the Hollywood elite - Cary Grant, Bob Hope, John Wayne, Steve McQueen, Kirk Douglas, Gov. Ronald Reagan even Mae West. Doris Day, who John loved, was also there. Frank Sinatra, Old Blue Eyes, was the emcee. John was amazed, as was I. We sat at a table with George Burns, whom we had bumped into two other times in the last week, and he quipped, "May, we gotta stop meeting like this or else they'll start talking about us."

As much as John was in awe of them, they were in awe of him. It was surreal as these bigger-than-life icons of the silver screen were coming over to talk with us. During one of the intermissions, Mick Jagger (who also loved the glamour of Hollywood) spotted us in the crowd and came over to our table to say hello. As they chatted, unbeknownst to us, Ron Galella was taking snaps.

As the photos began to appear in the press, John and I were surprised to see them as we didn't see him taking them. John said, "With all that Hollywood royalty, why would anyone take pictures of me?" When he learned these were taken by Ron Galella, the King of Paparazzi, John's expression went from surprised to impressed.

May Pang

August 2021

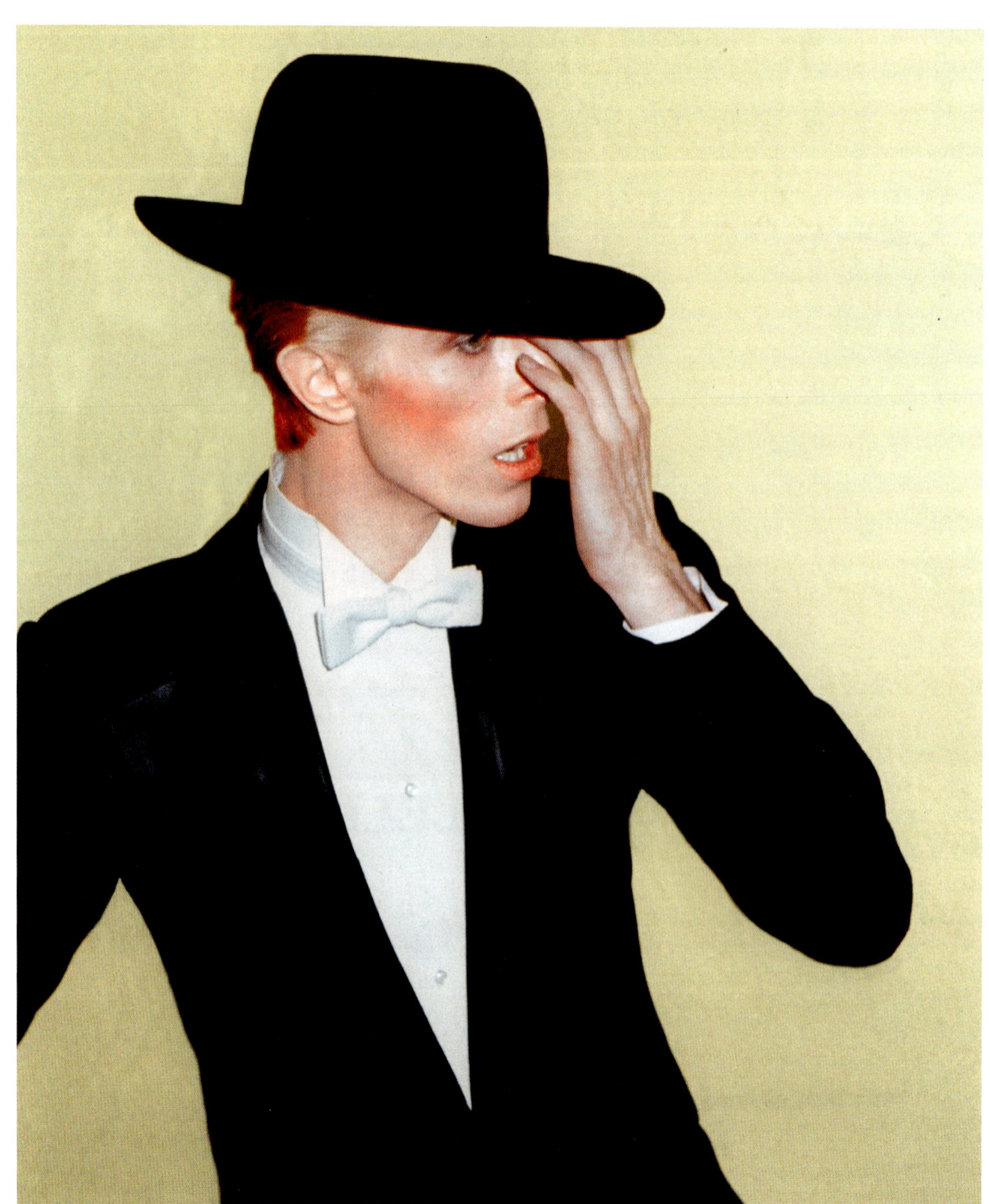

DAVID BOWIE
March 1, 1975 – New York City
17th Annual Grammy Awards at the Uris Theatre

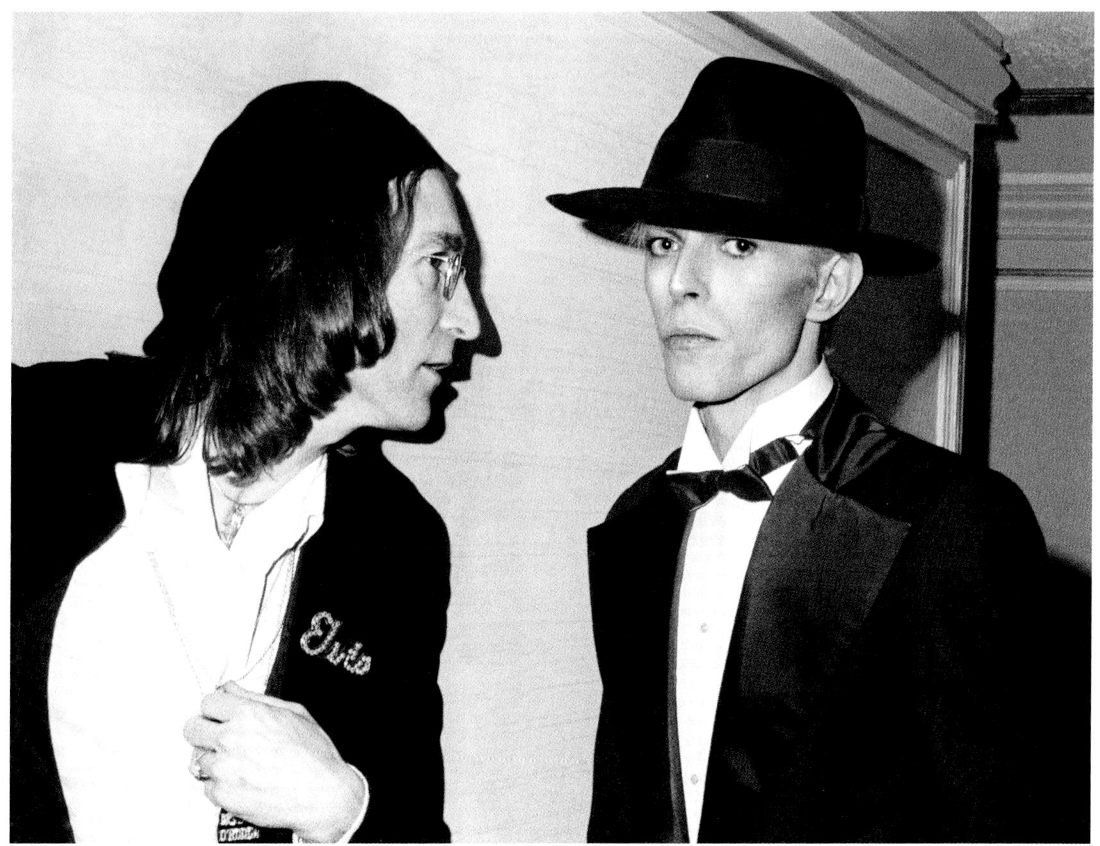

JOHN LENNON & DAVID BOWIE
March 1, 1975 – New York City
17th Annual Grammy Awards Party at the Essex House

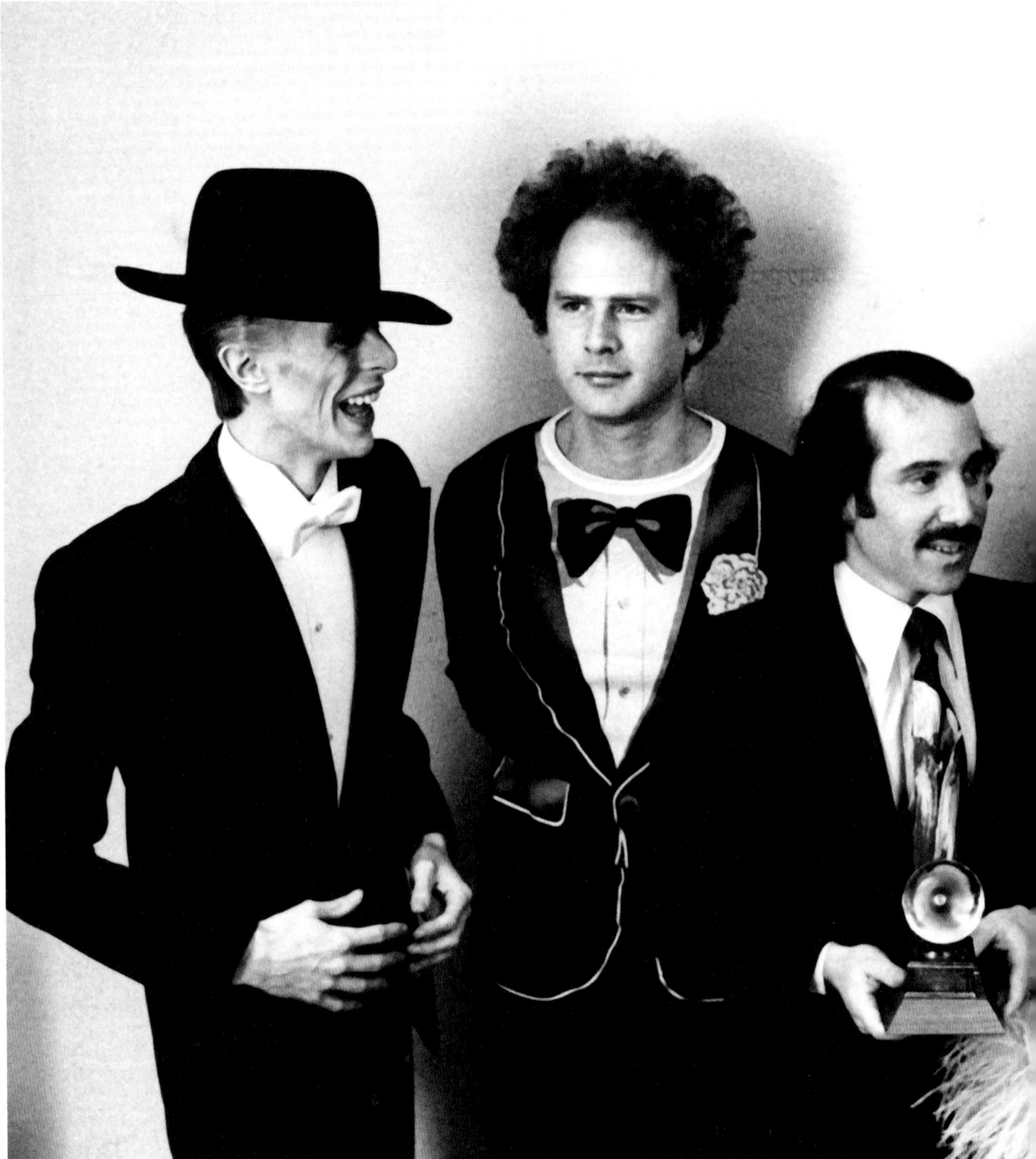

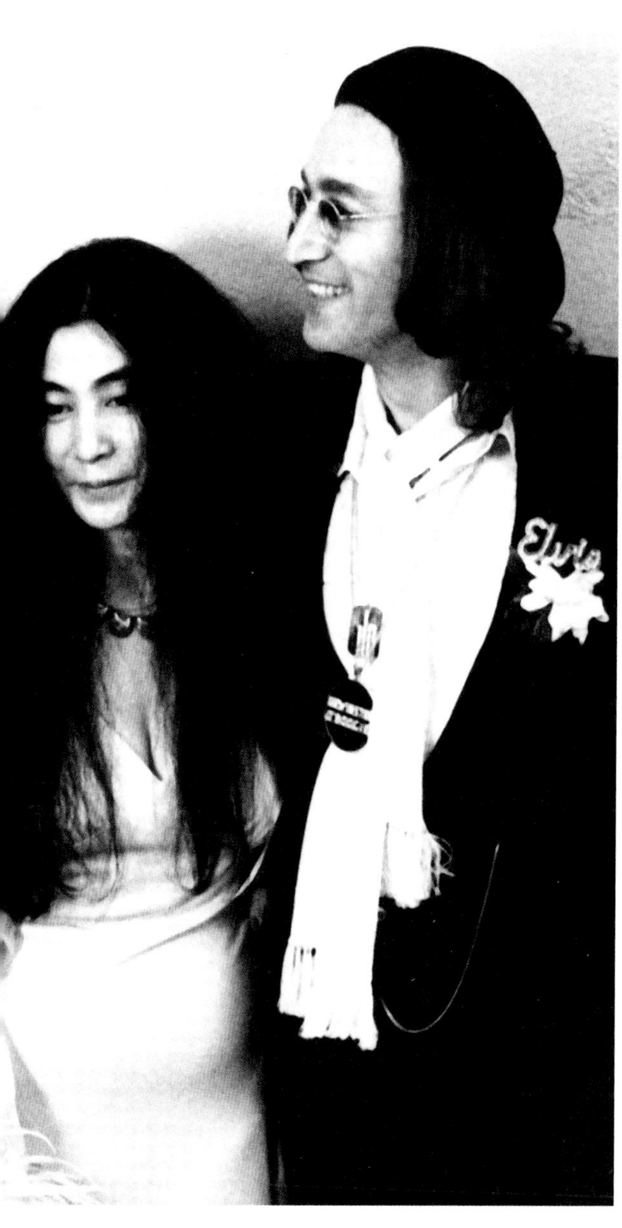

(L-R) DAVID BOWIE,
ART GARFUNKEL, PAUL SIMON,
YOKO ONO & JOHN LENNON
March 1, 1975 – New York City
17th Annual Grammy Awards
at the Uris Theatre

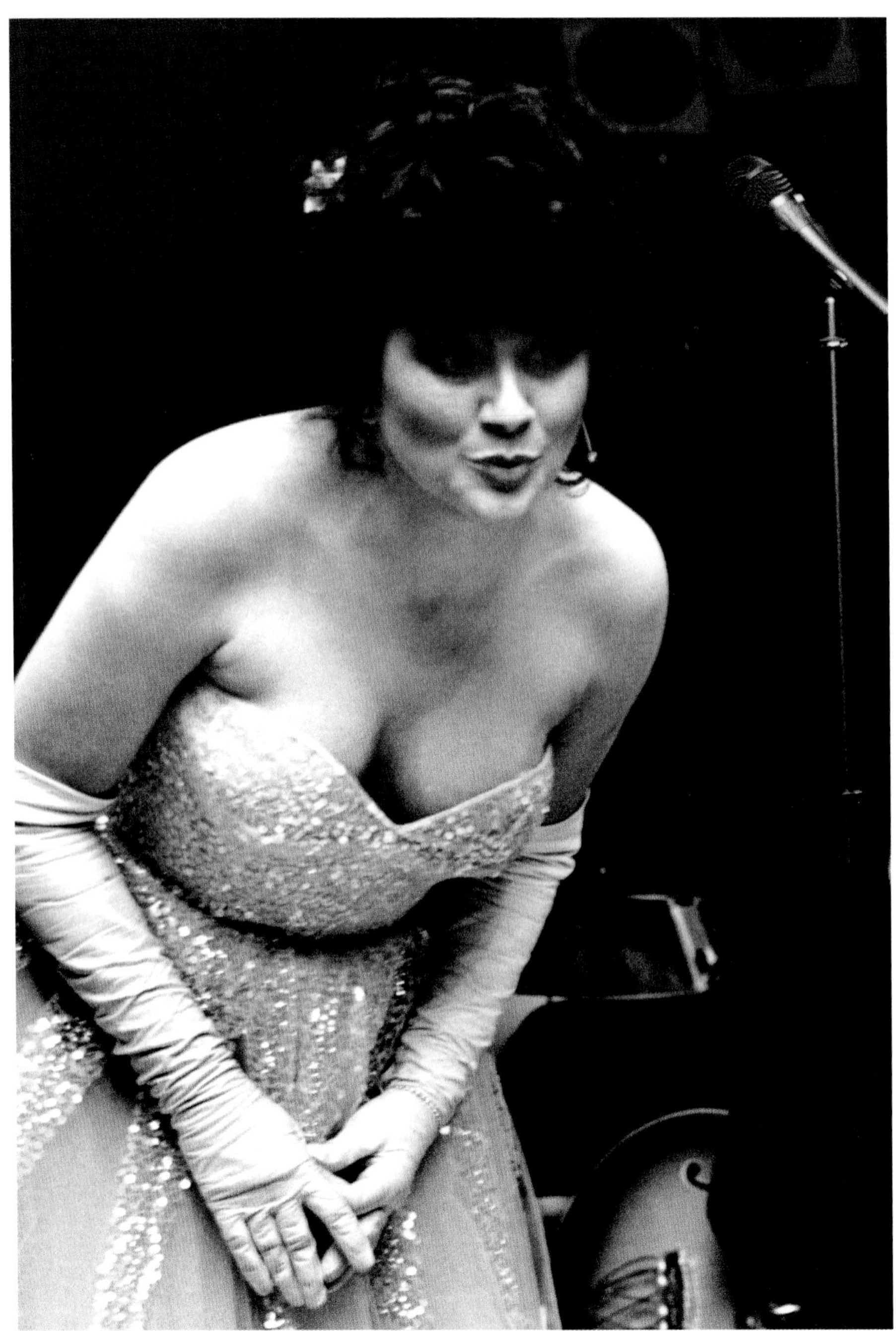

LINDA RONSTADT
October 24, 1985 – New York City
Dinner Dance Benefiting People For the American Way at the Puck Building

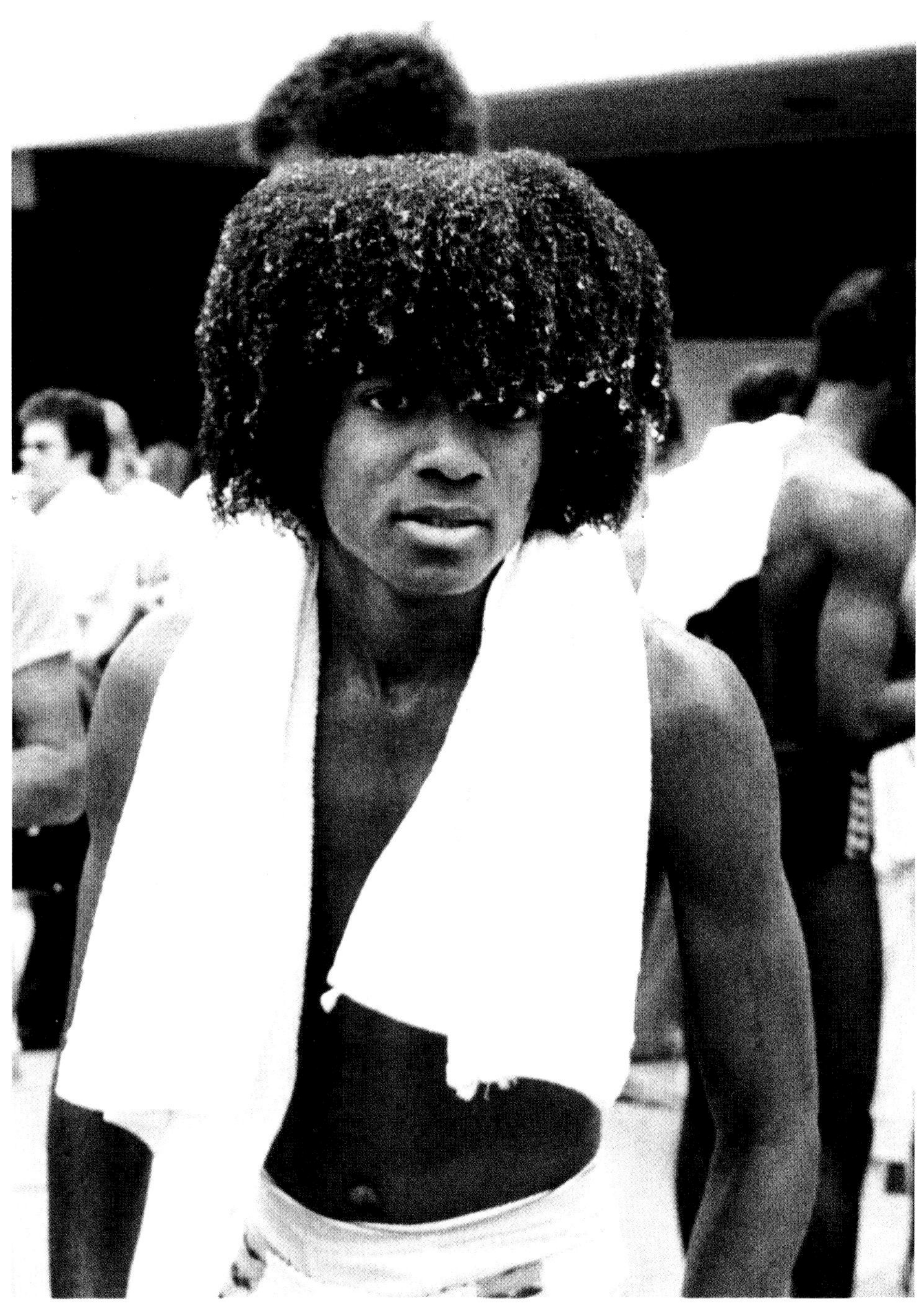

MICHAEL JACKSON
March 10, 1977 – Irvine, California
1st Annual Rock and Roll Celebrity Sports Classic at the University of California

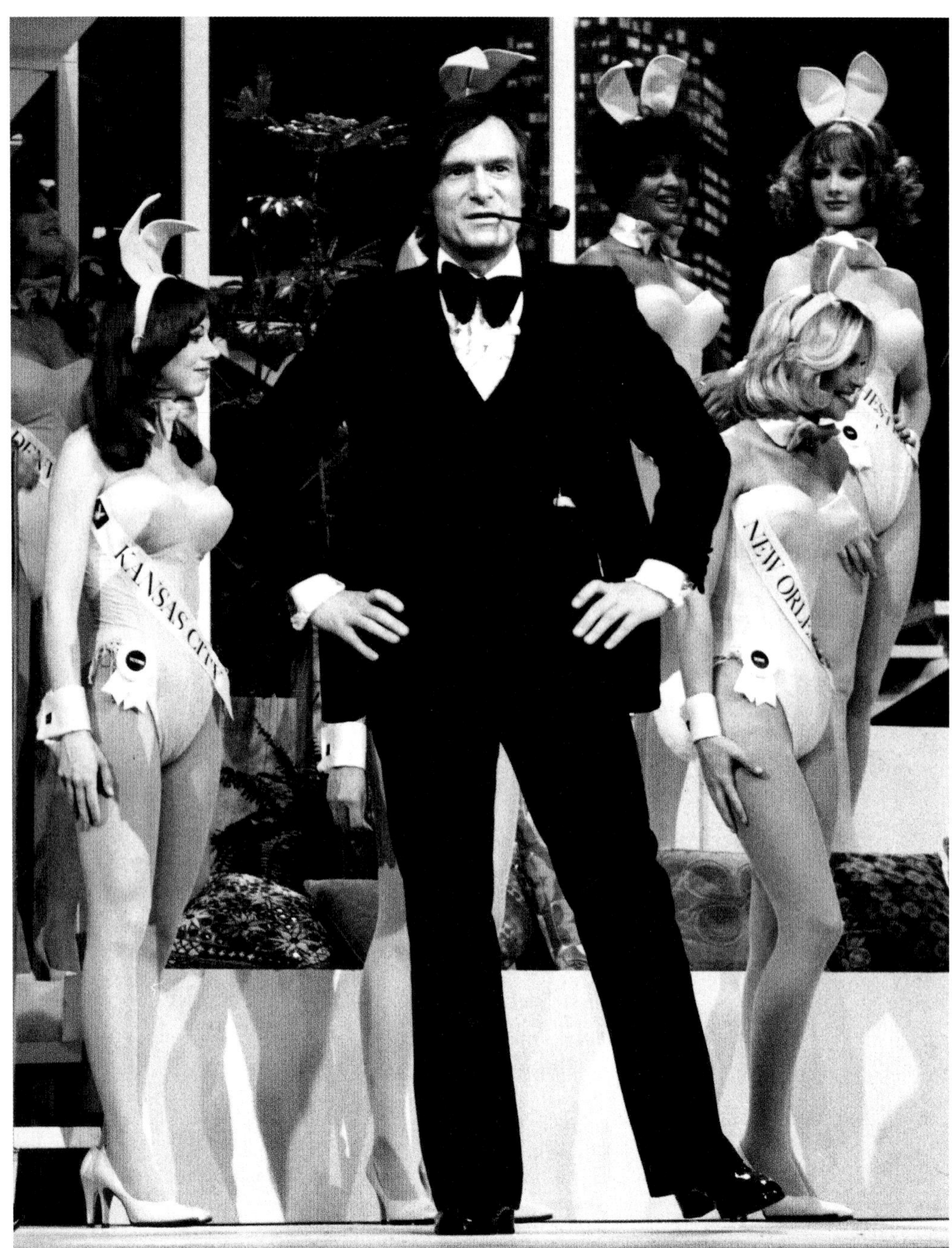

HUGH HEFNER
April 4, 1974 – Beverly Hills, California
5th Annual International Bunny of the Year Pageant at the Beverly Hilton Hotel

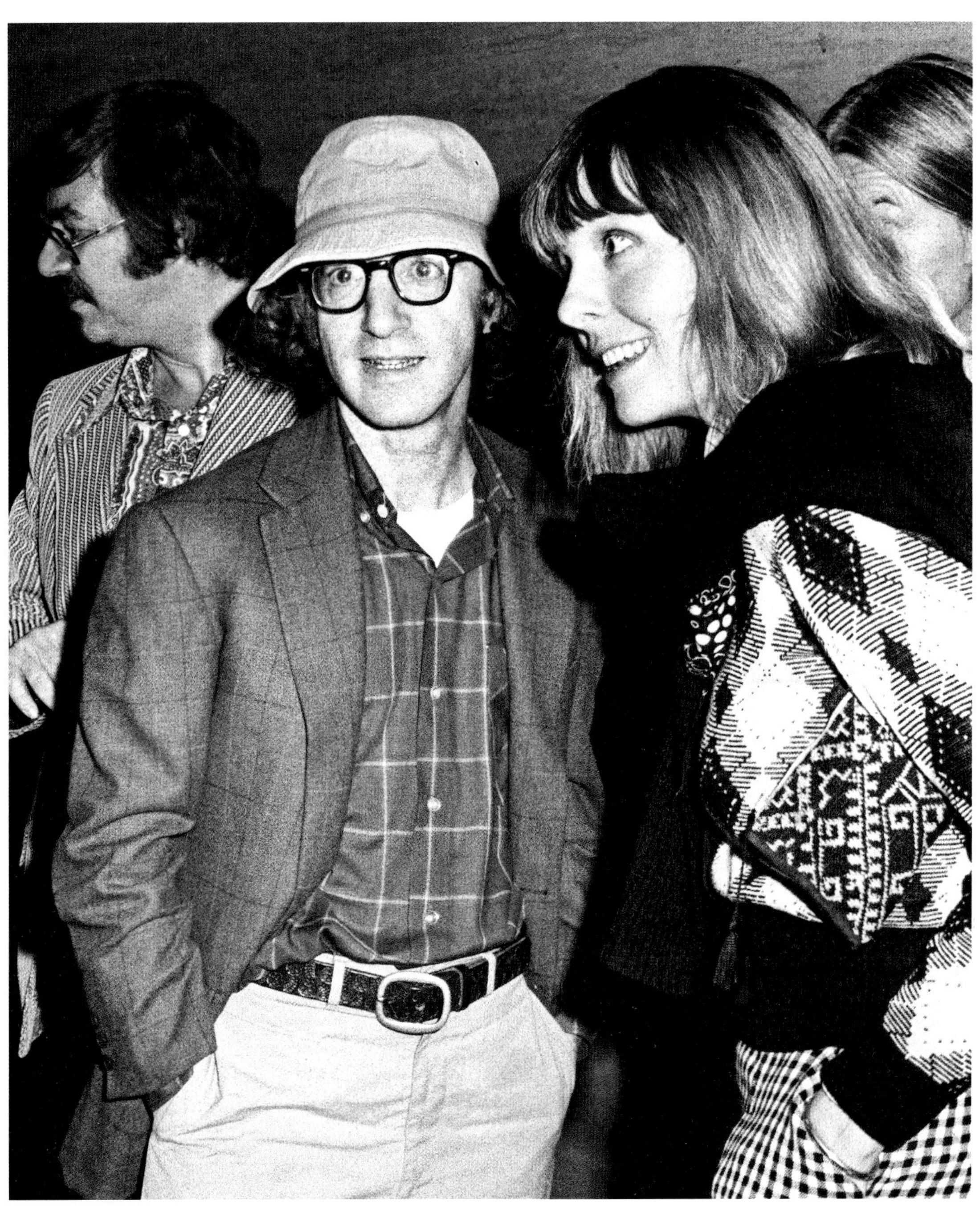

WOODY ALLEN & DIANE KEATON
September 12, 1972 – New York City
A Tracy and Hepburn Film Memoir Book Party at the New York Public Library

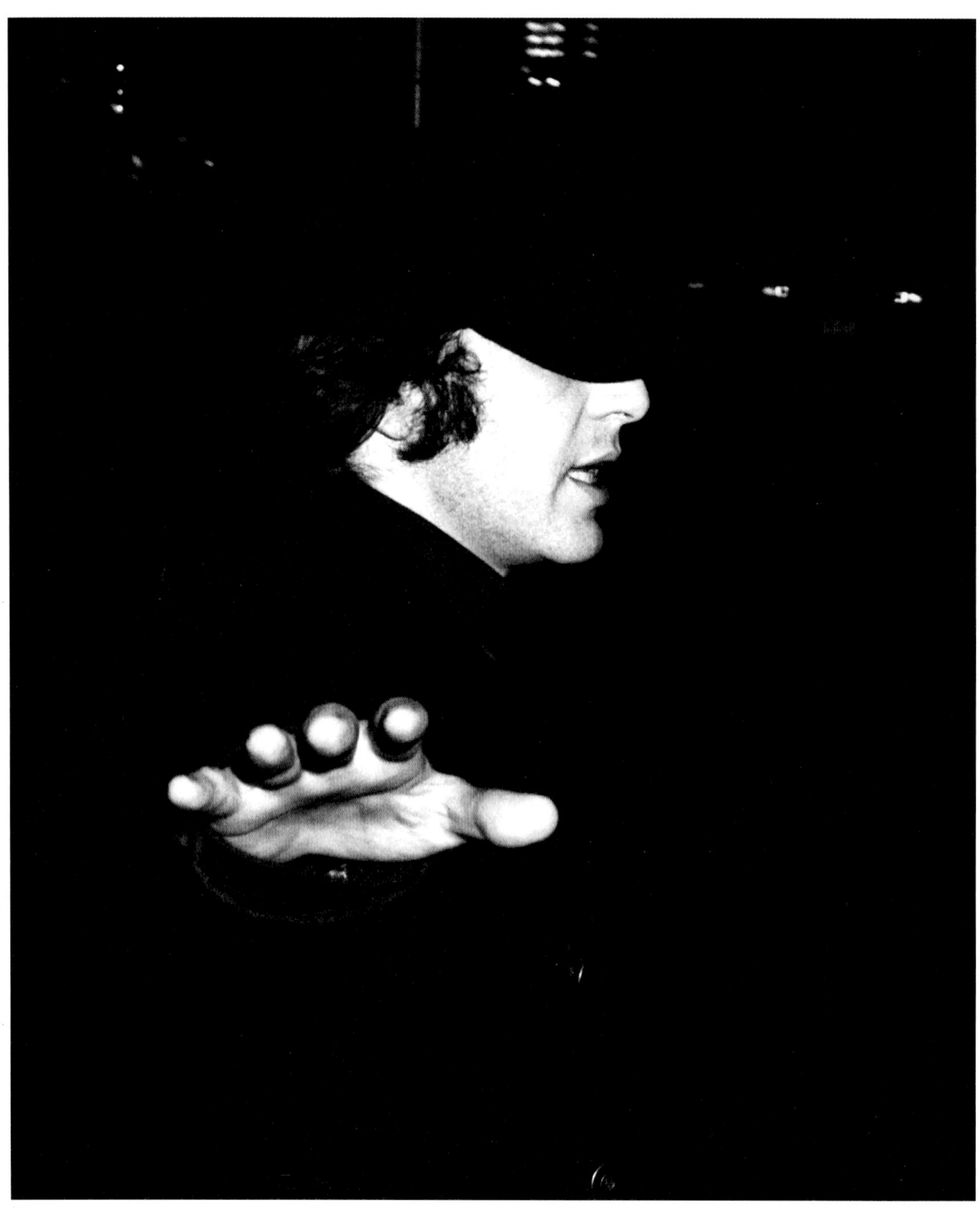

AL PACINO
December 9, 1974 – New York City
Elia Kazan's *The Understudy* Book Party at the Lyceum

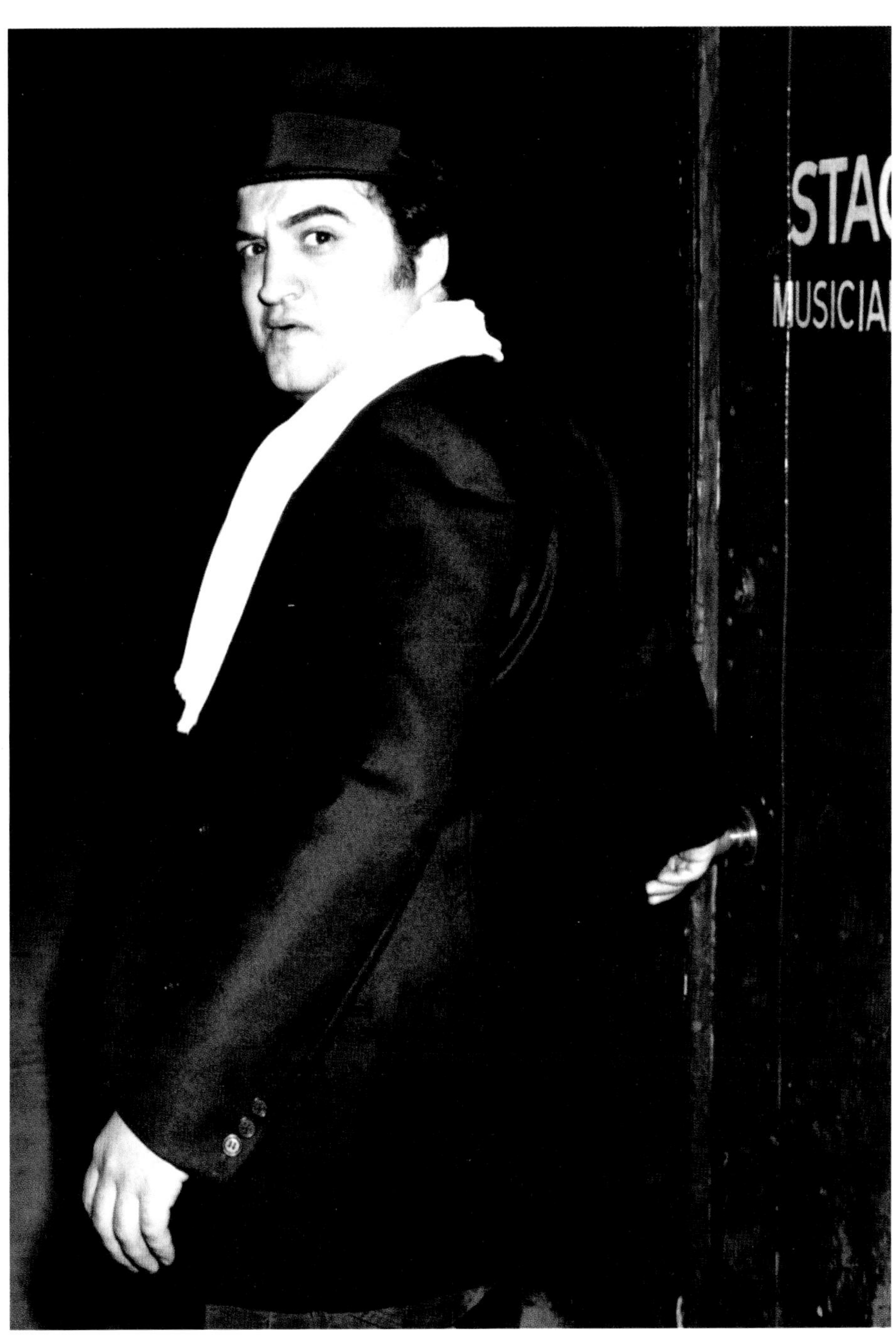

JOHN BELUSHI
April 7, 1978 – West Hollywood, California
The Roxy

74

BOB DYLAN
& WEST HOLLYWOOD POLICEMAN
March 11, 1977 – West Hollywood, California
Ronee Blakley Performance at The Roxy

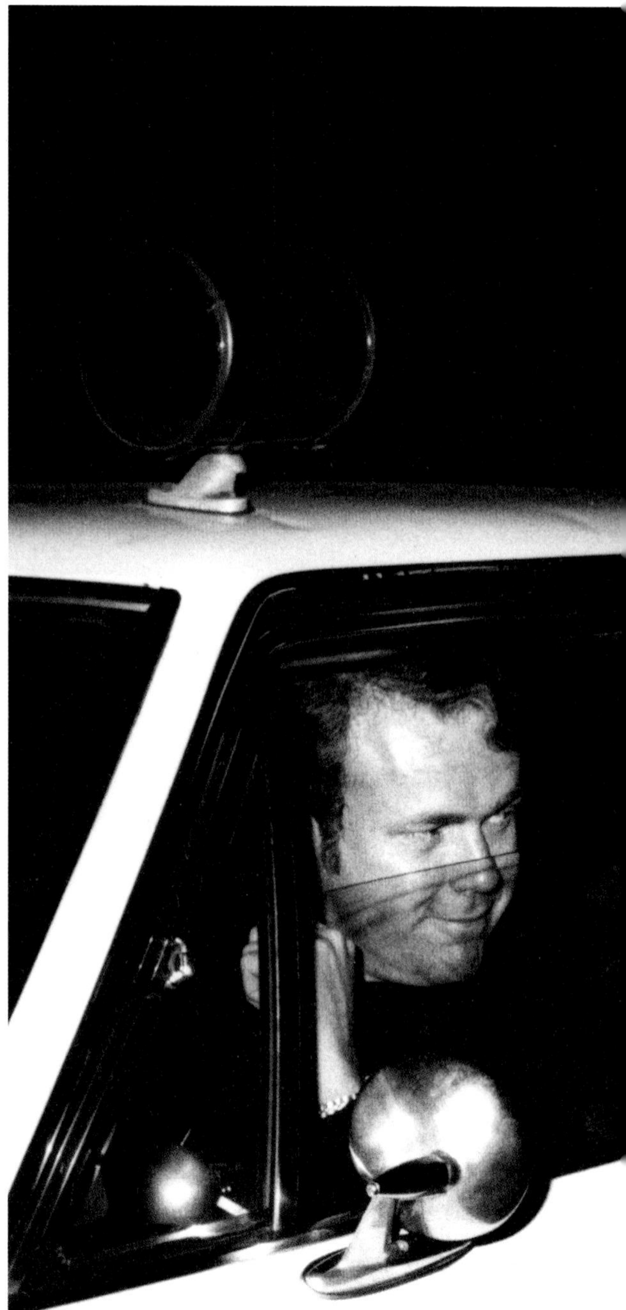

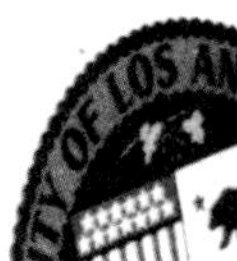

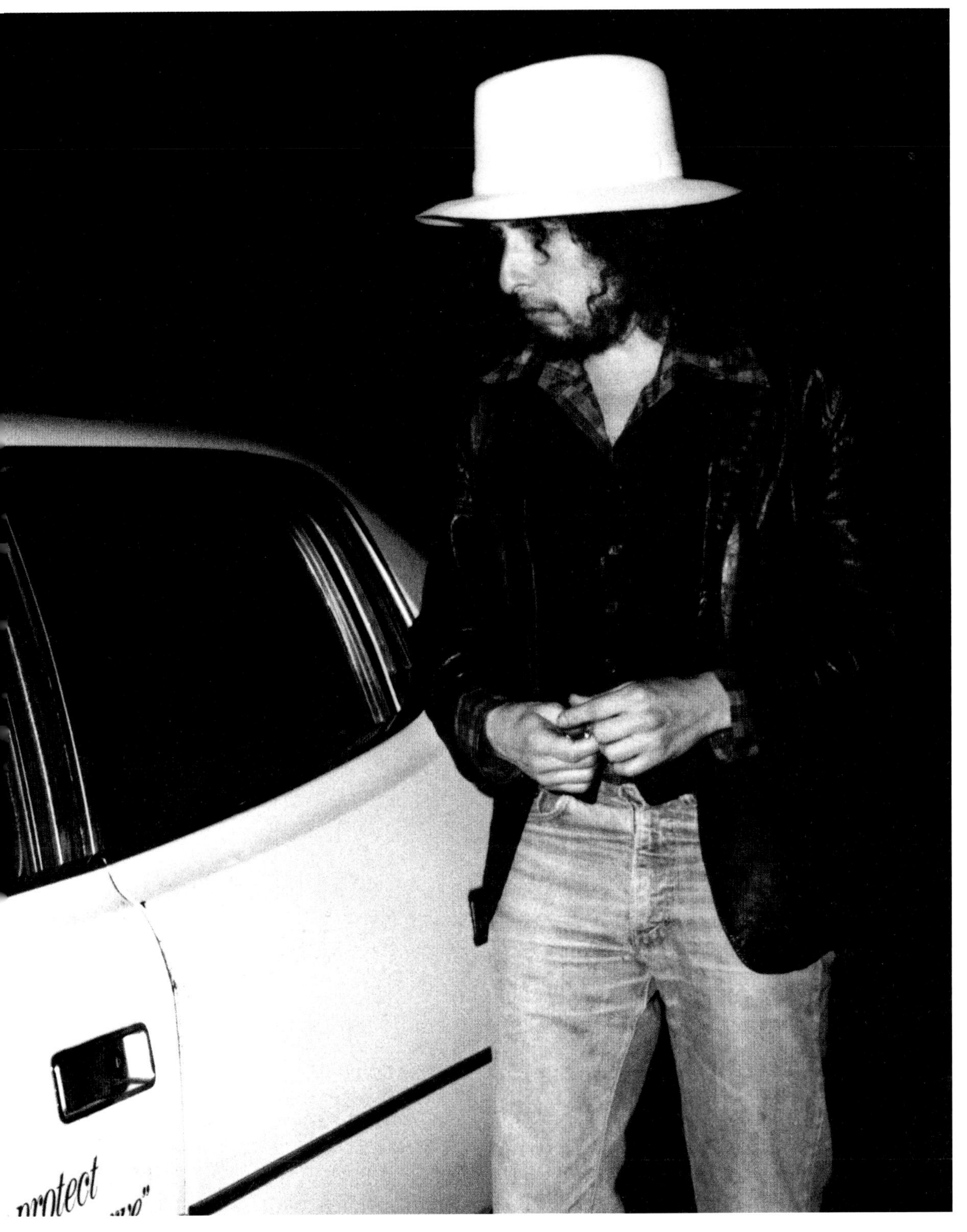
protect

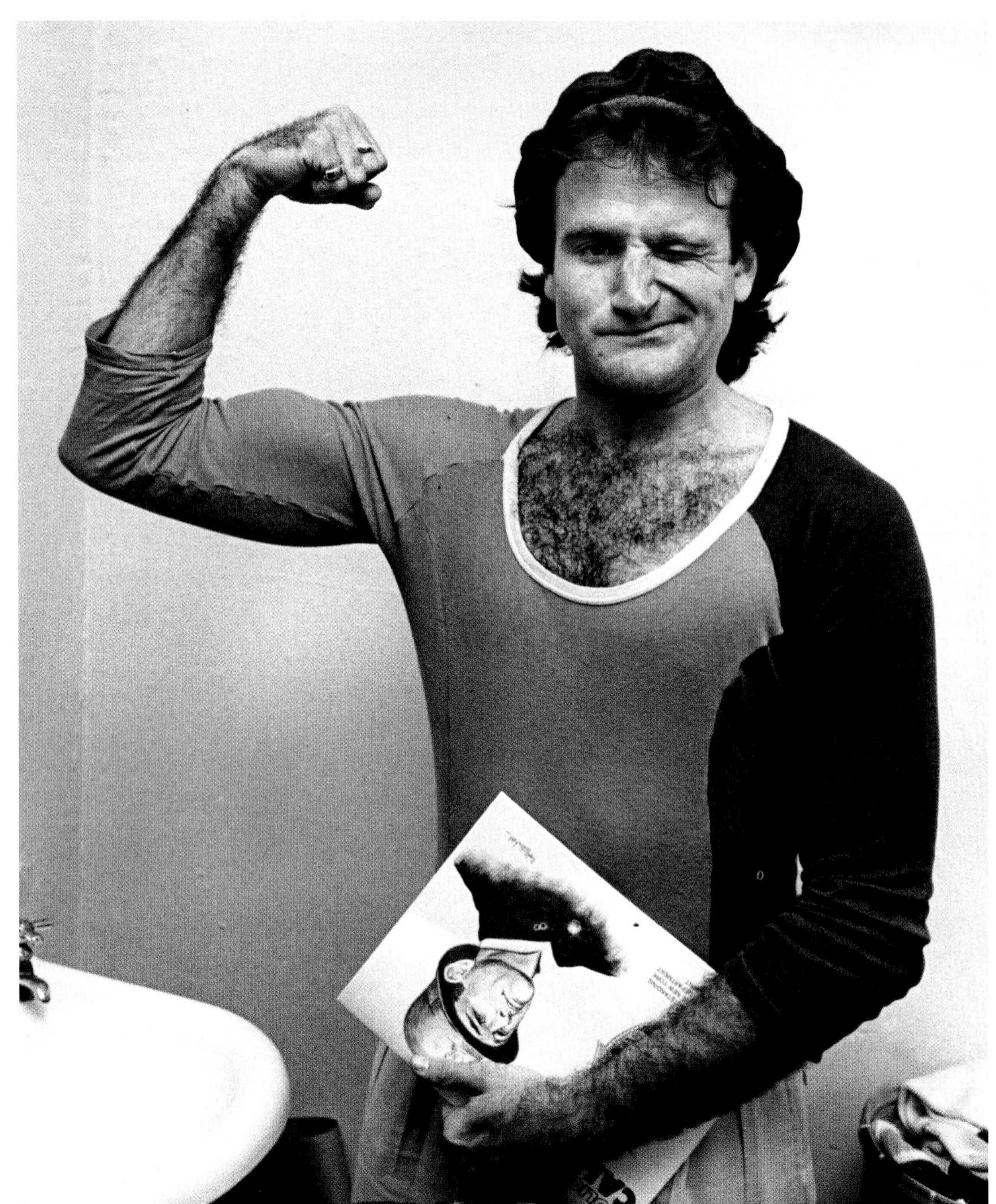

ROBIN WILLIAMS
April 22, 1979 – New York City
New York Police Bullet Proof Vest Benefit at the Schubert Theatre

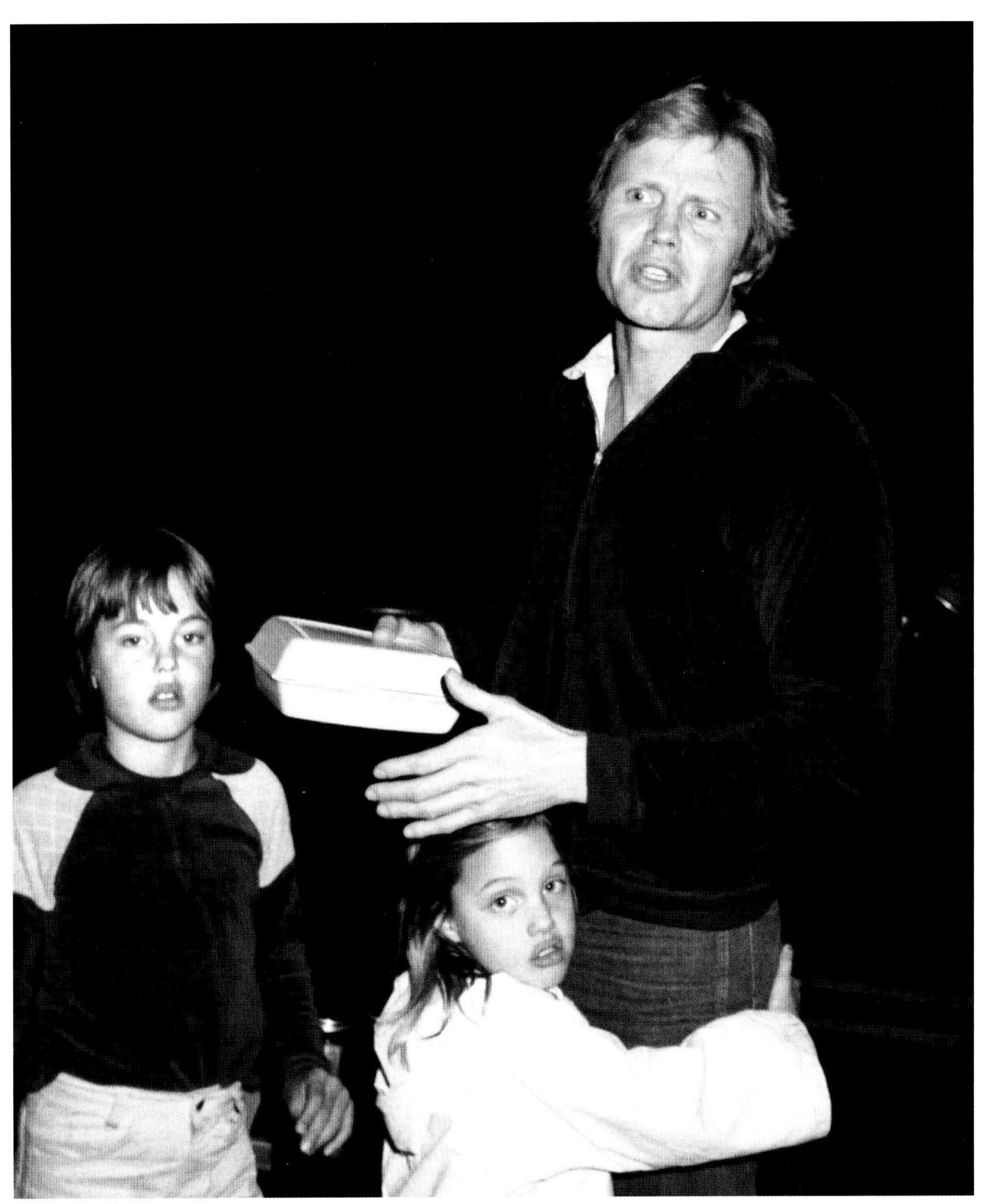

JON VOIGHT, SON JAMES HAVEN (AGE 8)
& DAUGHTER ANGELINA JOLIE (AGE 5)
January 9, 1981 – Beverly Hills, California

MARLON BRANDO & DICK CAVETT IN CHINATOWN

I read in Earl Wilson's column in the *New York Post* that Brando was scheduled as a guest on Dick Cavett's ABC talk show. The show was taped at five o'clock and then shown later that evening. Considering Brando was a recluse on his island in Tahiti, I thought I'd make the most of the opportunity and went to Cavett's office around noon for information and a possible take. But the office gave me nothing. On the way out, I noticed a limo parked in the front of the building and I asked the driver if he knew anything about Brando. He said, "Yes, he is coming in a helicopter." The driver did not know which heliport he was flying into. The heliport at the Pan Am building on the East River, between Sixty-first and Sixty-second Streets, seemed the most logical. The crew at the Pan Am depot knew a helicopter would be landing but did not know who was in it.

By four thirty, nothing was happening. I decided to leave so I could make the five o'clock taping at the ABC studios. On the way out, I saw a limo driving into the terminal and asked the driver if it was for Brando. The driver confirmed my suspicion—it was! I raced back upstairs to the heliport and got shots of Brando departing the plane. I quickly headed back to the studio but there was a frenzy of fans and photographers. I wasn't able to get any good shots.

After the taping, my friend and fellow photographer Paul Schmulbach and I followed Brando and Cavett to Chinatown. What I did not know then but found out later was that Brando told Cavett he knew I was following them. Cavett knew me but Brando didn't. Cavett explained to Brando that I was the photographer who'd gone to court with Jackie. As Paul and I snapped away, Brando asked Cavett, "Which one is Galella?" Cavett responded, "The tall one is Galella." Brando cautioned Cavett to keep his head down, telling Cavett, "Let them get the same pictures." Eventually, they reached the restaurant. Brando mumbled to me, "What else do you want that you don't have already?" I looked at Cavett since he knew me and was friendly. I said, "I'd like a picture without your sunglasses" (by this time the sun had set.) And then, without warning, SOCK! Brando punched me in my lower jaw. Regrettably, Paul did not get the picture. I placed my hanky to my mouth as it was bleeding profusely. I drove to Bellevue Hospital to get stitched up. As soon as the hospital finished mending my jaw, I went to the Showclub to cover an event. I ran into *New York Post* columnist Earl Wilson, who got the exclusive on the Brando punch. I learned the next day that Brando almost bled to death. Because he'd hit me so hard, five of my teeth had sunk into his knuckles, and his hand became infected. Cavett took Brando to New York's Hospital for Special Surgery, where he had to stay for three days to recover. I sued Brando and won a forty-thousand-dollar settlement.

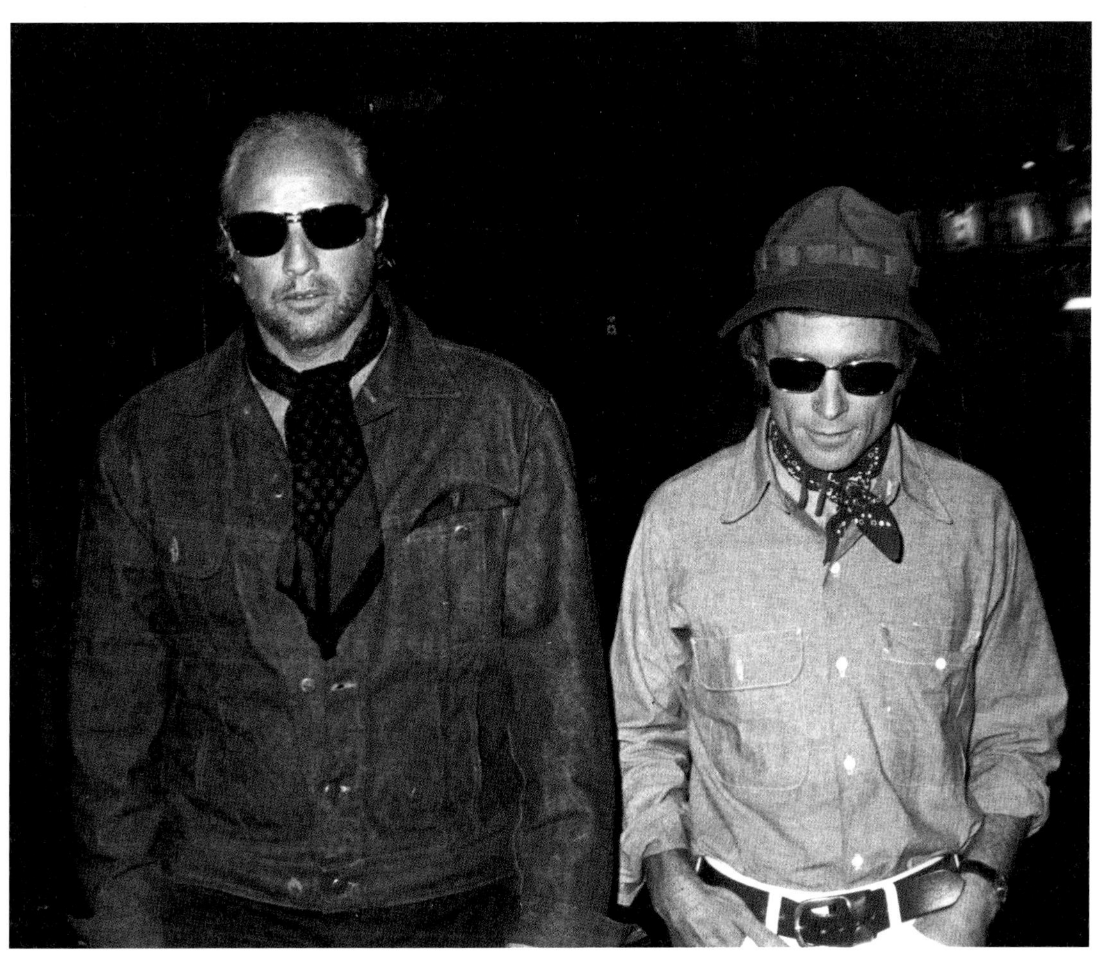

MARLON BRANDO & DICK CAVETT
June 12, 1973 – New York City
Chinatown

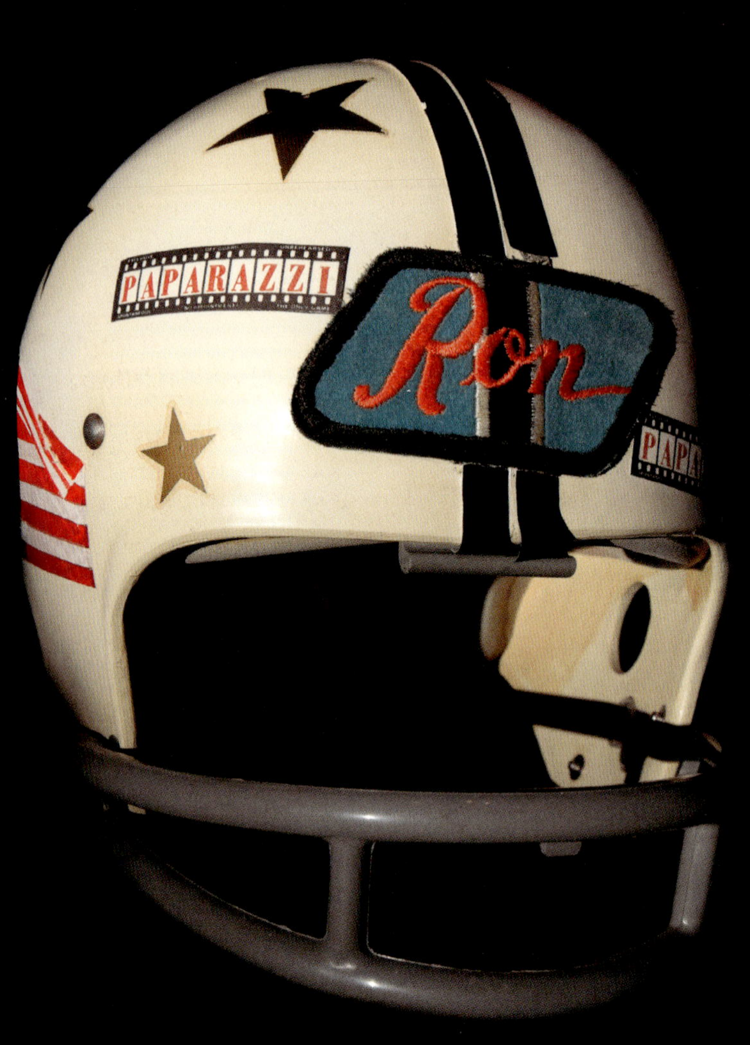
PAPARAZZI
Ron

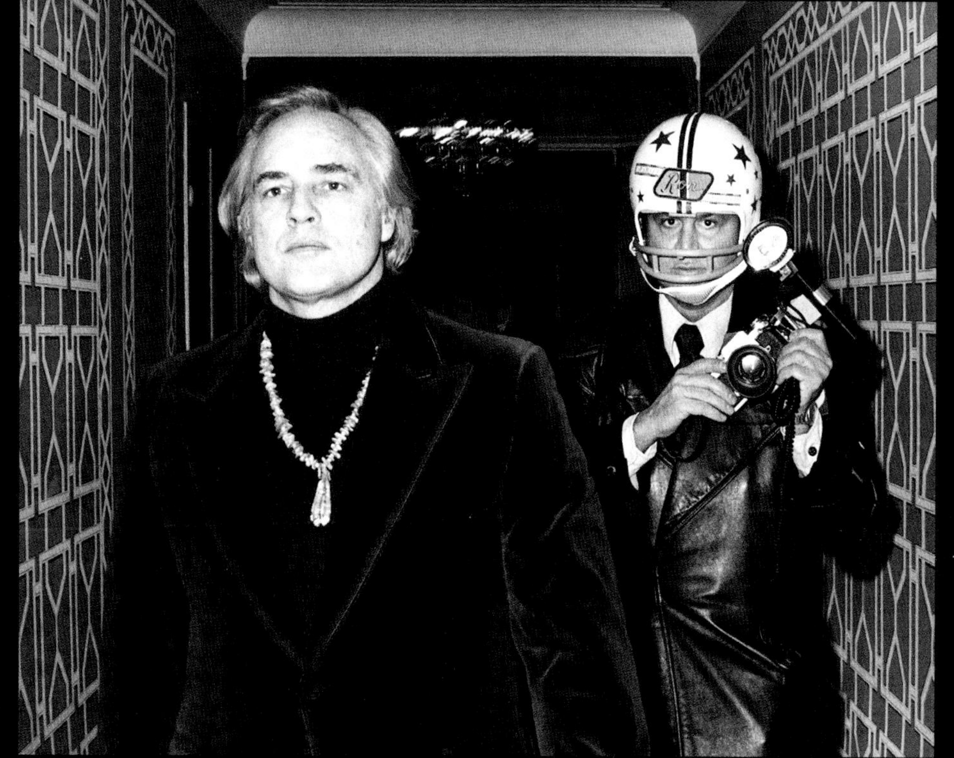

Photo Credit: Paul Schmulbach

MARLON BRANDO & RON GALELLA

A year after Brando punched me in Chinatown, he scheduled a press conference at the Waldorf-Astoria Hotel to announce a benefit for Native American Indians. This time I came prepared, wearing a helmet. Recalling in '73 that photographer Paul Schmulbach missed the shot of Brando punching me, as he arrived, I physically pushed Paul to take the picture of me wearing the helmet walking next to Brando. Brando was cool and did not react. The following week, this soon-to-be-iconic shot ran in People magazine as a double-page spread. This photo and the photo of me taken with Jackie by Joy Smith have become the two most famous and requested pictures of me with a celebrity. In response to this amusing photo, Cavett mentioned during an interview in the documentary, "Smash His Camera", "Ron has a cool sense of humor."

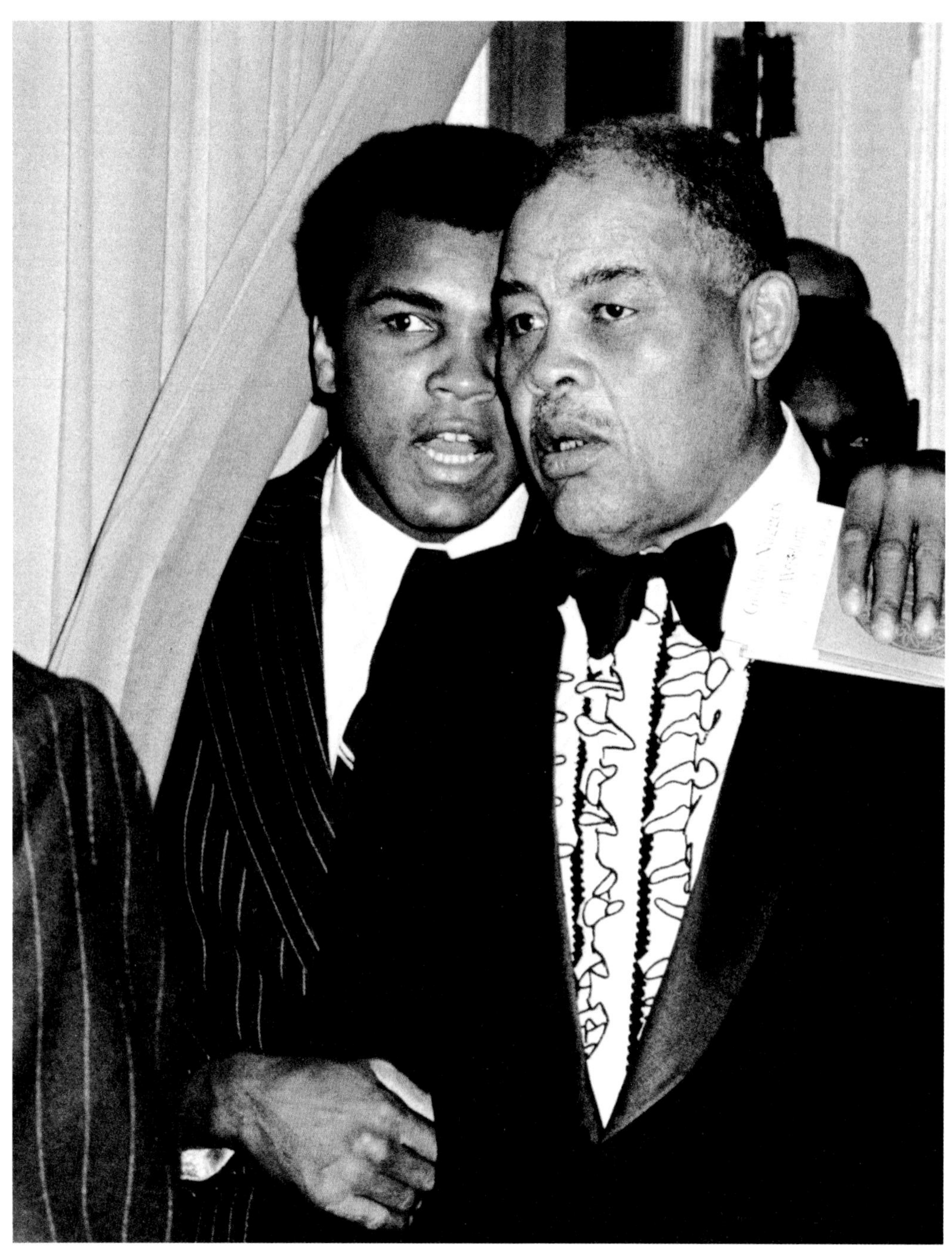

MUHAMMAD ALI & JOE LEWIS
May 18, 1975 – New York City
Boxing Writers Association Gala at the Plaza Hotel

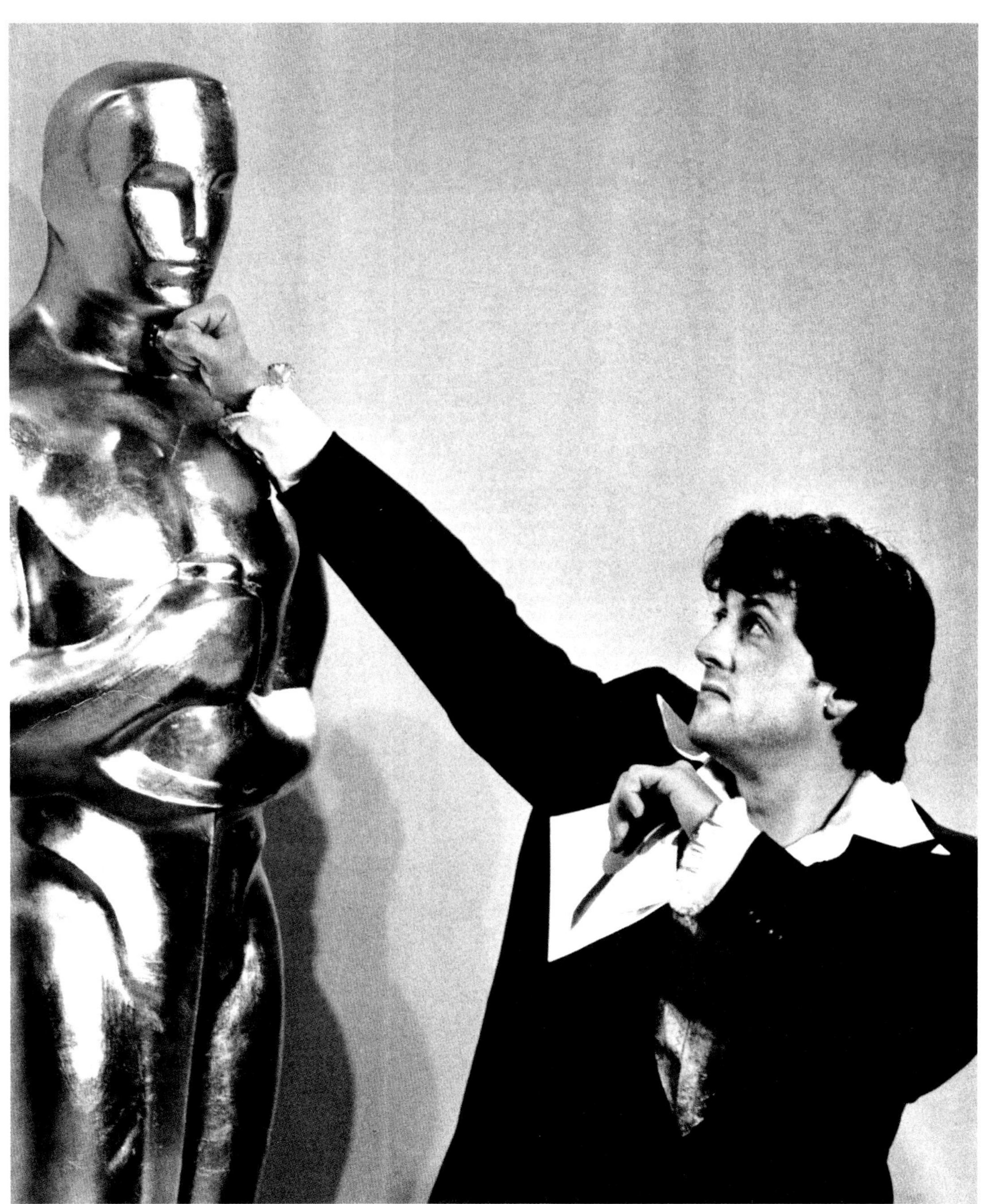

SYLVESTER STALLONE
March 28, 1977 – Los Angeles, California
49th Annual Academy Awards at the Dorothy Chandler Pavilion

SEAN PENN & ANTHONY SAVIGNANO

Bad-boy actor Sean Penn had a reputation for violence which included his dislike of photographers. I was among five photographers snapping away as Sean and Madonna left Lincoln Center after their workshop performance in David Rabe's "Goose and Tomtom". The unlikely married couple walked to the Ginger Man restaurant on West Sixty-fourth Street, which was on the same block as their apartment. After dinner, they left with a doggy bag and started the short walk to their building.

We all trotted after them. As soon as we arrived at their residence, my nephew Anthony Savignano and I stepped onto the courtyard entrance and Penn screamed, "That's it, now you're on my private property you motherf*ckers." Penn spat at me, then my nephew spat back at Penn. Penn swung his doggy bag, hitting Anthony in the face. A boxing match followed in the courtyard.

Madonna was standing in the courtyard yelling, "Stop, Sean, Stop, how could you do this?" Anthony fended off Penn's punches at arm's length. Penn caught Anthony in a headlock, with Anthony grabbing Penn by the throat. Madonna was hysterical, crying, begging them to stop. She approached freelance photographer Vinnie Zuffante and begged him to help Sean.

"Help him?, Help him? Your husband's a madman!" he replied. Madonna ordered the doorman, "Please stop them." He started swinging a broom, managing to separate them. All the photographers had started to leave when a crazed Penn walked up to Zuffante and sucker punched him the face, causing black and blue under his left eye. Luckily, no one was seriously injured.

The following year Sean was sentenced to sixty days after spitting and punching an extra on a film set who had taken his photo.

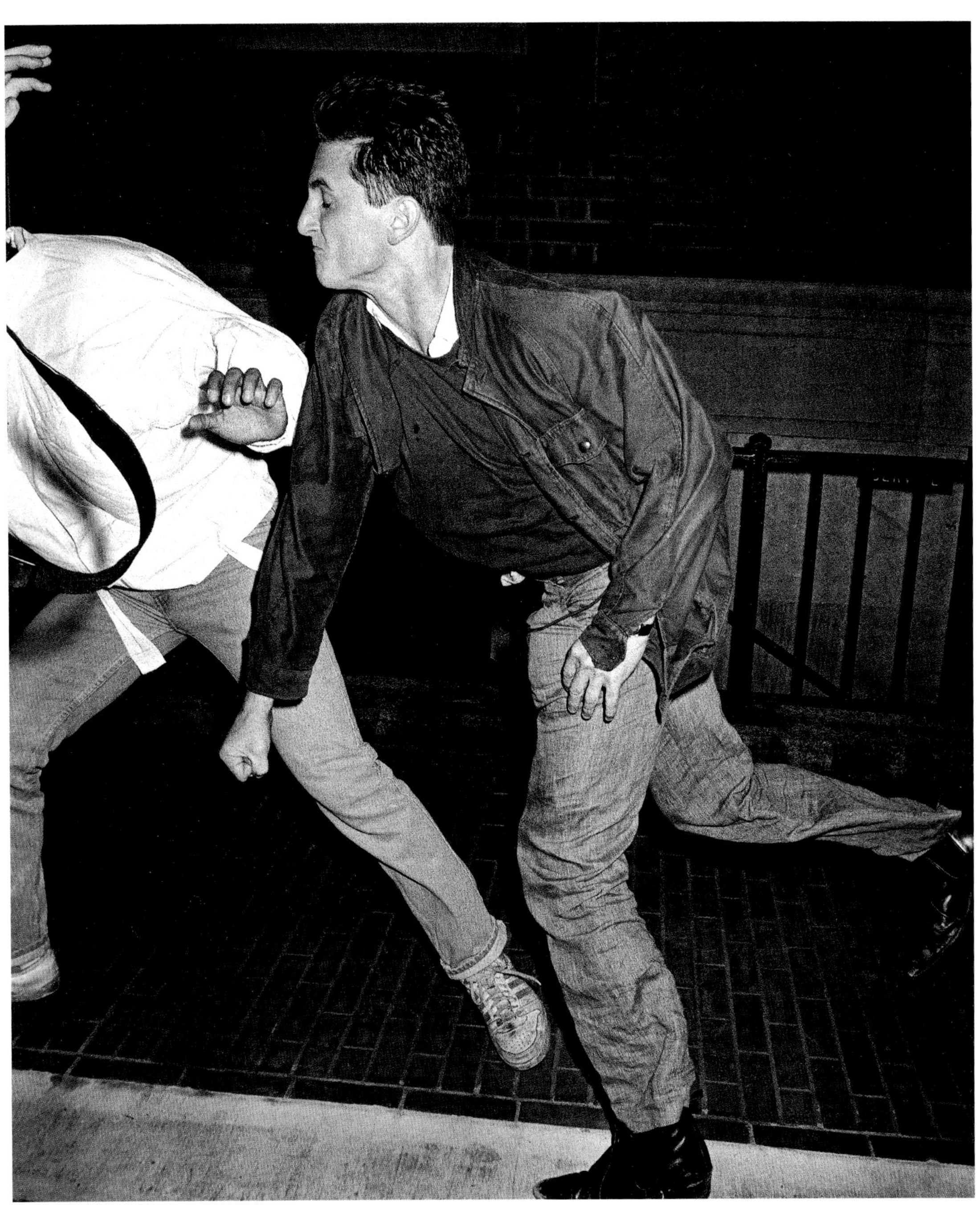

SEAN PENN & ANTHONY SAVIGNANO
August 29, 1986 – New York City
Madonna's courtyard on West 64th Street

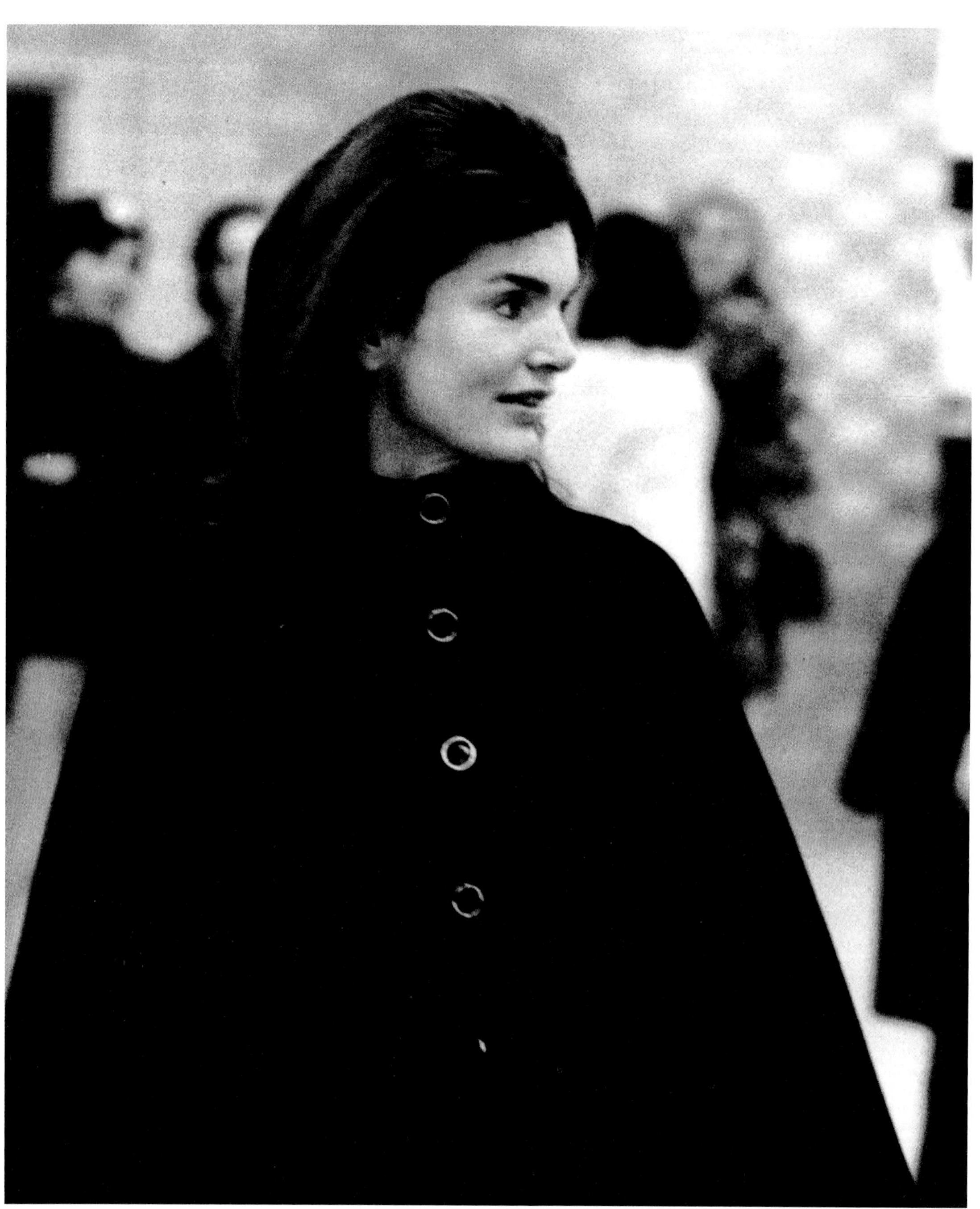

JACKIE KENNEDY ONASSIS
October 4, 1971 – New York City
John F. Kennedy International Airport

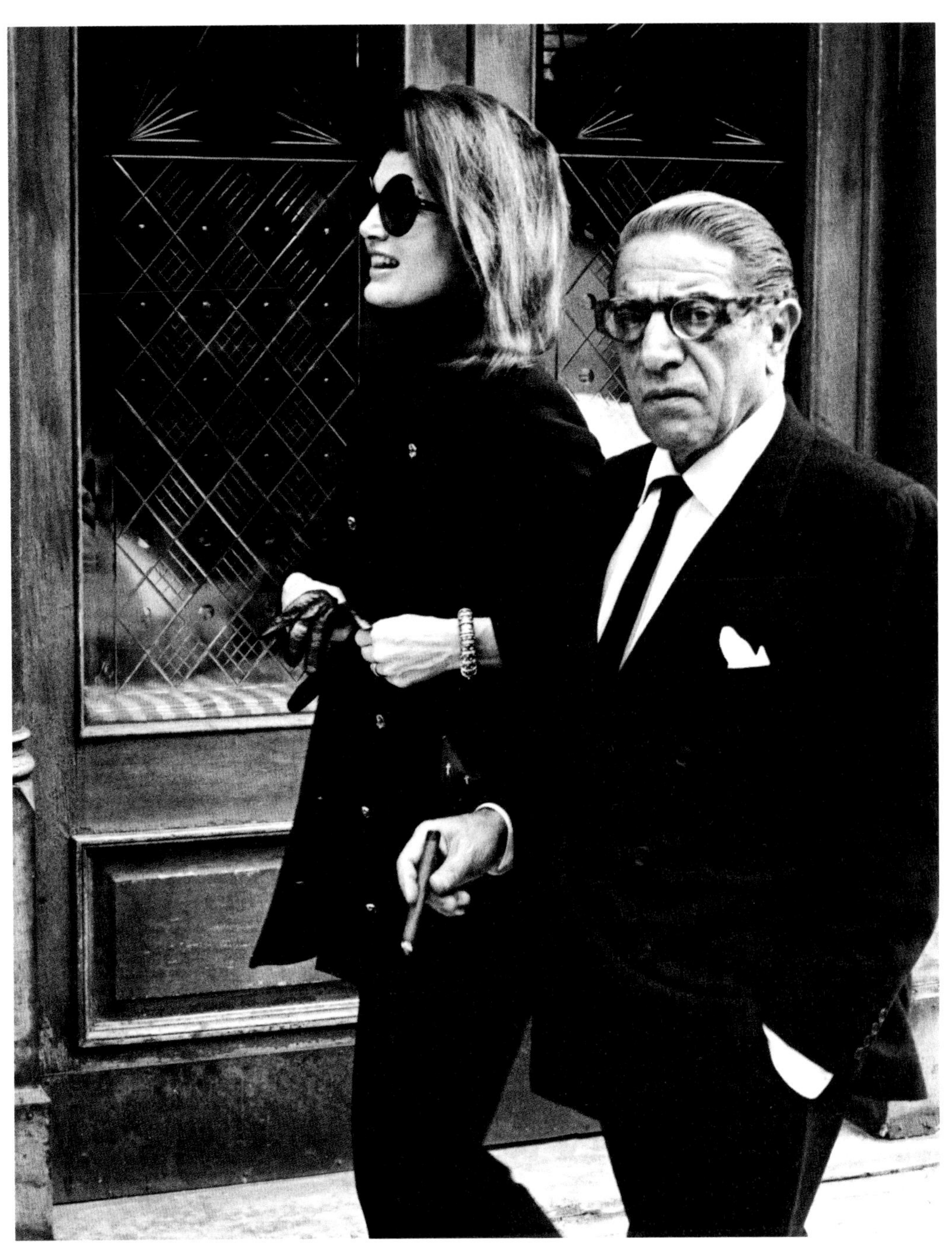

JACKIE KENNEDY ONASSIS & ARISTOTLE ONASSIS
January 17, 1971 – New York City
P.J. Clarke's

SMASH HIS CAMERA

On Wednesday, September 24, 1969, I showed up at Jackie's apartment. John Martin, a celebrity buff, was already there and I could see he was all worked up. "They're in the park," he said, very excited, "on bicycles." "What do you mean, 'they'?" I asked. "Jackie AND John,' he said. Jackie's doorman confirmed Martin's story.

I started up the pedestrian path and saw Jackie and John at the reservoir, nearing the path. I ran down the path, hopped over a guardrail and crouched behind a tree, prefocusing my 135mm lens to about forty feet away and setting the motor drive for 2–3 frames per second. As they whizzed down the path, I got one of my best takes! As Jackie reached the end of the path, she turned around and noticed me. As I hopped back over the fence, she remarked, "Oh, it's you again." Secret Service Agent John Connelly, who was also on a bike, said to me, holding his hands up, "You've had enough," blocking me from taking any more pictures. I managed to click a few more shots while Jackie looked for another agent, John Walsh, and she and John waited for the light to turn green. She then ordered her agent, "Mr. Connelly, smash his camera!" She also ordered agents John Walsh and James Kalafatis to take my film. Walsh slyly quipped to me, "She's breaking my balls!" I stubbornly refused to surrender my film, so they arrested me for harassment. I counter charged that I was the one being harassed. I was kept in the Secret Service car for at least twenty minutes in front of the police station. I feared that my car was being towed and my trunk forced open to get the film.

When the case came up for trial, the charge was dismissed in court, with the judge stating, "I'll say this. I am not certain who was being harassed; case dismissed." Winning this lawsuit, my lawyer advised me to bill Jackie for his legal fees of $450. She never responded. After almost a year of head-on encounters and incidents, my lawyer Mr. Brown and I decided to take the next step—to sue Jackie and the three Secret Service agents for malicious prosecution, false imprisonment, harassment, and interfering in the pursuit of my lawful occupation, photojournalism. This photo ran on the front page of the *Daily News* and in publications worldwide.

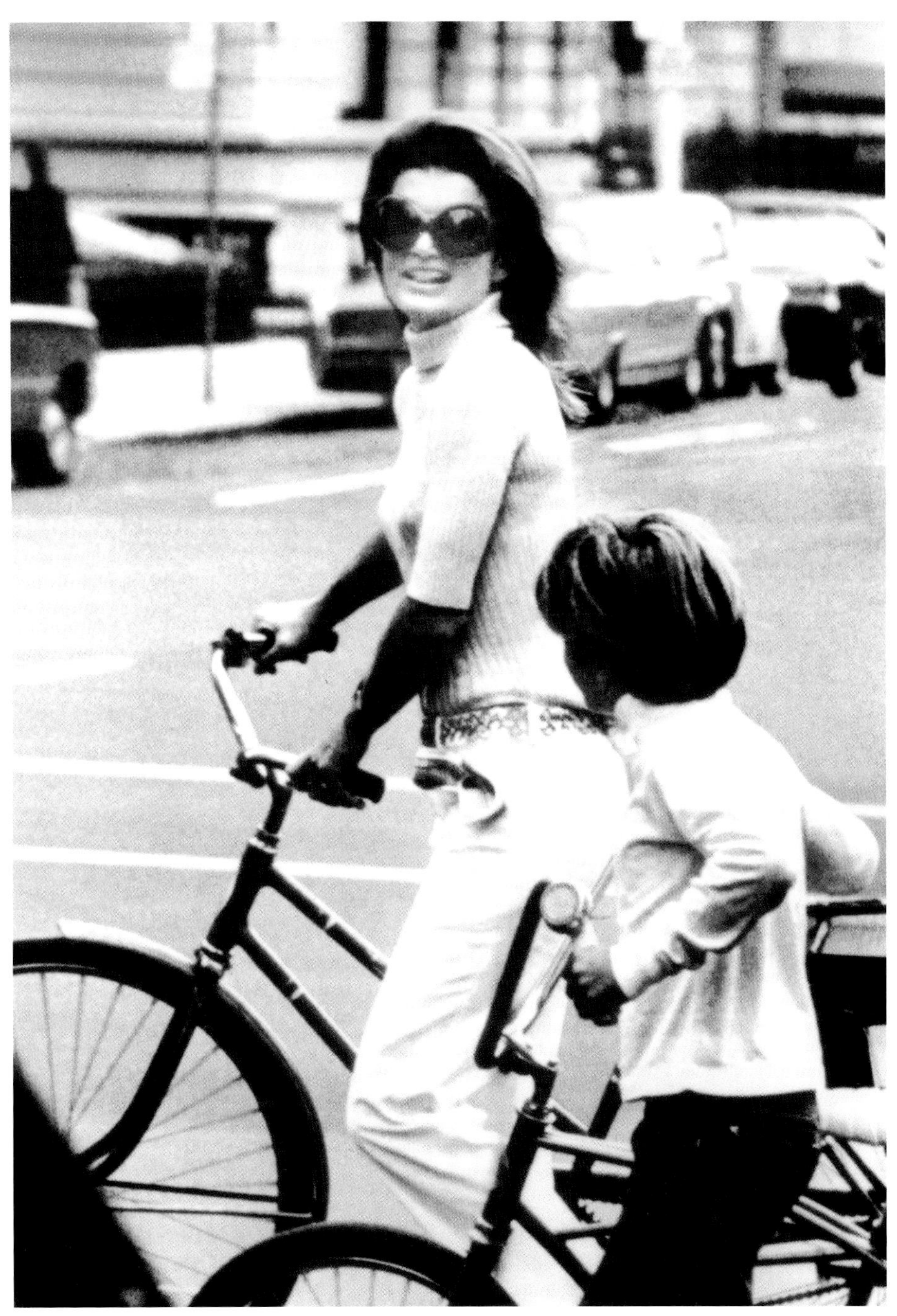

JACKIE KENNEDY ONASSIS & JOHN F. KENNEDY, JR.
September 24, 1969 – New York City
Central Park

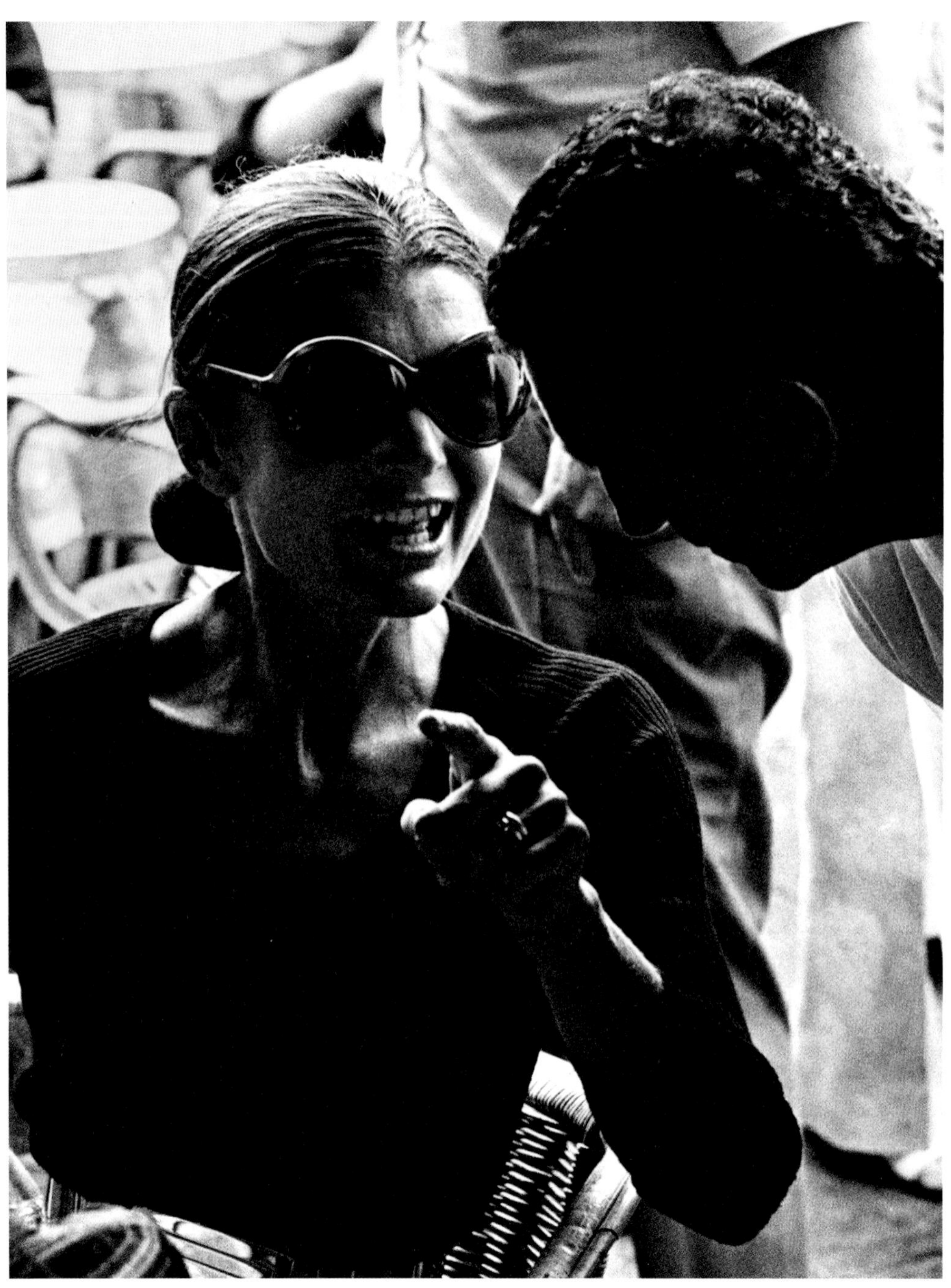

JACKIE KENNEDY ONASSIS
August 24, 1970 – Capri, Italy

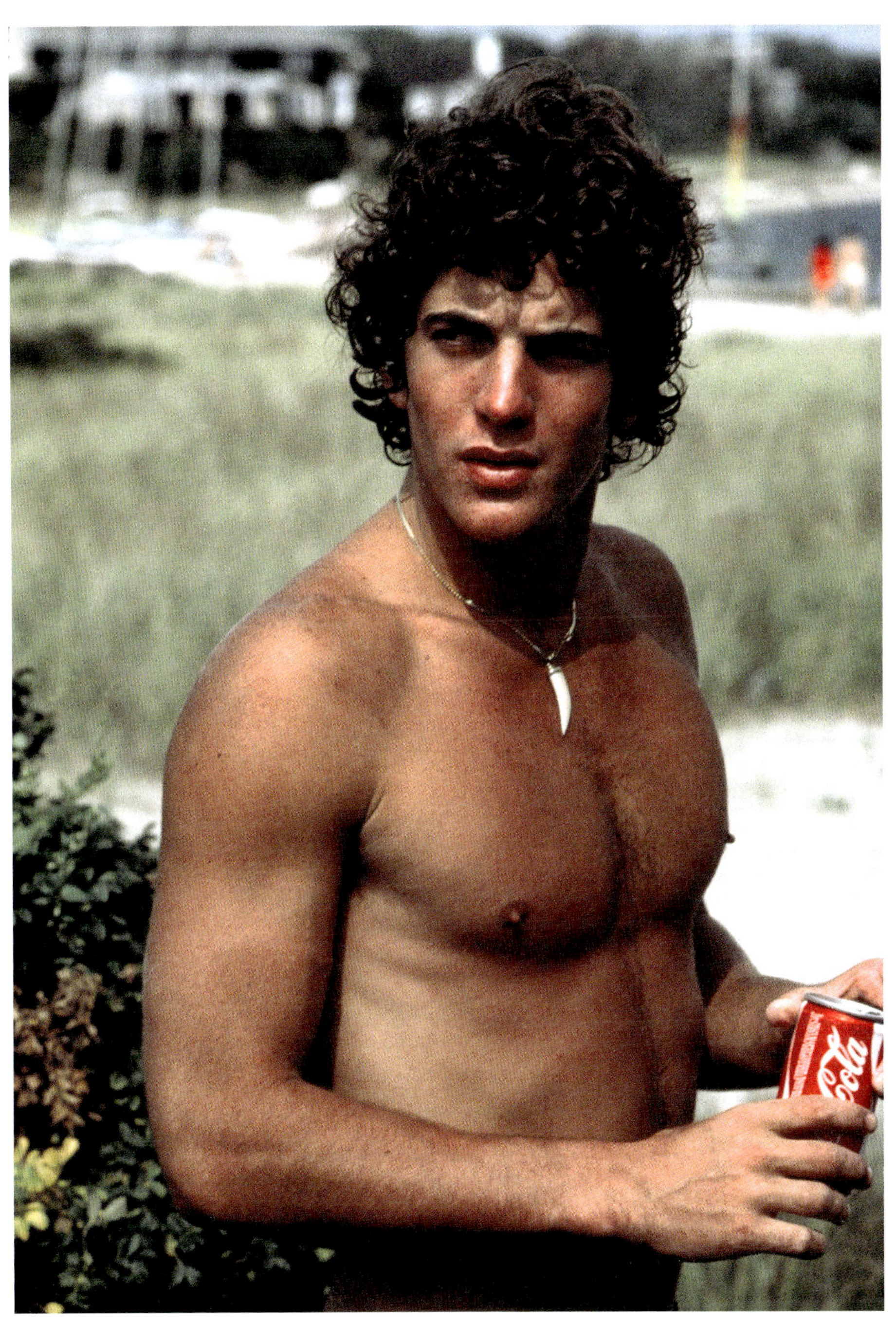

JOHN F. KENNEDY, JR.
August 31, 1980 – Hyannis, Massachusetts
Kennedy Family Labor Day Weekend Party

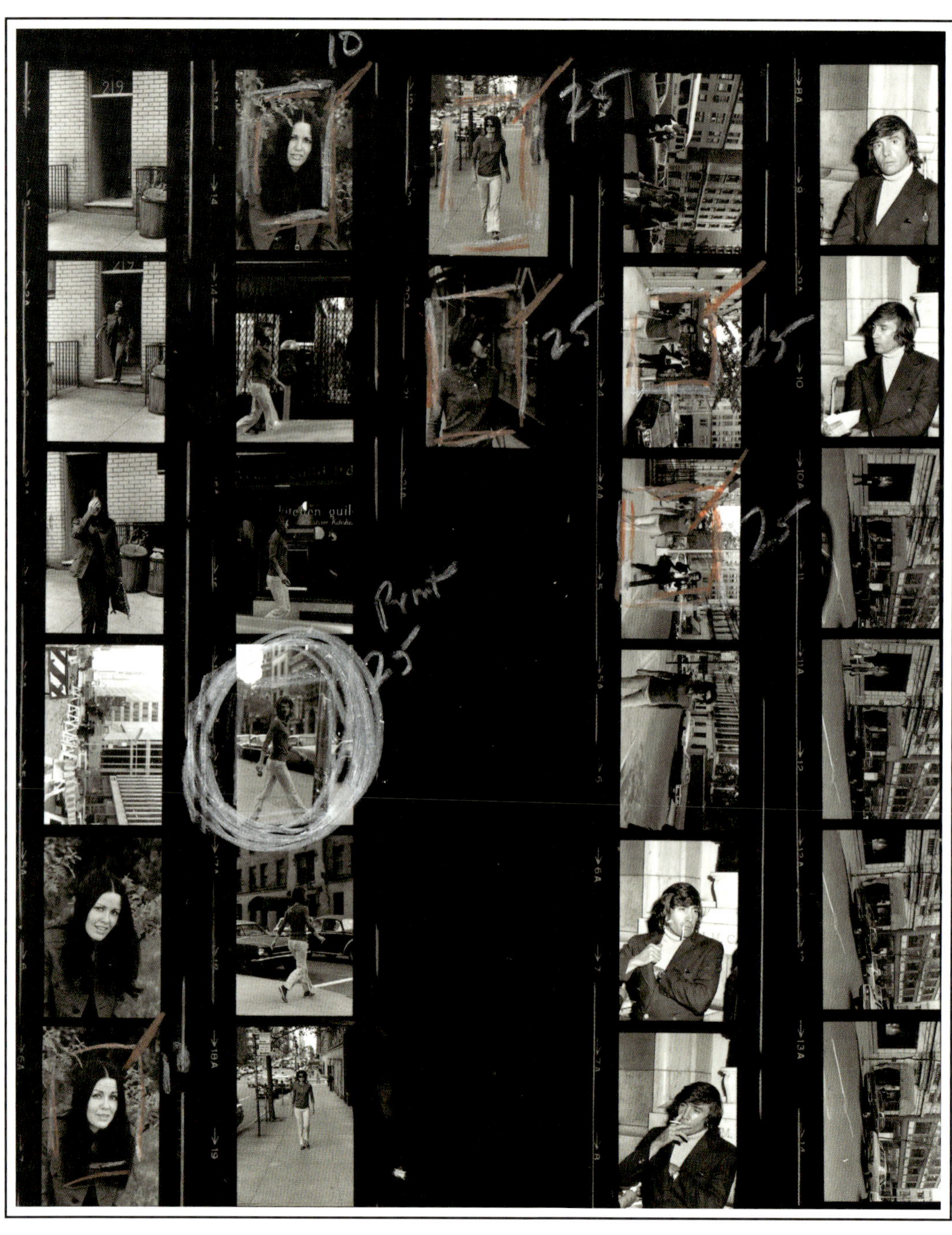

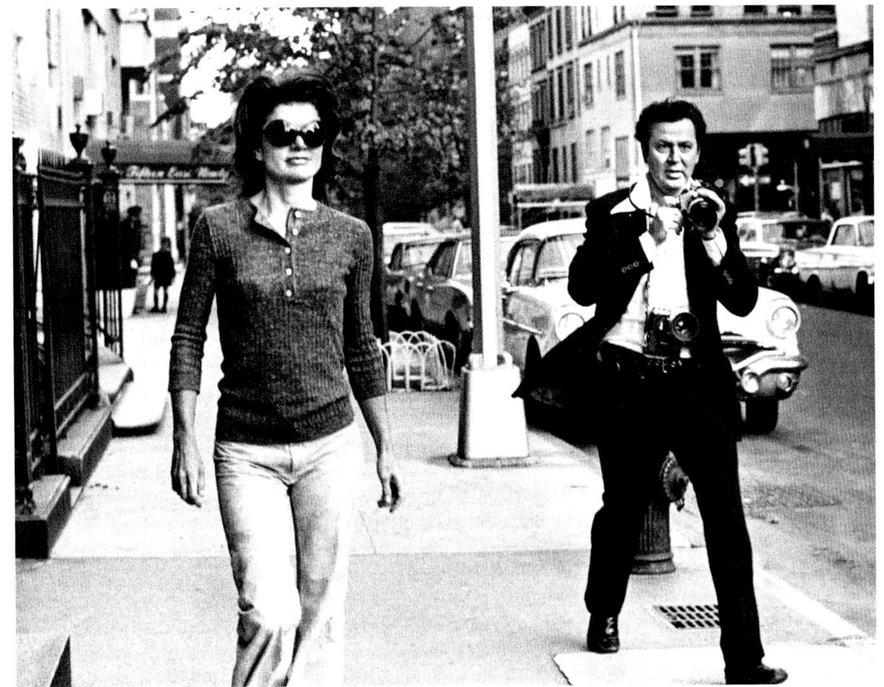

Photo Credit: Joy Smith

JACKIE KENNEDY ONASSIS & RON GALELLA

It was late in the afternoon, around four thirty, blue sky with a slight breeze. I had just finished photographing portfolio shots for Joy Smith, a pretty model who lived on East Eighty-eighth Street. A fool for beauty, I was not getting paid, so I figured I might as well shoot in Central Park across from Jackie's apartment in hopes of getting lucky - AND BOY DID I!

Upon leaving the park, we caught a glimpse of Jackie leaving her apartment through the back door on Eighty-fifth Street, heading toward Madison Avenue. Joy could not believe it was Jackie and I excitedly assured her that it was.

Walking a distance behind her, Joy and I followed Jackie on 85th Street to Madison Avenue, where Jackie made a left going north. I decided not to run in front of her because if I did she would have recognized me and put on those dark glasses. So with Joy, I decided to hop a cab to catch up to Jackie. "Follow that woman!" I told the cab driver. When we caught up with her between Eighty-ninth and Ninetieth Streets, I rolled down the rear window and shot two profiles of her walking. She did not see me or hear the shutter click due to the noisy New York traffic. Suddenly and without me asking, at the corner of Ninetieth Street, the cab driver blew his horn! Jackie turned and I pressed the shutter release for the third time, creating what Henri Cartier-Bresson called a decisive moment.

The father of photojournalism, Cartier-Bresson is one of my favorite photographers and the crème de la crème of street photographers. He was an early adopter of the 35mm format and candid photography. This decisive moment photo, which I titled, Windblown Jackie, is my favorite, most published picture and the best-selling print of all time at my fine art galleries worldwide. It's a superior picture, like DaVinci's most famous painting, the Mona Lisa. It embodies all the qualities of my paparazzi approach: exclusive, unrehearsed, off-guard, spontaneous, no appointments—the only game. Jackie has a slight smile on her lips as well as in her eyes. The dramatic, soft backlighting and the over-the-shoulder composition show Jackie at her finest. She was casually dressed, wore no makeup, and her hair was windblown, which added to her raw, natural beauty. With a bit of luck, and all the elements working with me, I captured this iconic photo outside, in the street, from a cab; it could never have been produced in the sterile environment of a photo studio. Jackie responded casually, not knowing it was me, as my camera covered my face. Then, after I got out of the cab, she recognized me and immediately put on her sunglasses.

After capturing this iconic image, I photographed her from Ninetieth Street to Ninety-first Street. I handed one of my prefocused cameras with a wide-angle lens to Joy and asked her to try and photograph Jackie and me together, which she did. Both Joy and I were laughing and clicking away until a furious Jackie turned toward me and said, "Are you pleeeased with yourself?" I knew then it was time to stop and said, "Yes, thank you," and we left.
Clearly, at the time I did not know it was going to become the most purchased, most recognized, most talked about, most significant photo I ever captured.

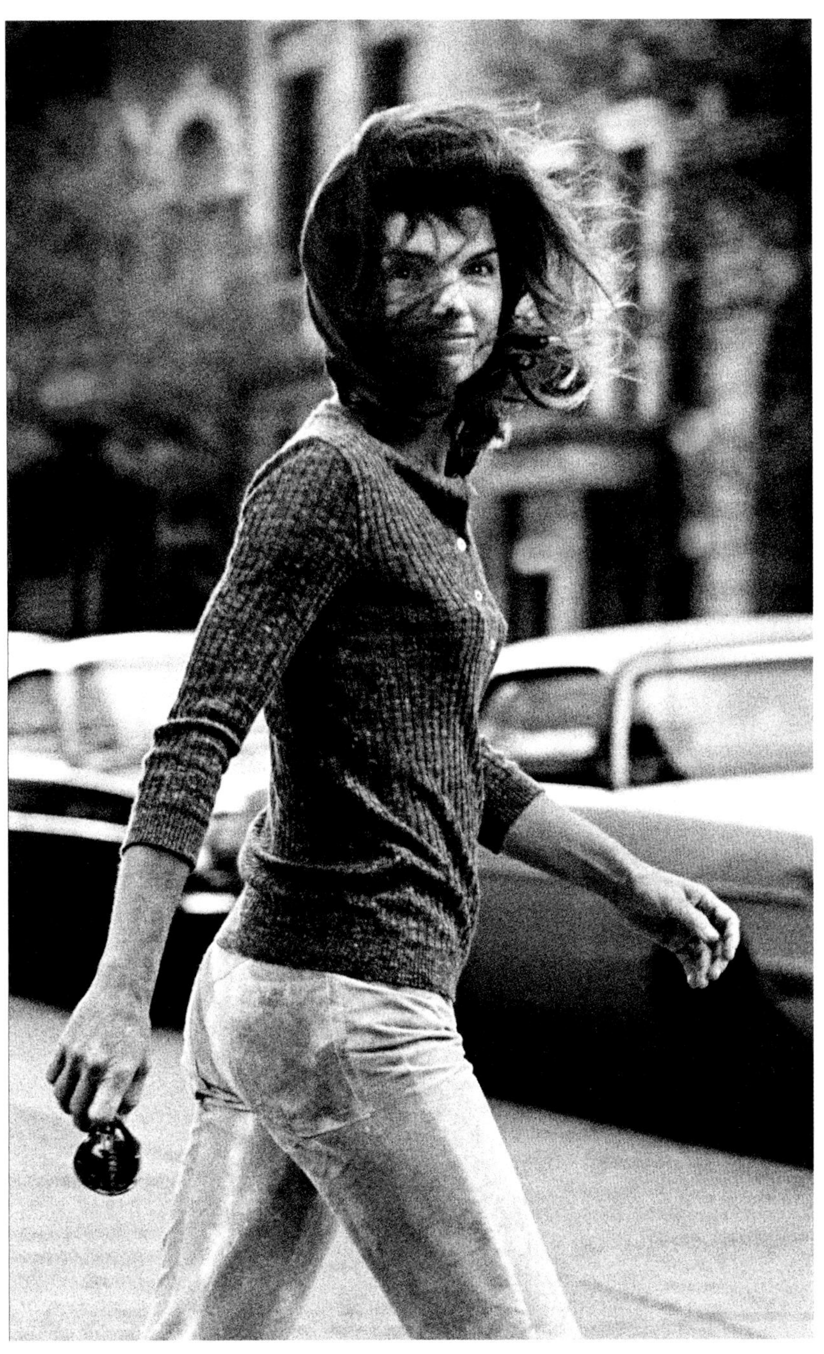

WINDBLOWN JACKIE
October 7, 1971 – New York City
Madison Avenue

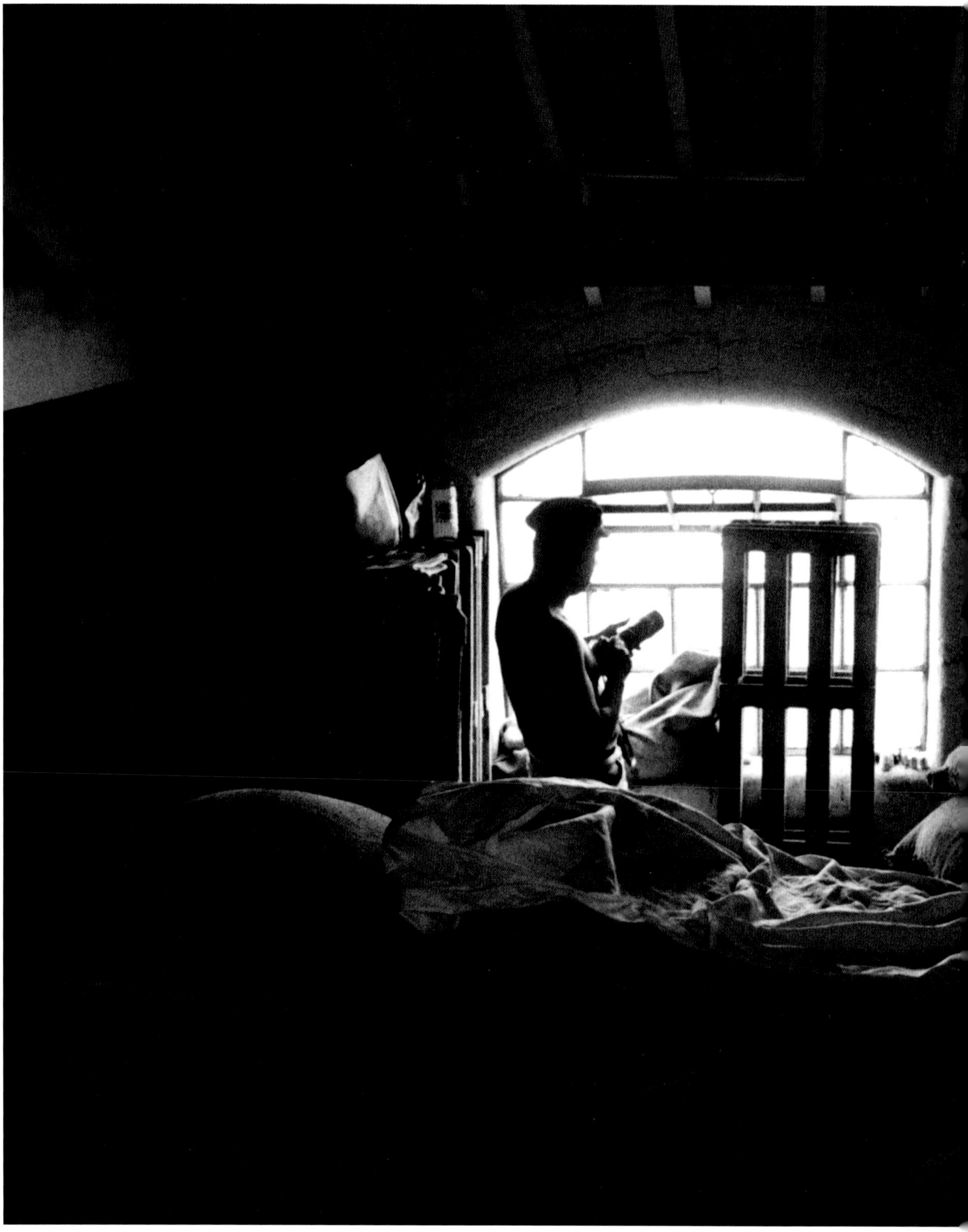

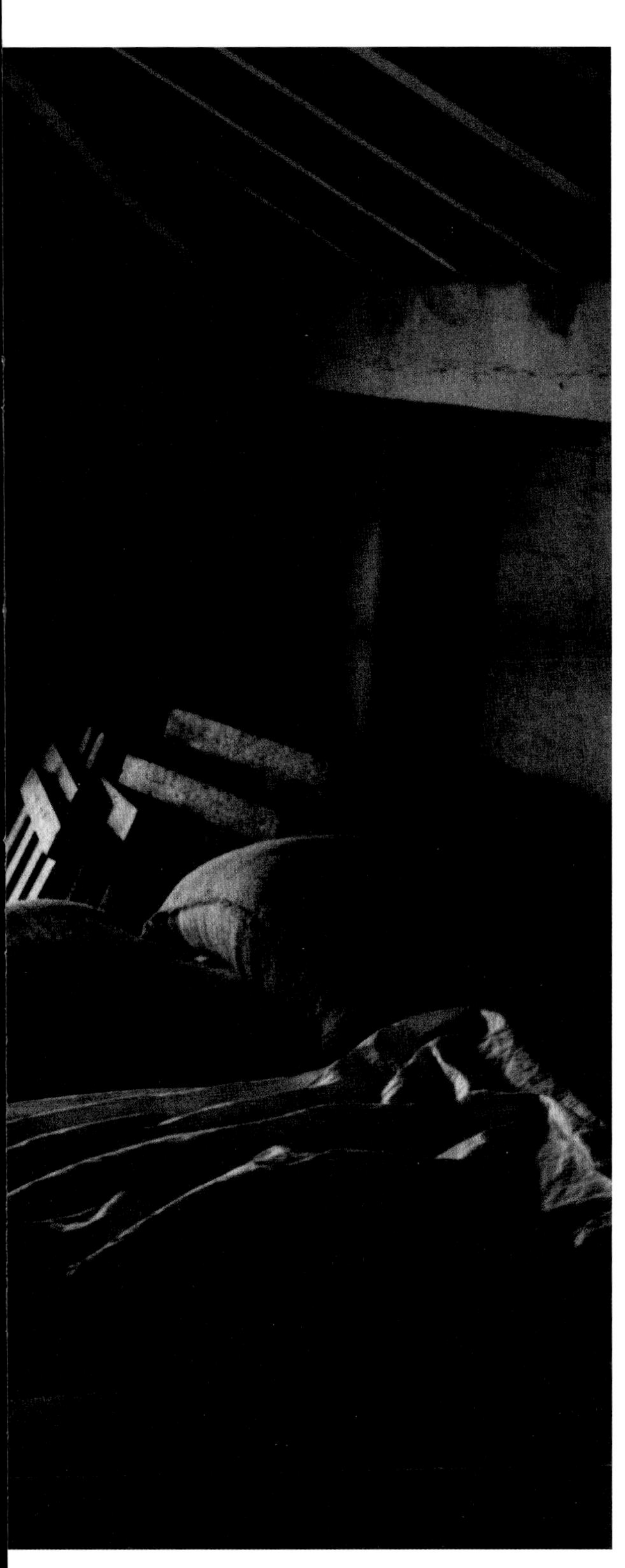

RON GALELLA
August 1, 1969 – London, England
Self-Portrait inside warehouse
along the River Thames waiting for
Elizabeth Taylor and Richard Burton

ELIZABETH TAYLOR & RICHARD BURTON ON THEIR YACHT KALIZMA

My most memorable and unusual take in August was of the Burtons on their yacht Kalizma, named after their daughters, Kate, Liz, and Maria. The boat was moored in the Thames. They would visit it on weekends to see their dogs, which were quarantined on the boat because of British health laws. Adjacent to the yacht was a dock with a big five-story customs warehouse that stored sugar, cinnamon, cocoa, butter, and coffee. The Kalizma floated 150 feet from the warehouse. I spoke with the warehouse watchman and he said I could go in and shoot from the windows Monday through Friday, as the building was closed from Friday afternoon until Monday morning. Instead, I developed a plan to spend a weekend in the warehouse, but I needed to be sure what weekend the Burtons would be spending time there. I spoke with one of the Portuguese sailors who worked on the yacht and he mentioned that "some event" was planned for the following weekend. So, I prepared myself for the three-night stay by buying a sleeping bag. On Friday afternoon around four, I bought a whole shopping bag of food and soft drinks and paid the watchman fifteen dollars to lock me in the warehouse. He wouldn't be back to let me out until about nine on Monday morning.

The warehouse had bars on the windows, so there was no way to get out. Climbing up the stairs, I saw rats, which became the worst part of this bazaar stakeout. That first night, fearing the rats, I slept on the roof. Saturday morning, I put my sleeping bag on top of sacks of coffee, facing the window, on the fifth floor. The spices combined with the coffee created a sweet, chocolaty fragrance, helping me stay alert. The window acted as my TV, with only one station, which I watched constantly in order to catch the Burtons coming aboard. Nothing happened Friday, but on Saturday afternoon they started parading in. There was Elizabeth Taylor; lawyer, Aaron Frosch; a bride and groom; and other minor actors. I found out later Richard and Elizabeth had been best man and maid of honor at the wedding of their secretary, Bob Wilson. The wedding took place at the Dorchester, which of course I missed, but I wouldn't have been able to get in there anyway. All I would have gotten was them coming out of the Dorchester at the end of the ceremony. I soon realized that what I had was much more valuable–exclusive pictures of the wedding reception. Best of all, it took place right in front of me, on the Burtons' yacht.

But the best shot wasn't from the wedding at all. This yacht was like a landmark; tourist boats would pass by and I could hear the tour guides say with their megaphones, "This is the Kalizma, the Burtons' yacht and when the American flag is flying, Elizabeth is on board and when the British flag is flying, Burton is on board." My best picture–and the best-selling picture–was one of a tourist boat passing by while Elizabeth and the yacht's steward, Raymonde, were hanging up gauze curtains for privacy. The tourists were there with their cameras unaware that Elizabeth Taylor was right in front of them. The screen blocked the tourists from taking pictures, but I got the best shot! *The National Enquirer* published a two-page layout of nine pictures titled, Exclusive Photos: Liz Hangs 'Curtains' on Her Yacht to Hide from Gawking Sightseers. I was paid the normal rate of four hundred dollars. I did not have time to bargain since making a long-distance call from London was time-consuming and, as always, my goal was to shoot nonstop. Thinking back, I should have been paid at least four thousand dollars, but I did receive high praise from the *The National Enquirer* at a later date.

Pictures of Elizabeth and Richard were hot; they always sold. On a balmy September day outside London's Dorchester Hotel, I almost got socked by Richard Burton. Elizabeth, her son Michael Wilding Jr., and daughter Liza Todd went to Trader Vic's at the Hilton Hotel for lunch, which was a few blocks from where they were staying at the Dorchester. Burton joined them, arriving late due to filming "Anne of a Thousand Days". After lunch, they left through the back exit of Trader Vic's to head back to the Dorchester. Burton had had too much to drink and was staggering. Elizabeth helped him walk. When we'd almost reached the hotel, Burton yelled to me, "Sweetheart, come here." Then, pointing to me, he said in his Shakespearean voice, "You've had enough, one more and I'll…" He then raised his fist in an attempt to sock me and Elizabeth held him back. This stopped me from shooting and I missed the shot with his fist up. Burton's chauffeur Gaston must have felt a bit of loyalty to Burton because as I was leaving he hit me on the shoulder and chased me away.

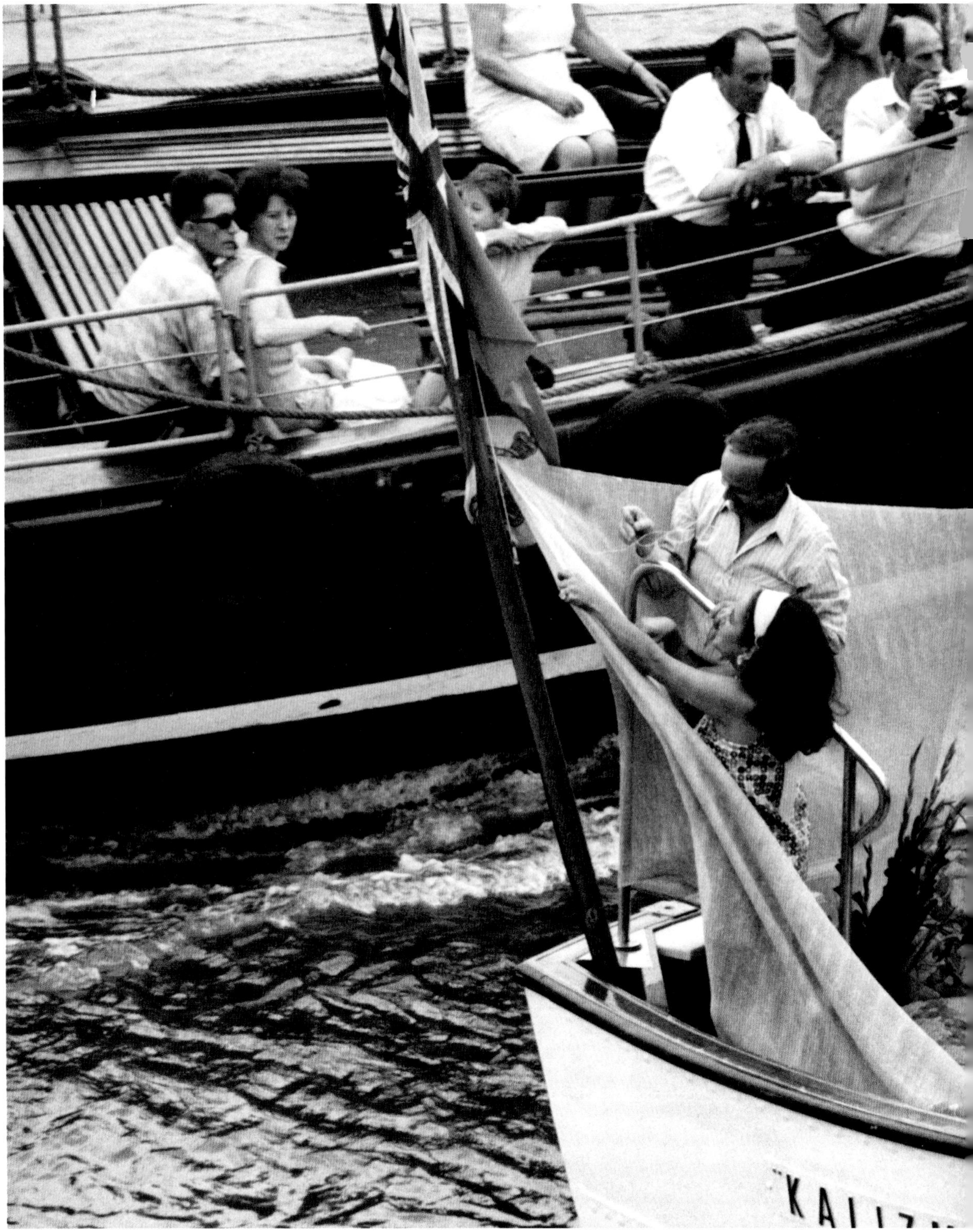

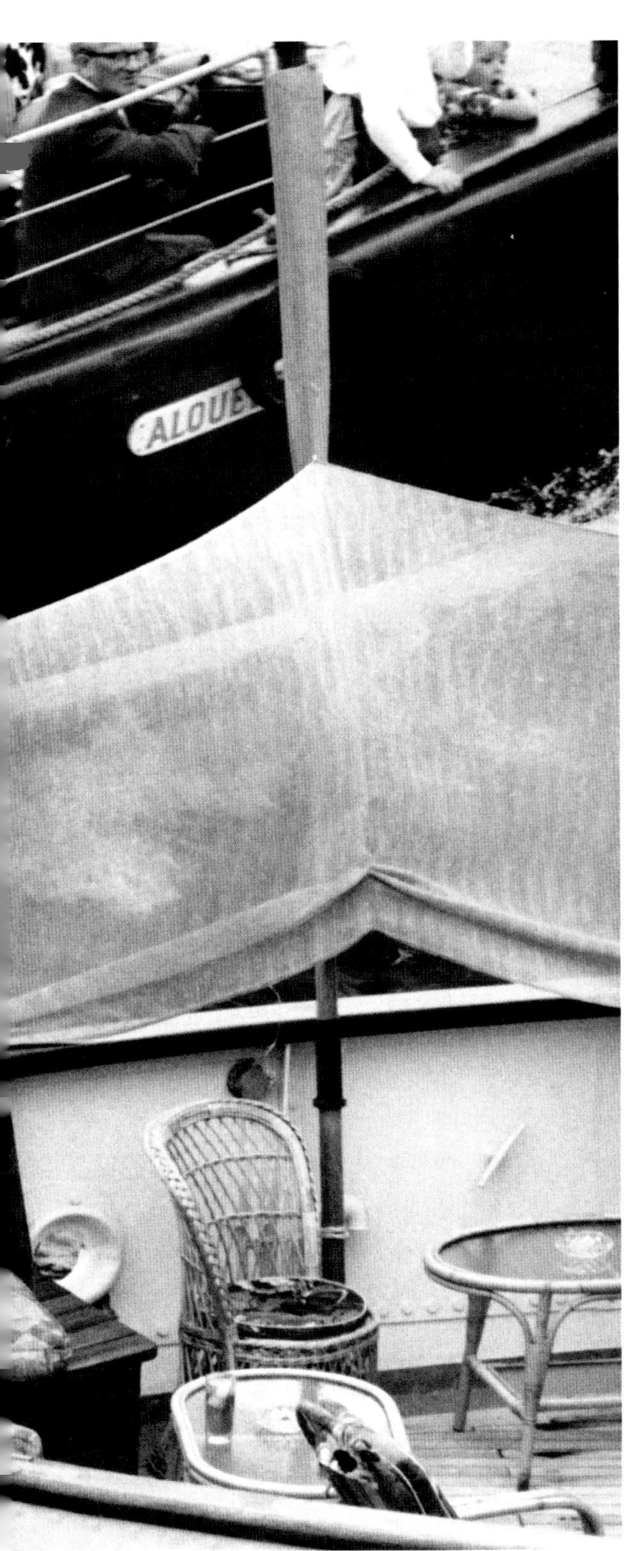

ELIZABETH TAYLOR

August 1, 1969 – London, England
aboard Kalizma on the river Thames

102

RICHARD BURTON
& ELIZABETH TAYLOR

August 11, 1970 – Le Havre, France

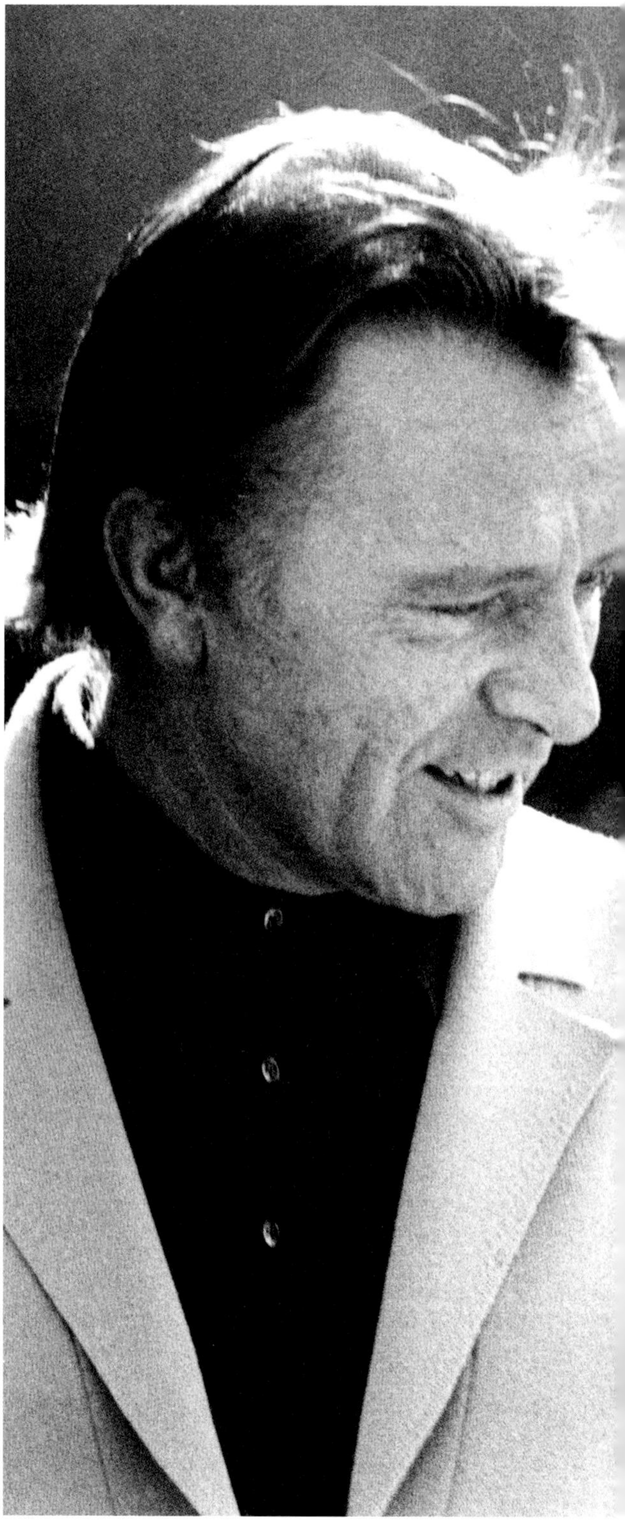

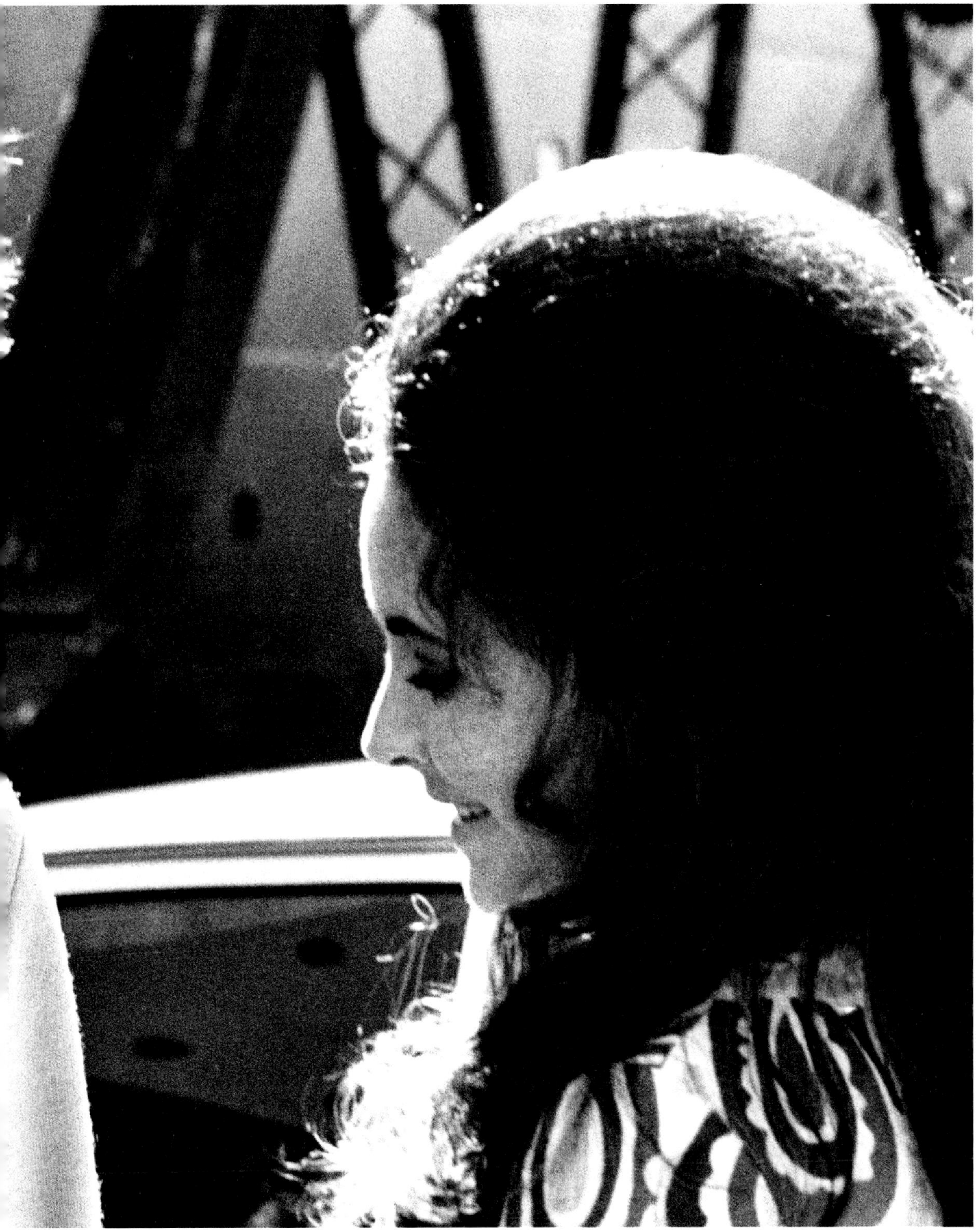

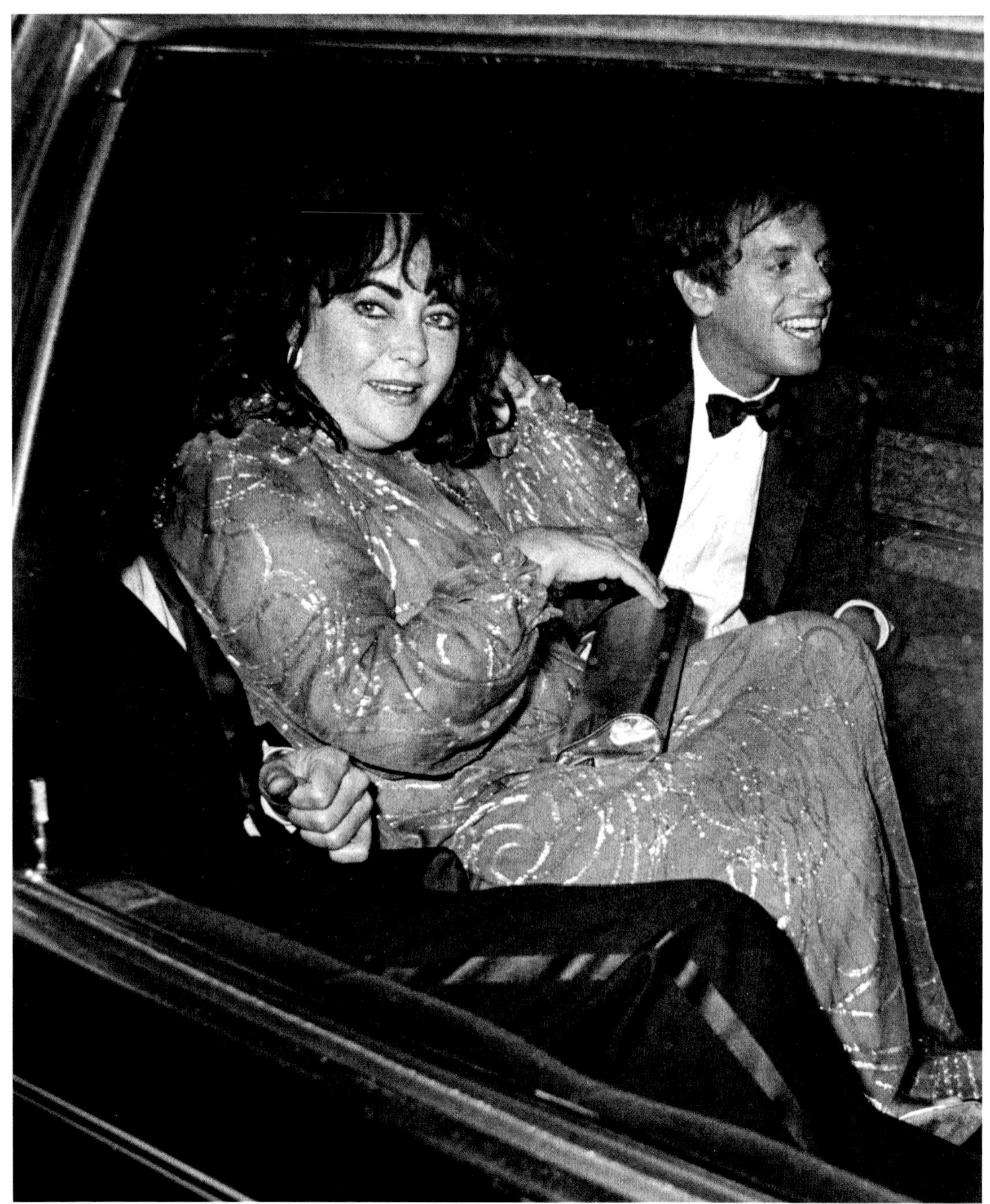

ELIZABETH TAYLOR & STEVE RUBELL
May 21, 1979 – New York City
Martha Graham Awards Gala Honoring Halston at Studio 54

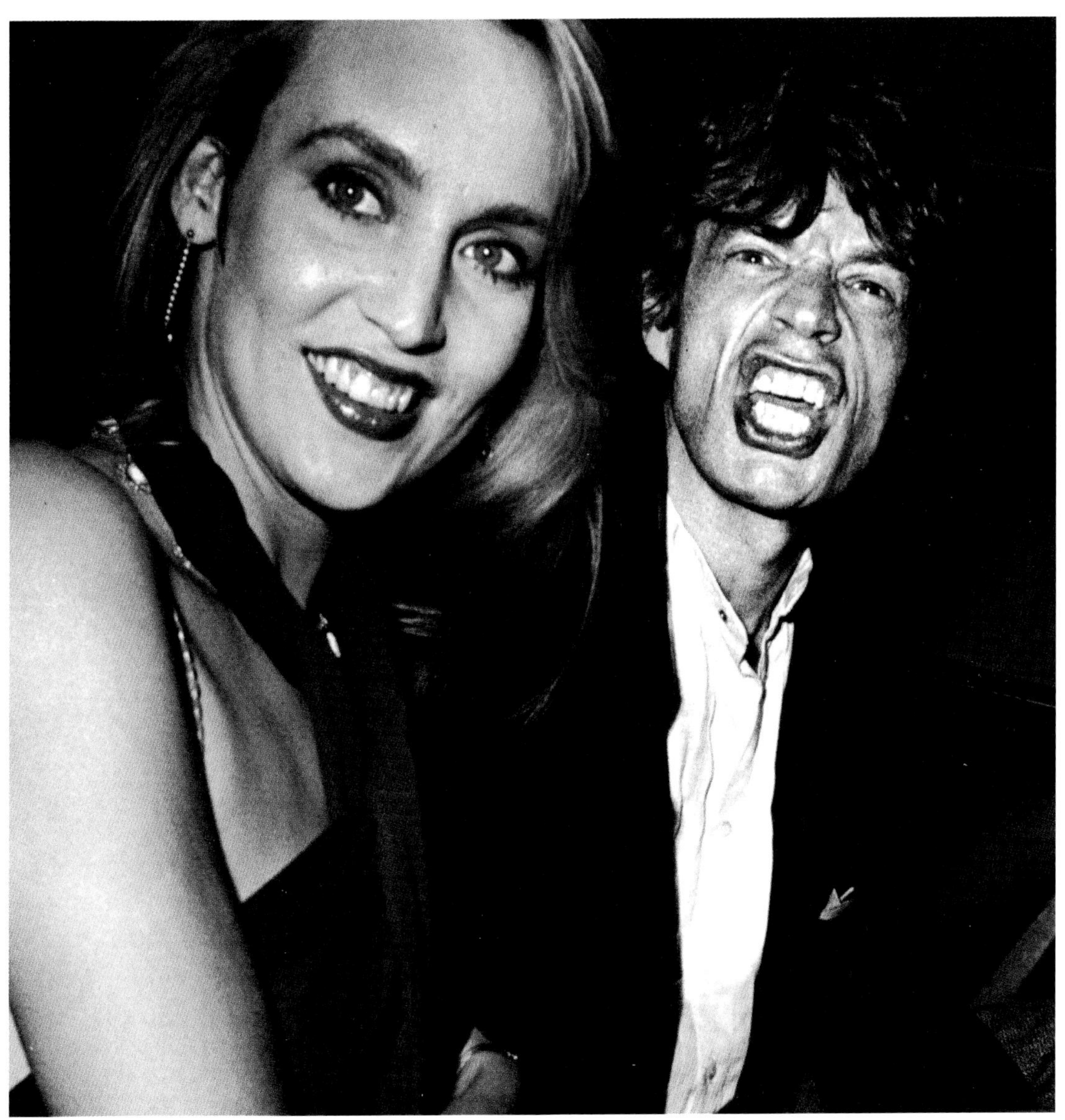

JERRY HALL & MICK JAGGER
September 19, 1984 – New York City
Party for Reid Rogers at the Limelight

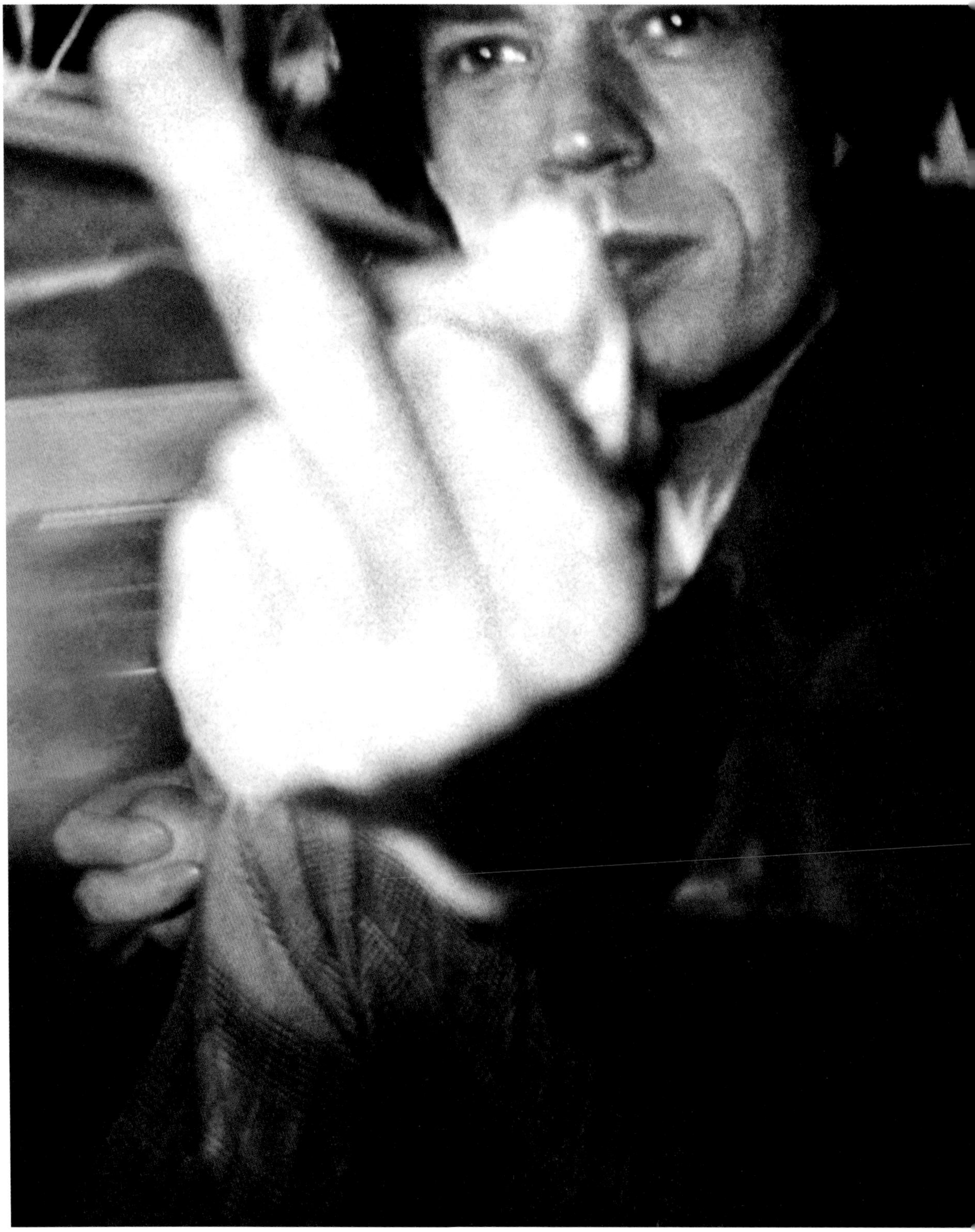

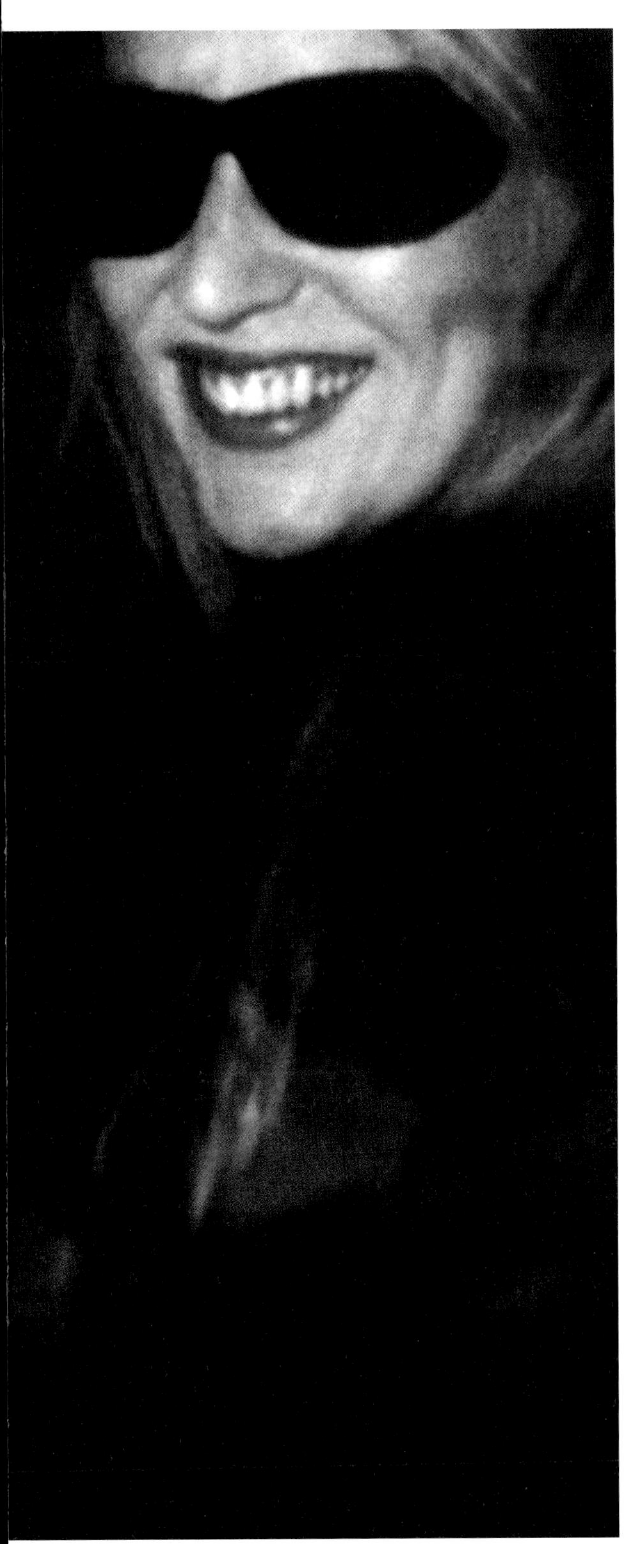

MICK JAGGER & JERRY HALL 107
January 16, 1983 – Los Angeles, California
Mizuno Gallery Opening

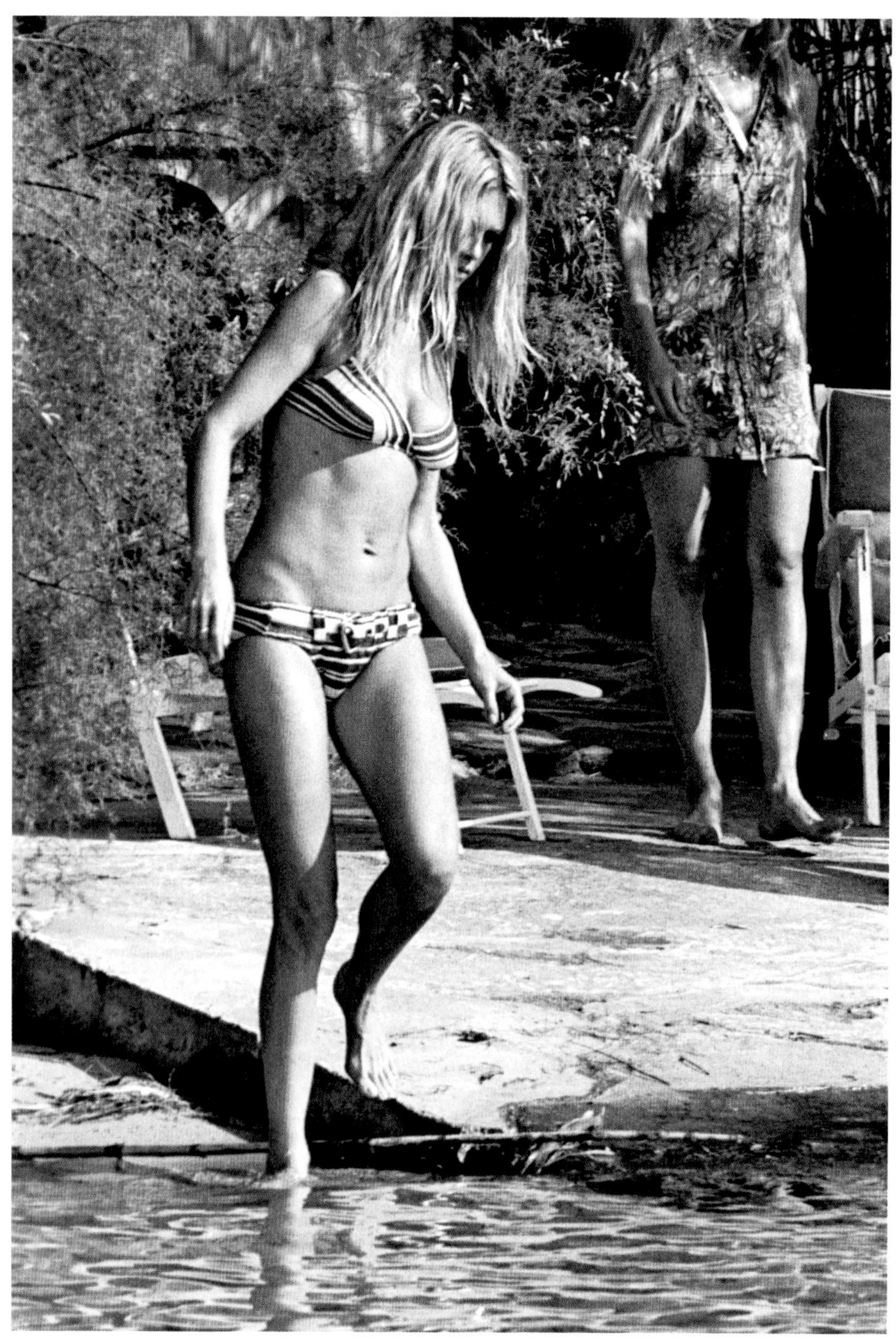

BRIGITTE BARDOT
September 15, 1968 – St. Tropez, France

BRIGITTE BARDOT

On September 11, arriving at the Nice airport, I met actor George Sanders, who lived in St. Tropez. As I was taking a few shots of him, he said, "Why are you photographing me? You should be going after Brigitte Bardot."

The following day, I was determined to get pictures of Bardot in St. Tropez. With my cameras exposed, I asked a taxi driver to take me to her house and he refused. It was obvious I was a photographer and he wanted to protect Bardot's privacy. I then hid my cameras in my leather mailbag and asked another driver. He assumed I was a mailman and drove me to Bardot's house on the Mediterranean shore. I rolled up my trousers and waded in the water adjacent to her property to view Bardot and her boyfriend water-skiing. After I'd taken a dozen beautiful photos of Brigitte in her bikini, her angry boyfriend attempted to hose me with water. At that point I departed without getting wet!

JULIE CHRISTIE

During their seven-year romance in the late sixties and early seventies, Julie Christie and Warren Beatty were the most celebrated couple in Hollywood. All the national and international newspapers and magazines wanted photos of the beautiful young duo. I decided to stake out Christie's Pacific Coast Highway home, in hopes of catching them together. I spotted Julie leaving the house alone and followed her along the Pacific Coast Highway. Unfortunately, I lost Julie's BMW due to the poor performance of my rented Volkswagen Beetle. Later, I spotted her car at a Malibu market and caught her shopping for groceries barefoot, no doubt planning to share them with her boyfriend, the handsome young actor Warren Beatty.

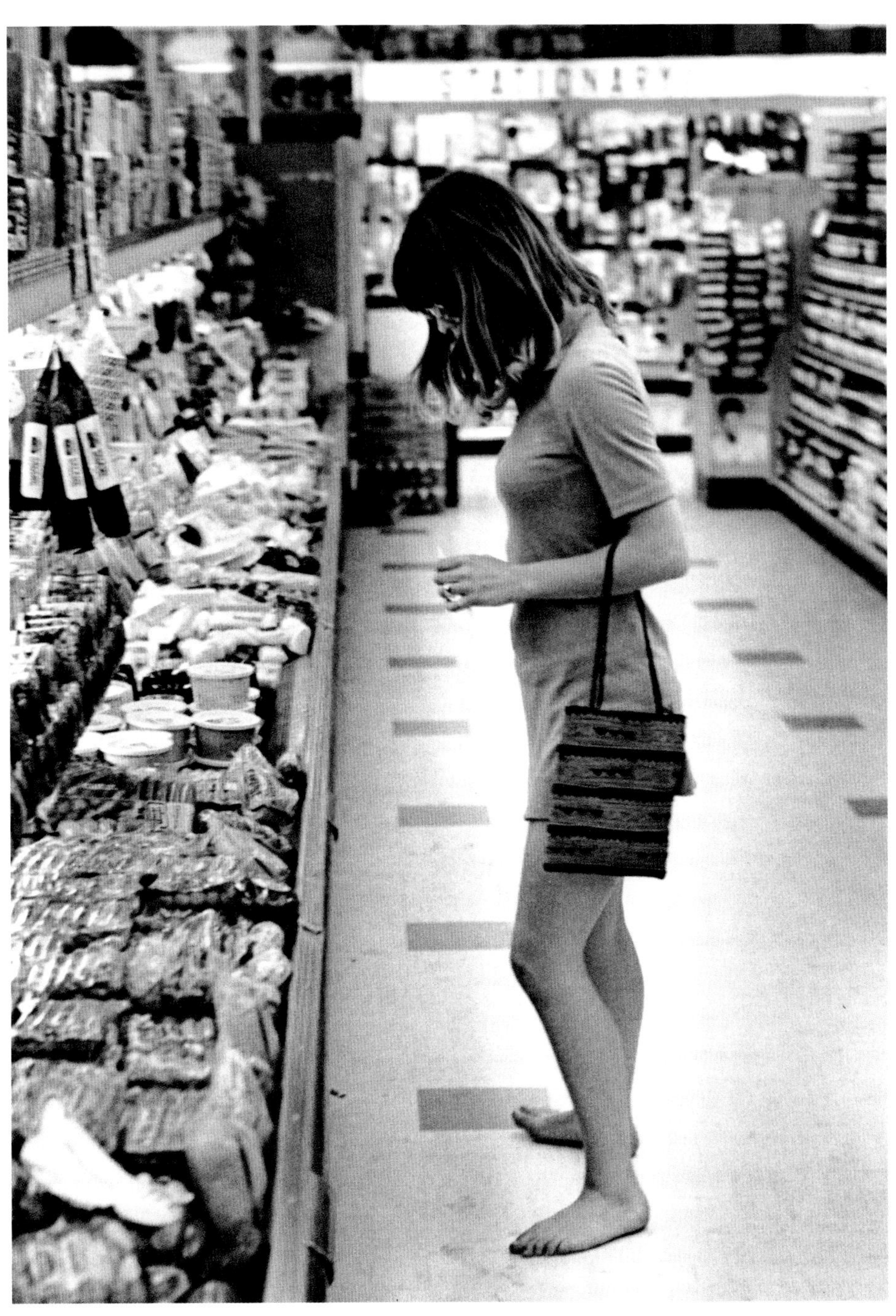

JULIE CHRISTIE
April 12, 1968 – Malibu, California
Malibu Supermarket

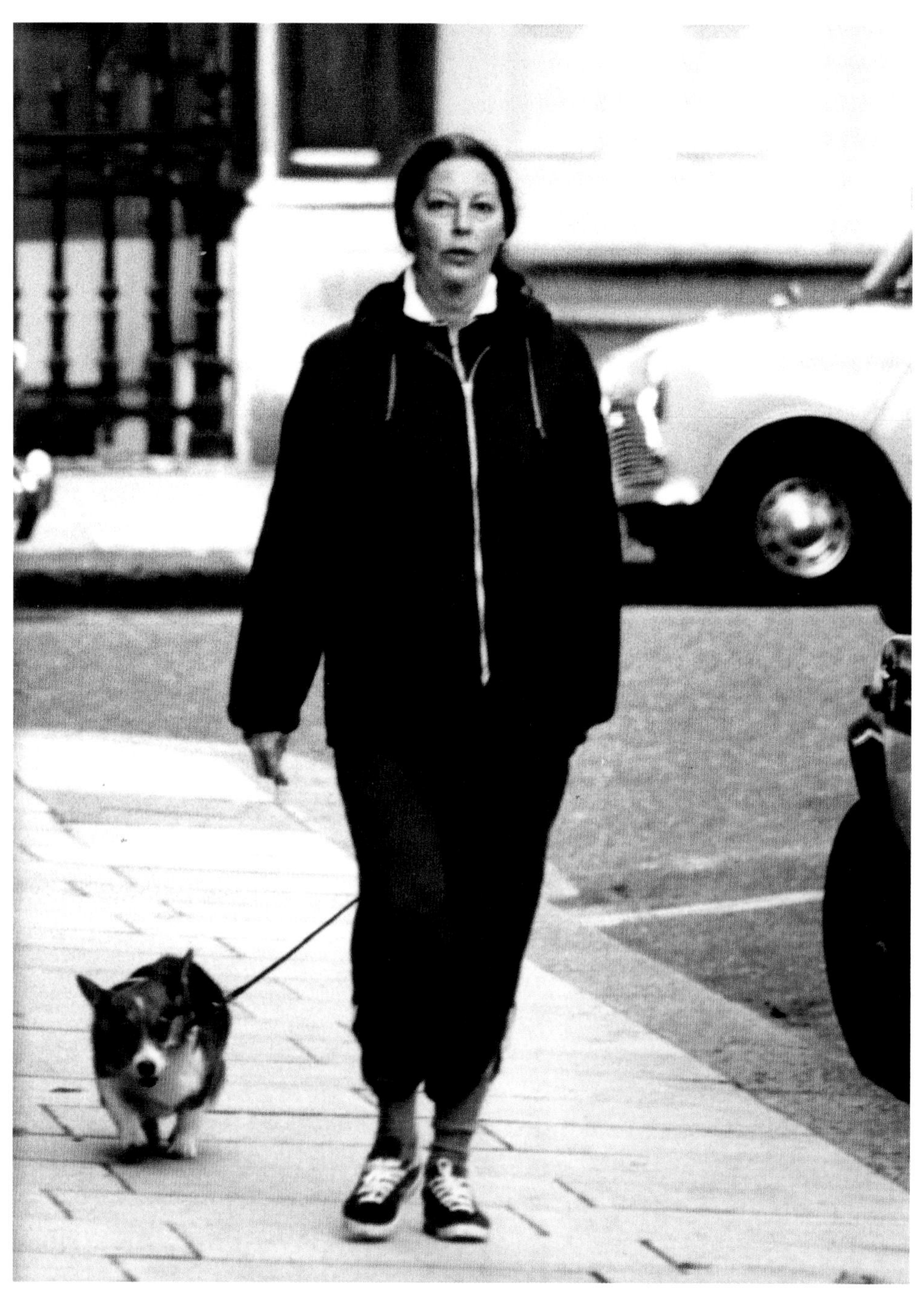

AVA GARDNER
October 17, 1976 – London, England
Walking her dog

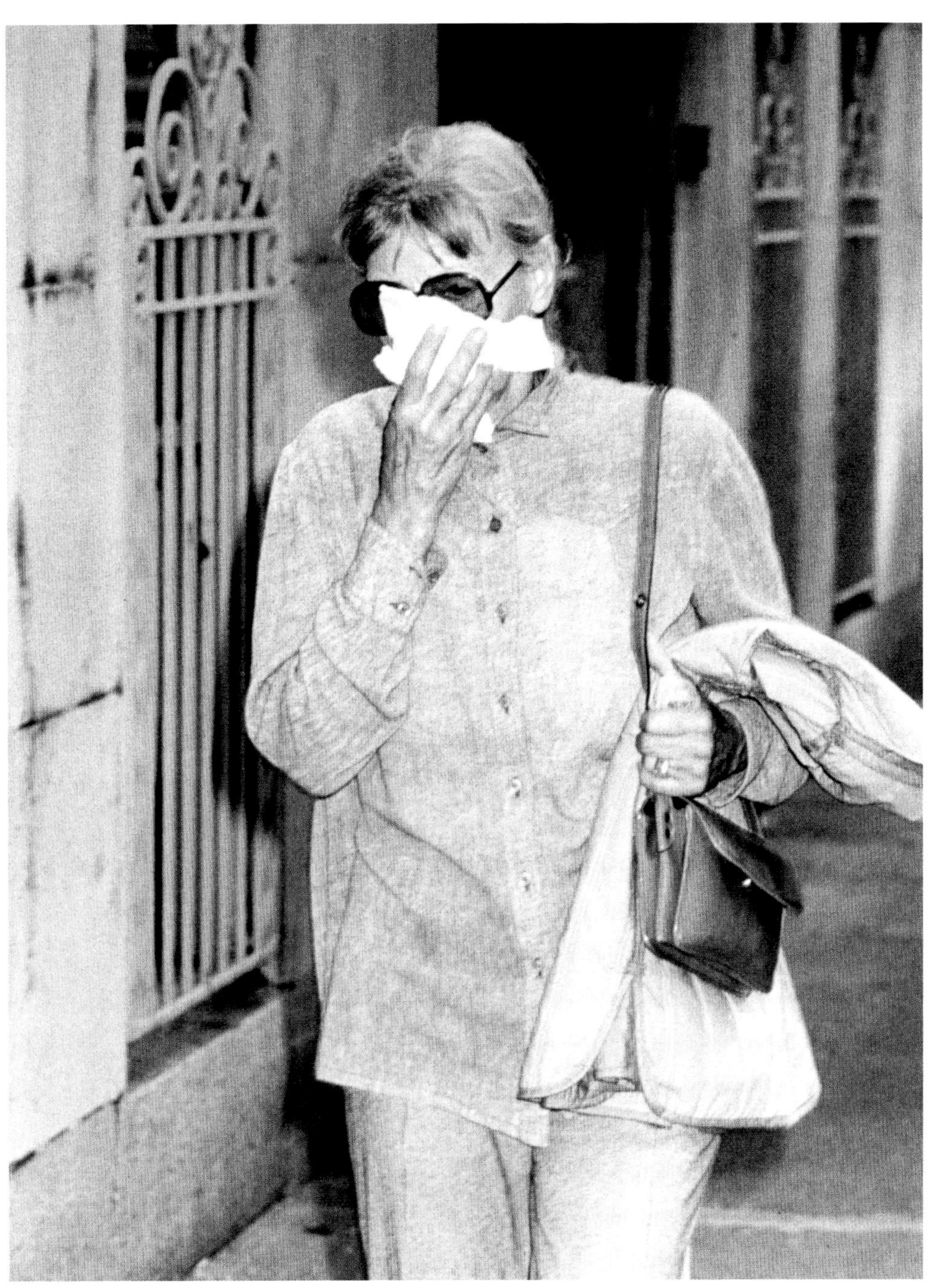

GRETA GARBO
June 1, 1978 – New York City
East 52nd Street

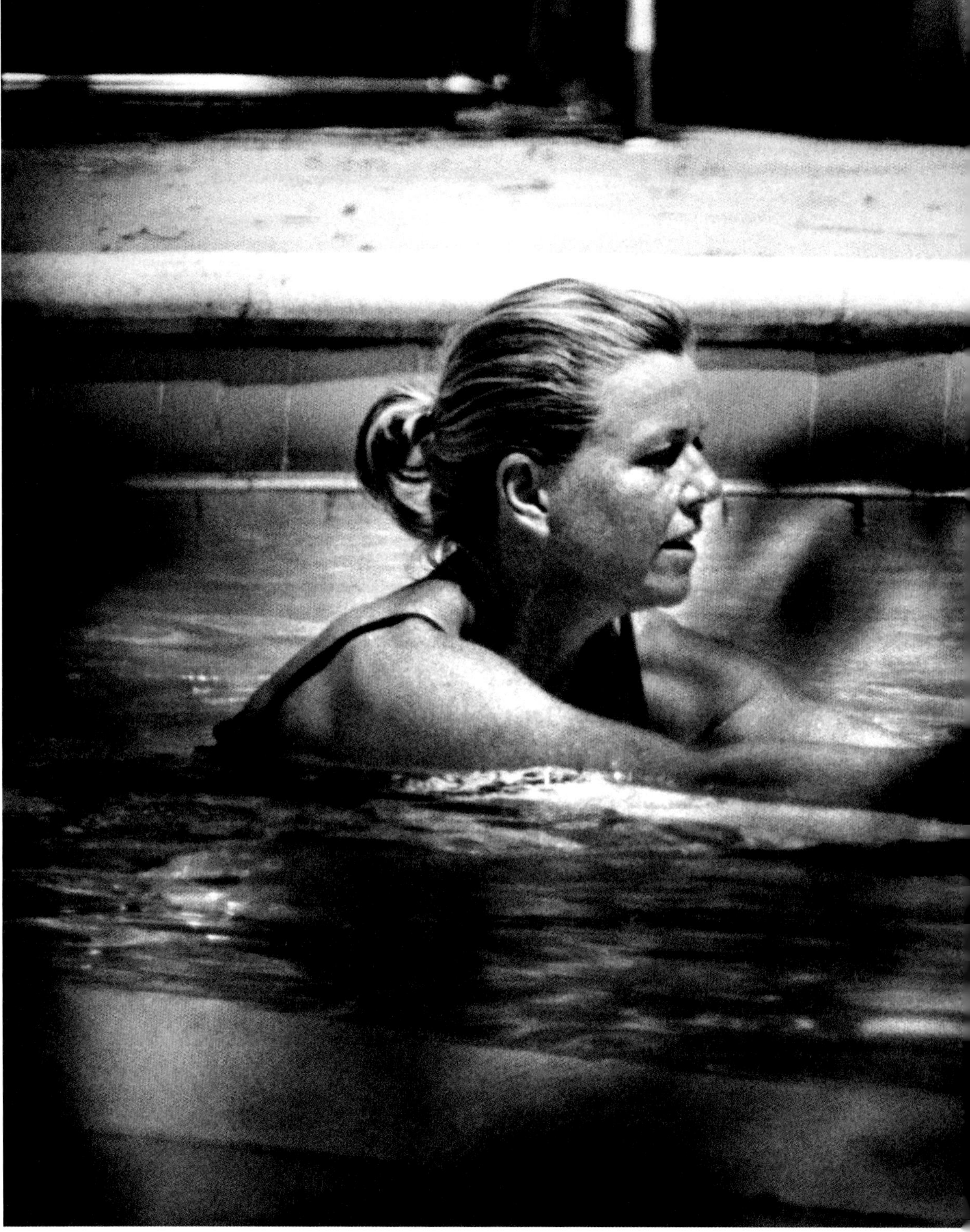

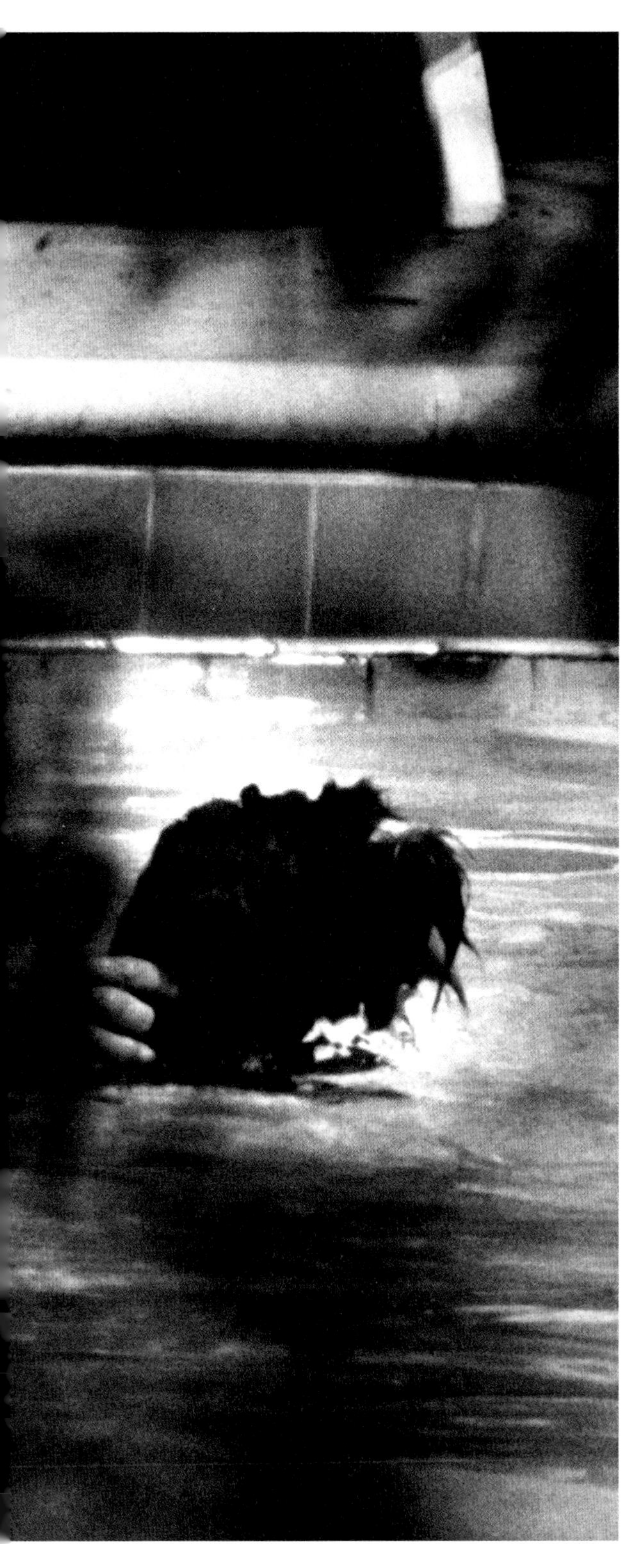

DORIS DAY

April 22, 1971 – Beverly Hills, California
Swimming in her backyard pool

116

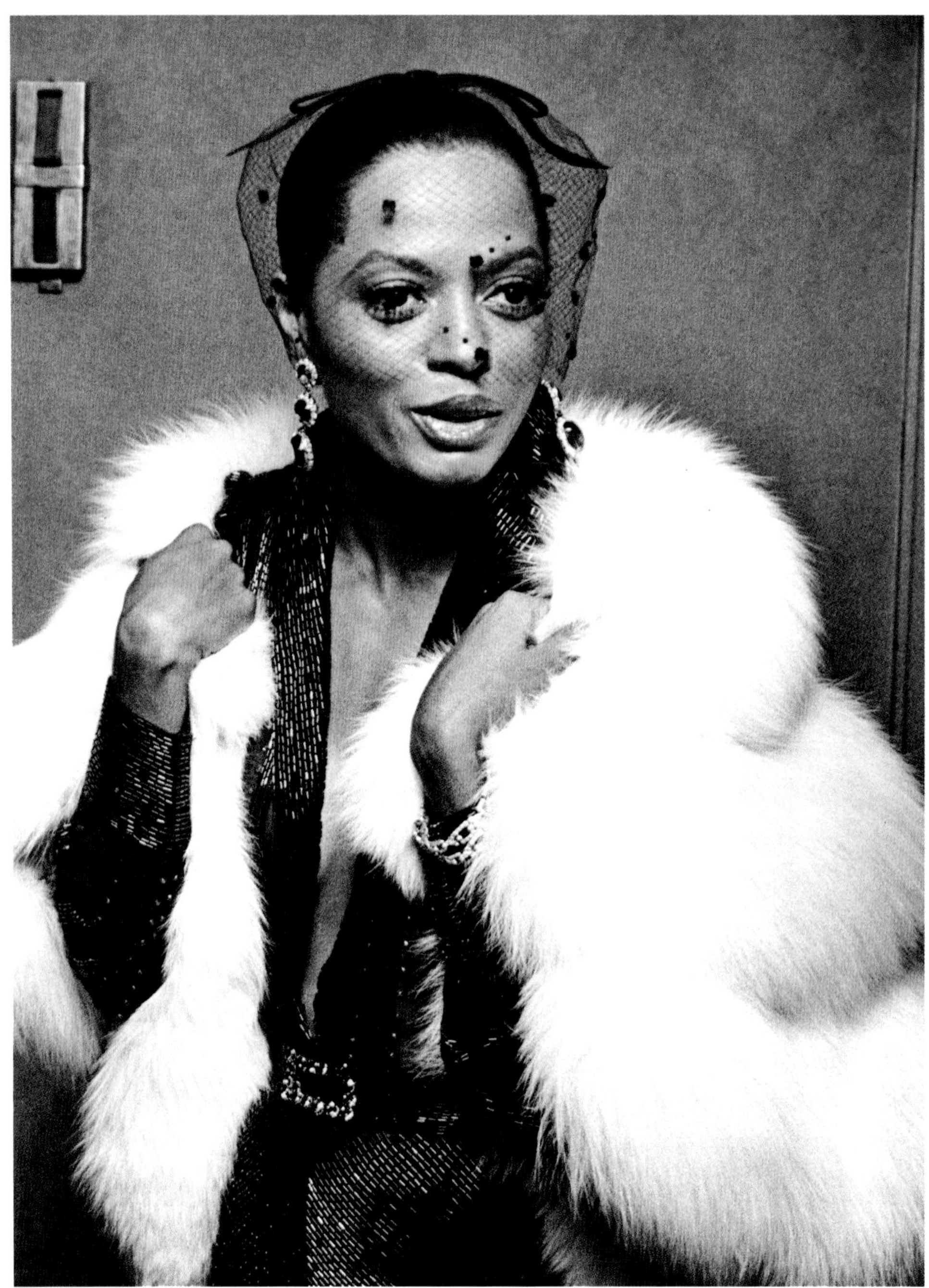

DIANA ROSS
October 16, 1978 – New York City
Motion Picture Award Of The Year Gala Honoring Jule Styne
at the Waldorf-Astoria Hotel

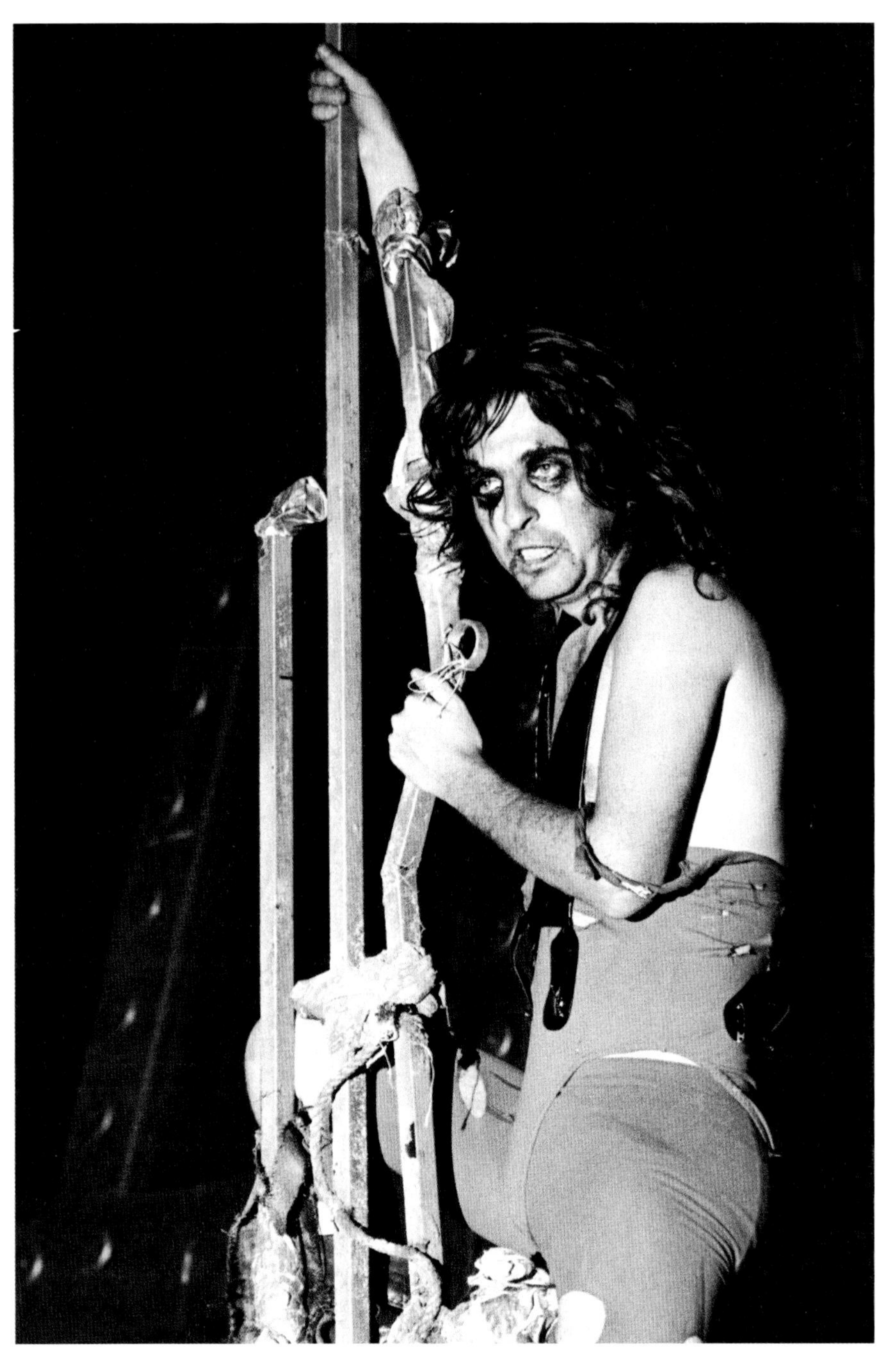

ALICE COOPER
May 5, 1975 – New York City
Performing in concert at Madison Square Garden

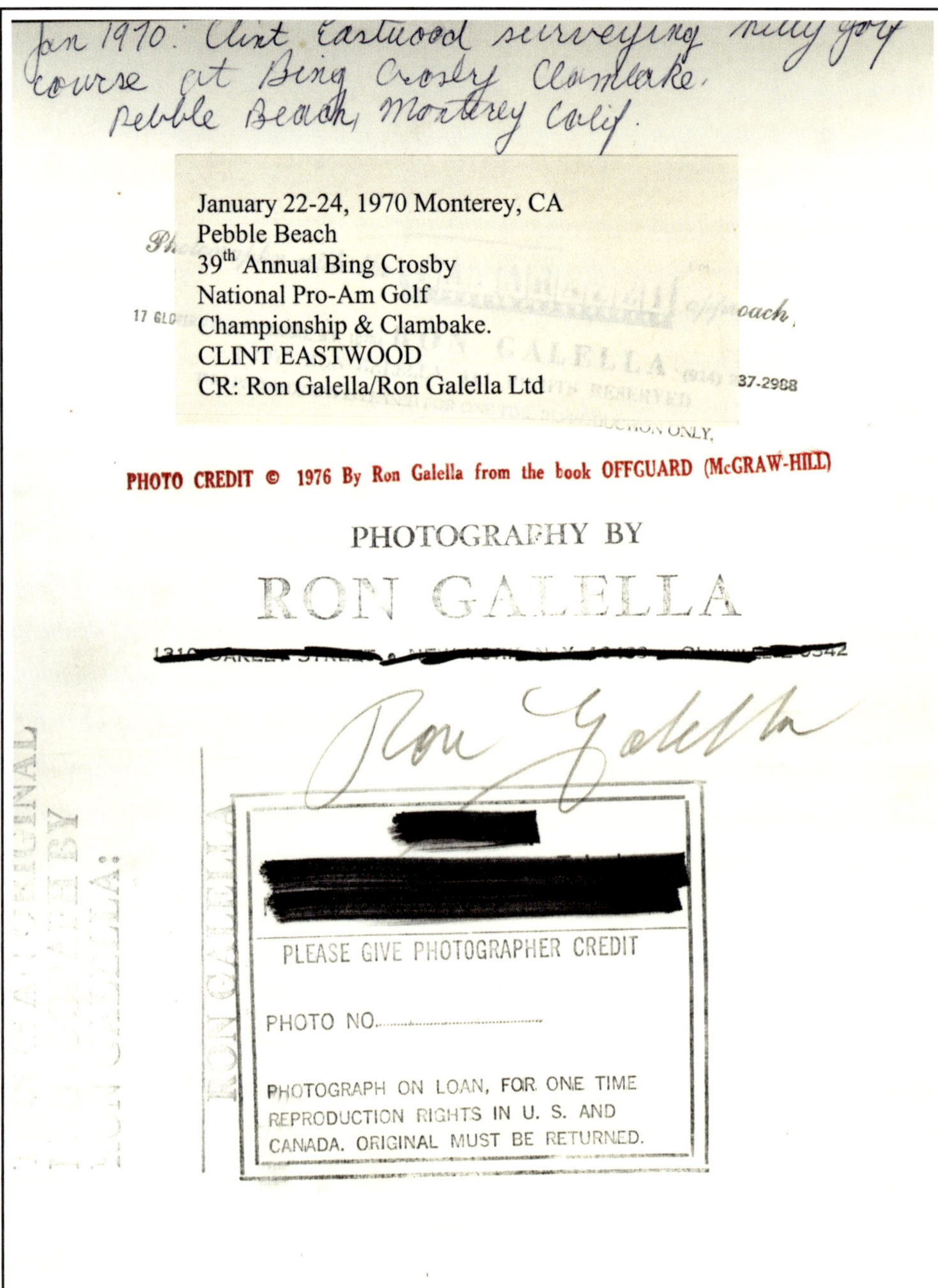
Jan 1970: Clint Eastwood surveying hilly golf course at Bing Crosby Clambake. Pebble Beach, Monterey Calif.
January 22-24, 1970 Monterey, CA
Pebble Beach
39th Annual Bing Crosby
National Pro-Am Golf
Championship & Clambake.
CLINT EASTWOOD
CR: Ron Galella/Ron Galella Ltd
PHOTO CREDIT © 1976 By Ron Galella from the book OFFGUARD (McGRAW-HILL)
PHOTOGRAPHY BY
RON GALELLA
Ron Galella
RON GALELLA
PLEASE GIVE PHOTOGRAPHER CREDIT
PHOTO NO.
PHOTOGRAPH ON LOAN, FOR ONE TIME REPRODUCTION RIGHTS IN U. S. AND CANADA. ORIGINAL MUST BE RETURNED.

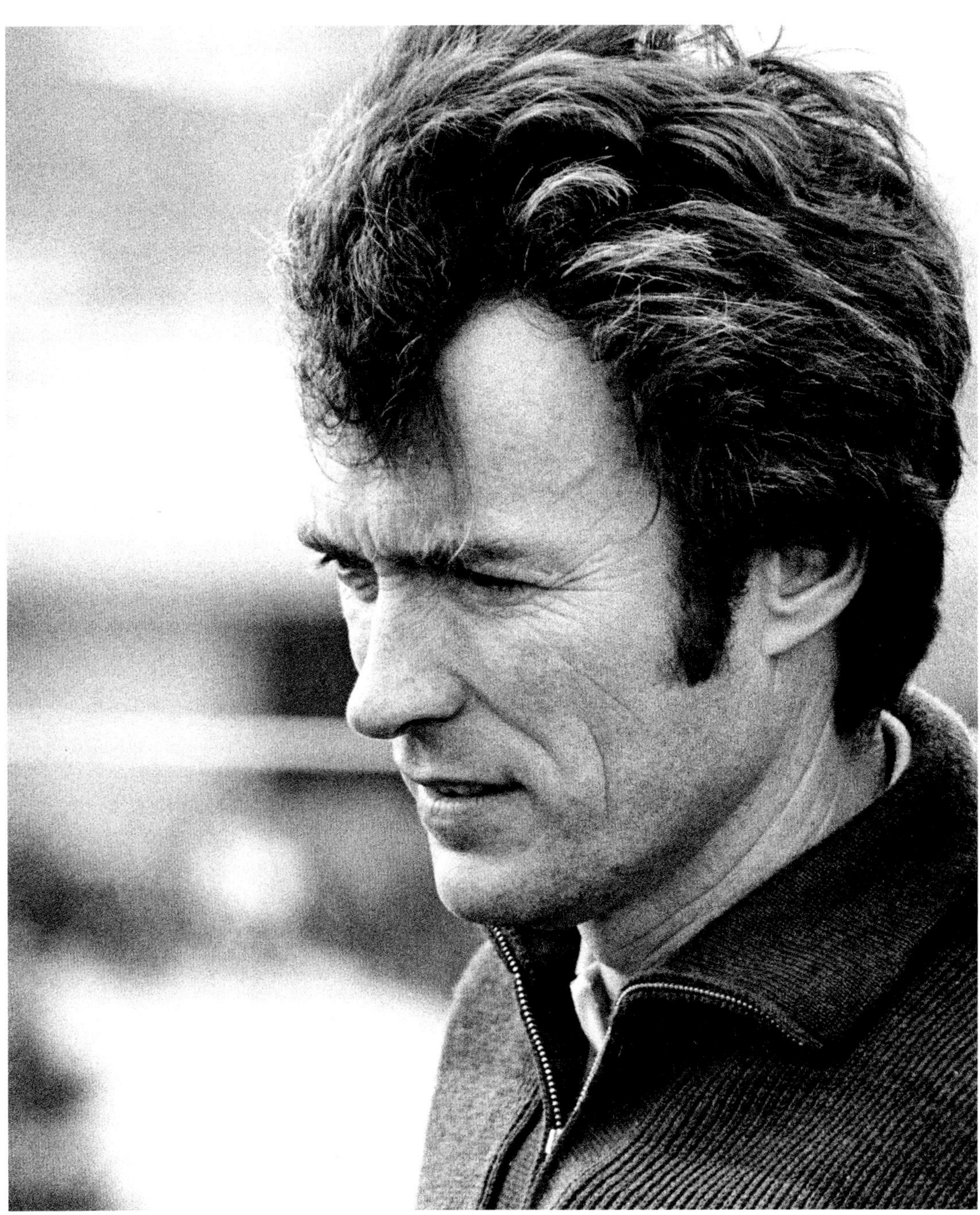

CLINT EASTWOOD
January 22, 1970 – Pebble Beach, California
29th Annual Bing Crosby National Pro-Am Golf Tournament & Clambake Weekend

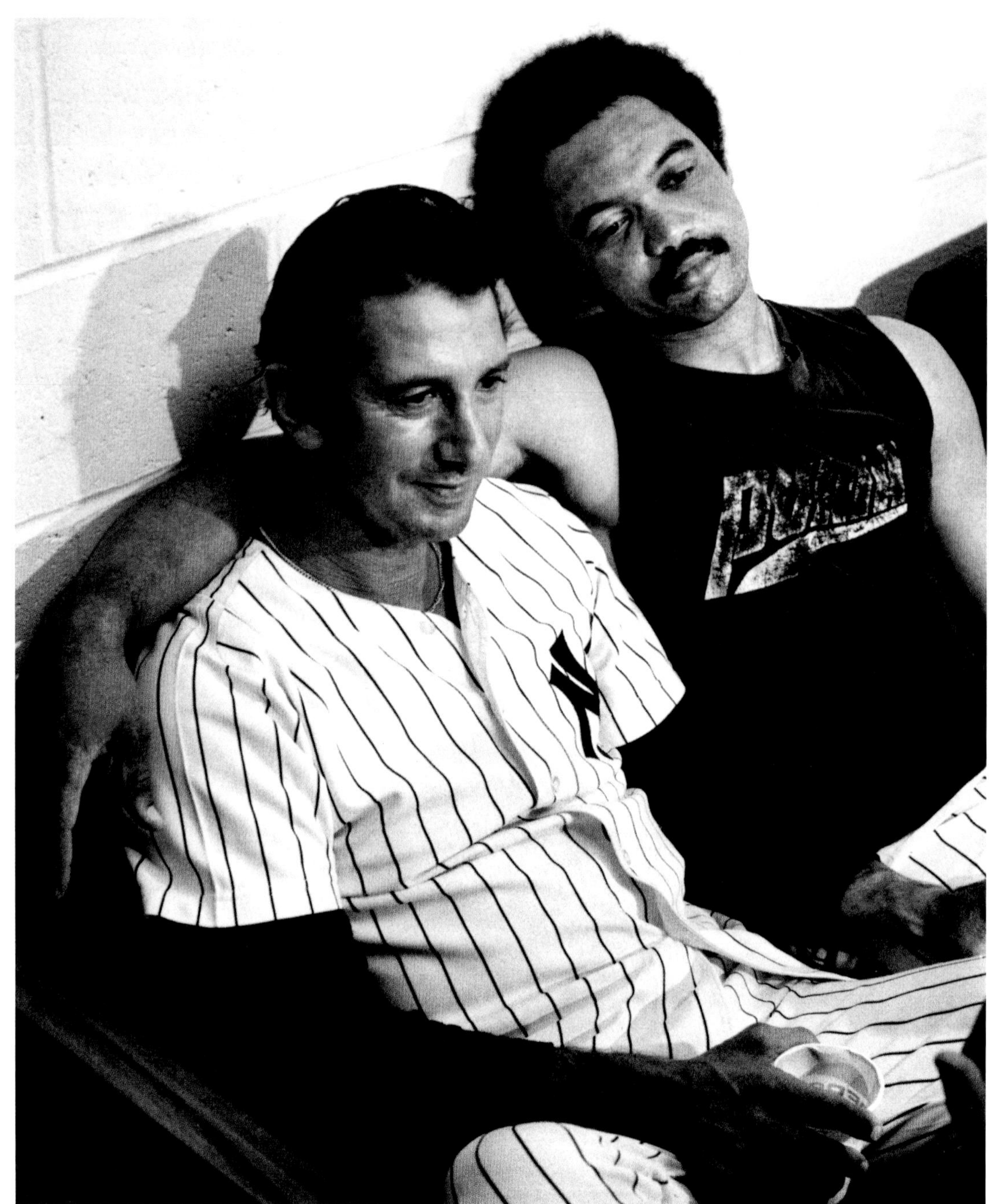

BILLY MARTIN & REGGIE JACKSON
October 18, 1977 – Bronx, New York
Yankees vs. Dodgers World Series Game at Yankees Stadium

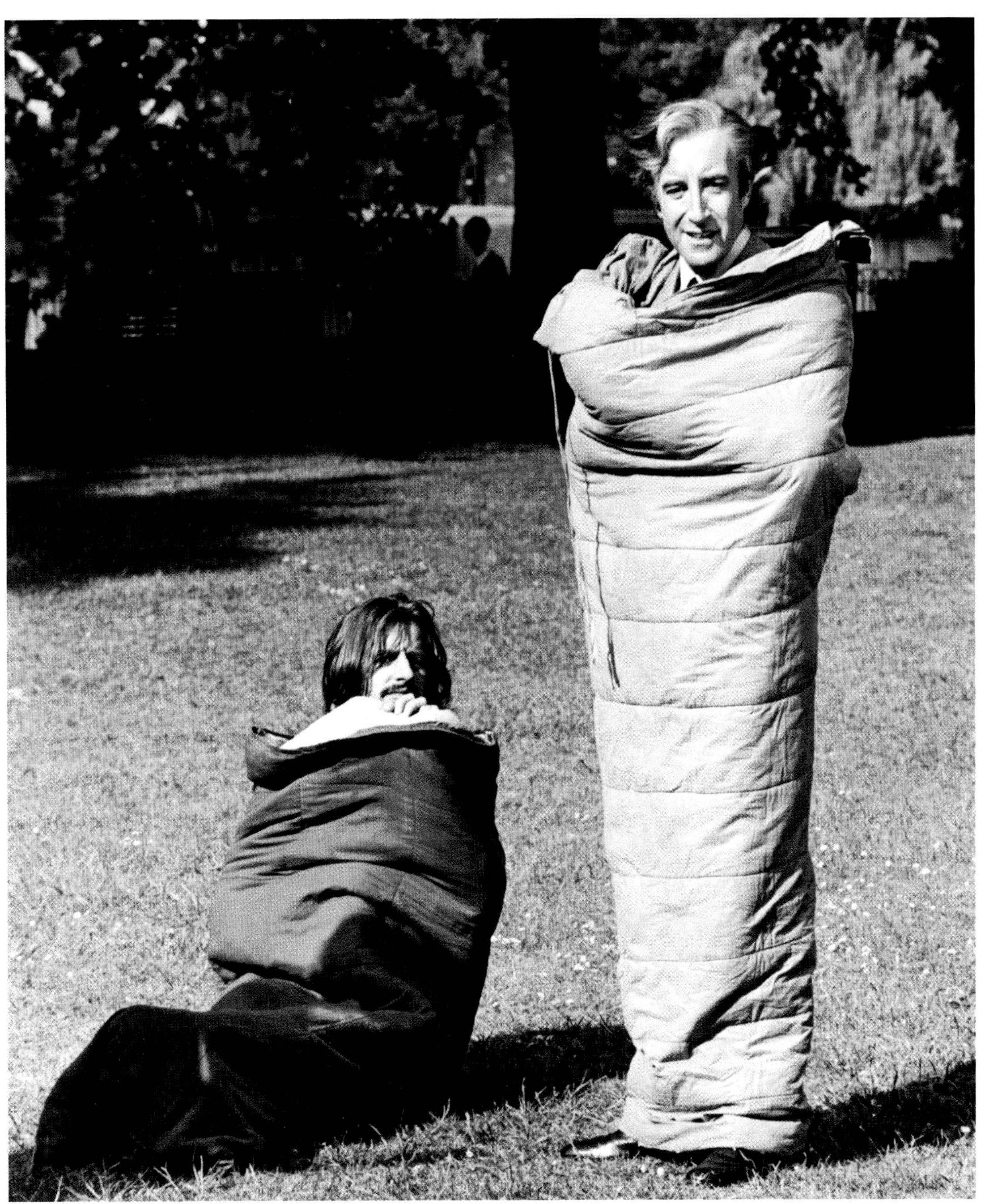

RINGO STARR & PETER SELLERS
September 1, 1969 – London, England
On Location Filming "The Magic Christian" at St. James's Park

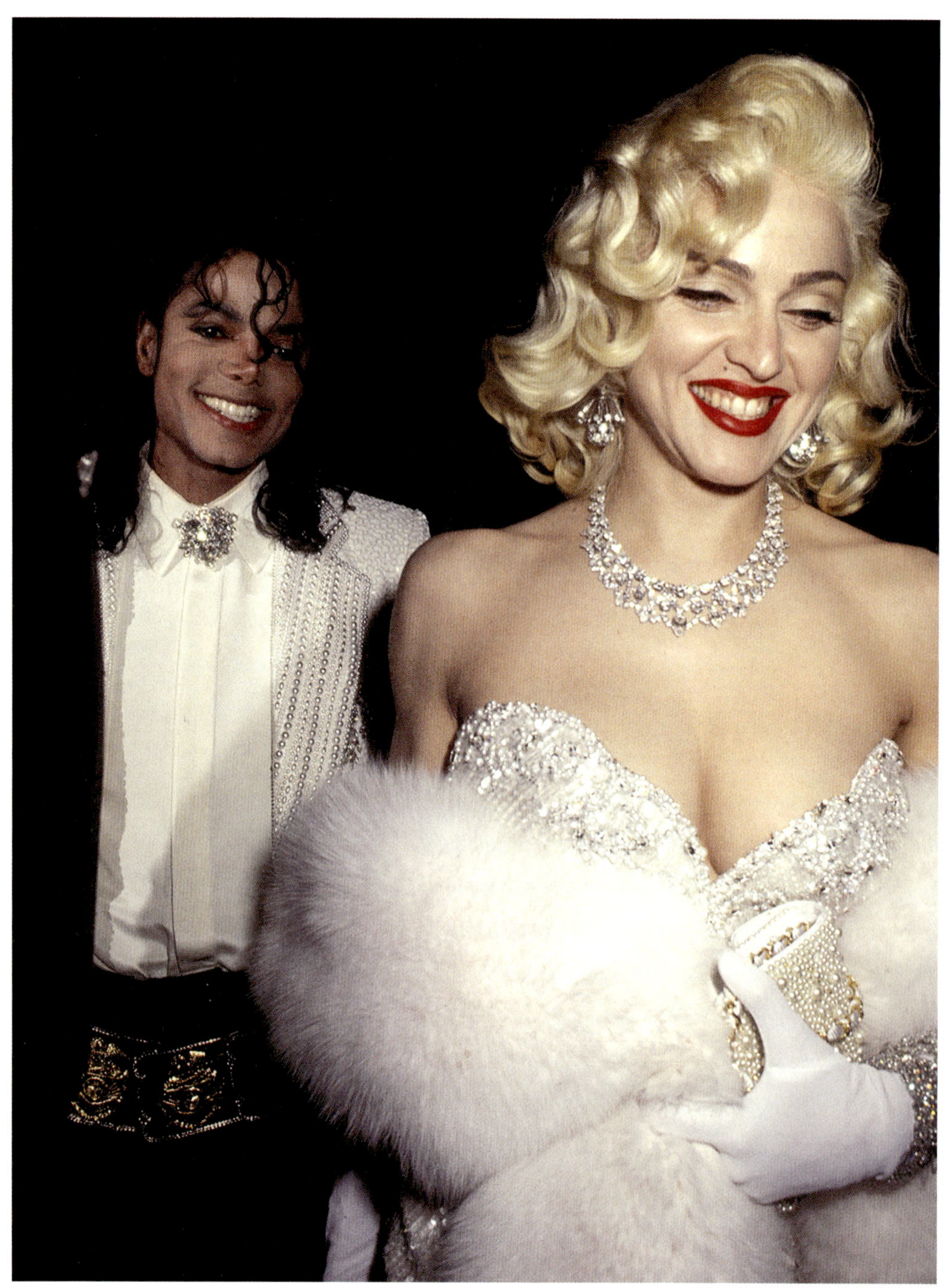

MICHAEL JACKSON & MADONNA
March 25, 1991 – West Hollywood, California
Party for 63rd Annual Academy Awards at Spago

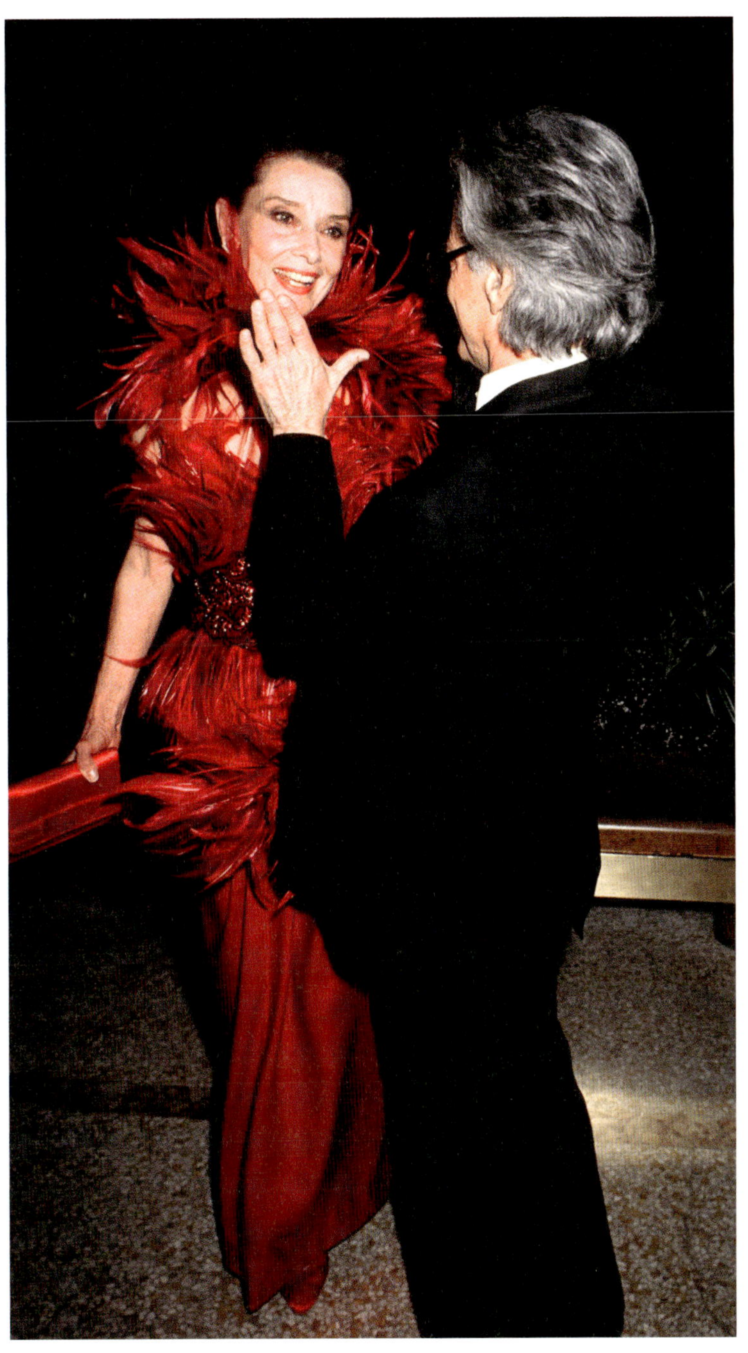

AUDREY HEPBURN & RICHARD AVEDON
January 9, 1989 – New York City
8th Annual Council of Fashion Designers of America Awards
at the Metropolitan Museum of Art

ELVIS PRESLEY & HIS BODYGUARDS

When Elvis departed the Philadelphia Hilton for his concerts at the Spectrum Stadium, he and his twelve to fifteen bodyguards habitually left and entered the hotel through the hotel's rear kitchen exit, where the loading dock is, to avoid being noticed. This time Elvis turned to me and said, "Who are you with, cat?" and I replied, "I'm freelance!" This was the first and only time Elvis spoke to me. Elvis knew about me as I featured him in a chapter in my second book, *Off-guard: A Paparazzo Look at the Beautiful People*, in 1976. My secretary at the time, Ann Marie McKenna, wanted Elvis to autograph the book. This was accomplished through one of Elvis's bodyguards, who stayed with the King on the top floor of the hotel, where they occupied the whole wing.

After the concert, I followed Elvis and his entourage to the Philadelphia International Airport. Upon arriving, I jumped out of my 1975 yellow Pontiac Firebird and rushed to the entrance to get photos of Elvis Presley, his dad Vernon, Linda Thompson, and the bodyguards leaving on Elvis's plane for Columbus, Ohio. I missed Linda Thompson boarding the plane but did get shots of Elvis and his dad.

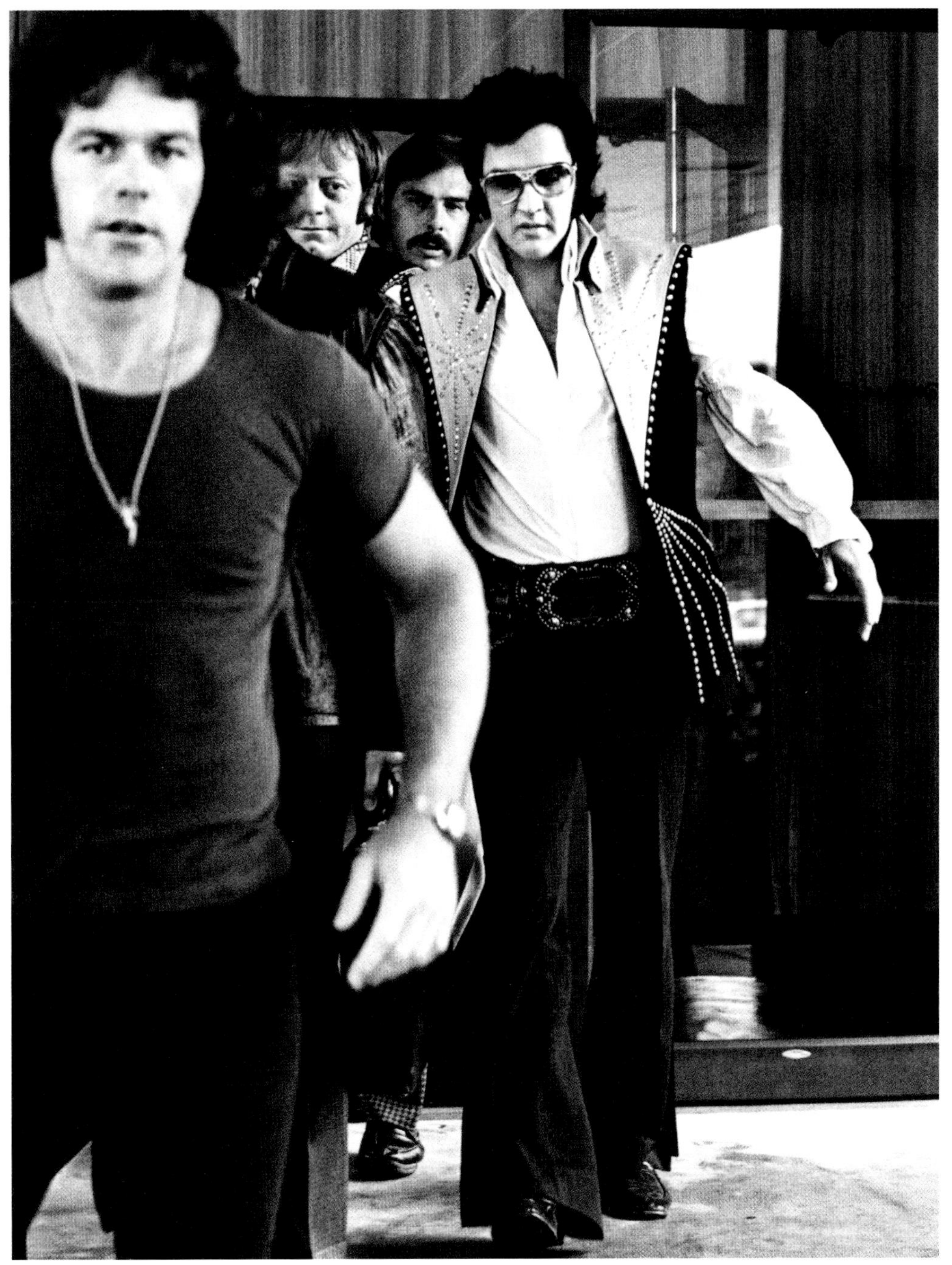

125

ELVIS PRESLEY
June 25, 1974 – Philadelphia, Pennsylvania
The Philadelphia Hilton Hotel

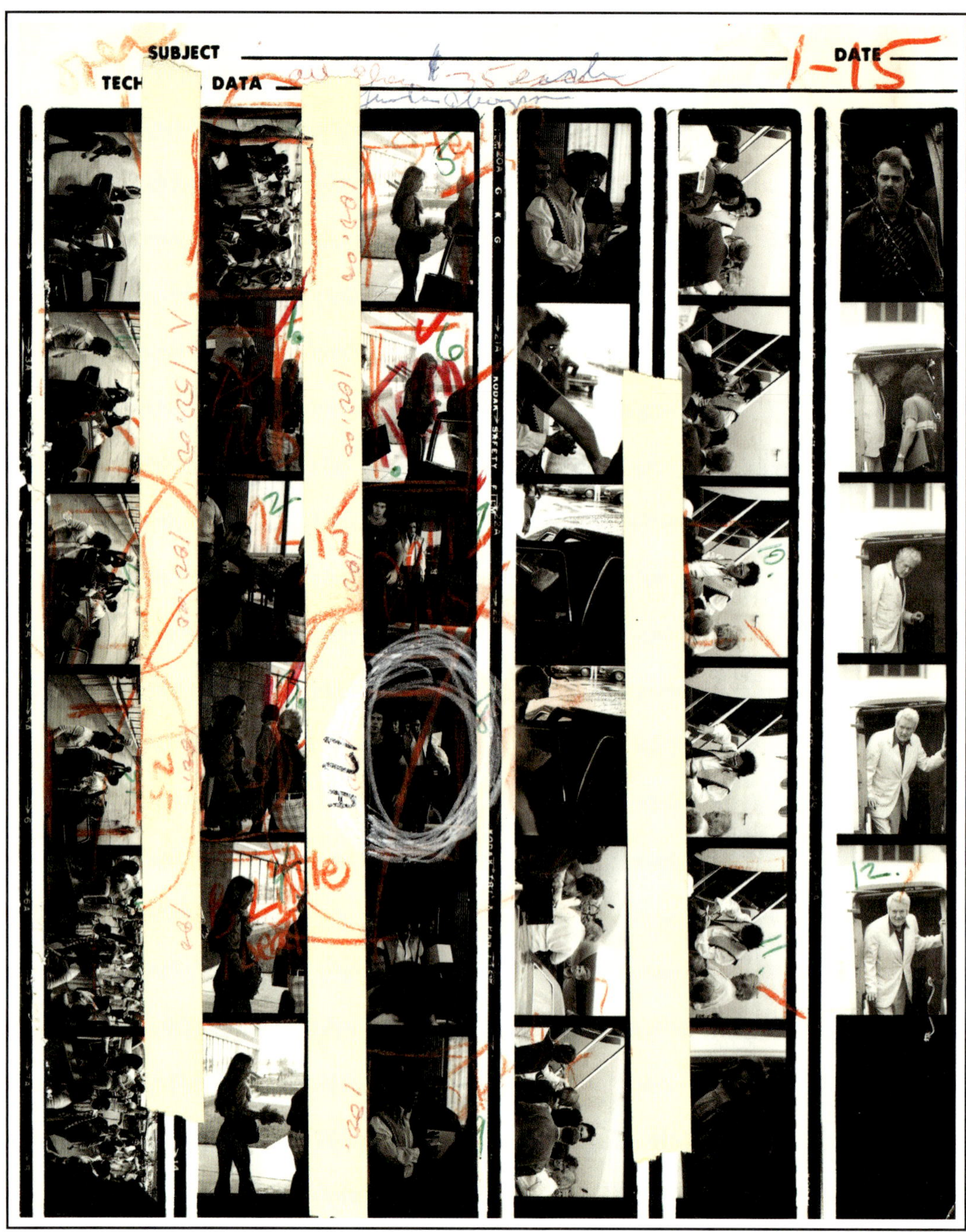
SUBJECT
TECH
DATA
1-15
DATE

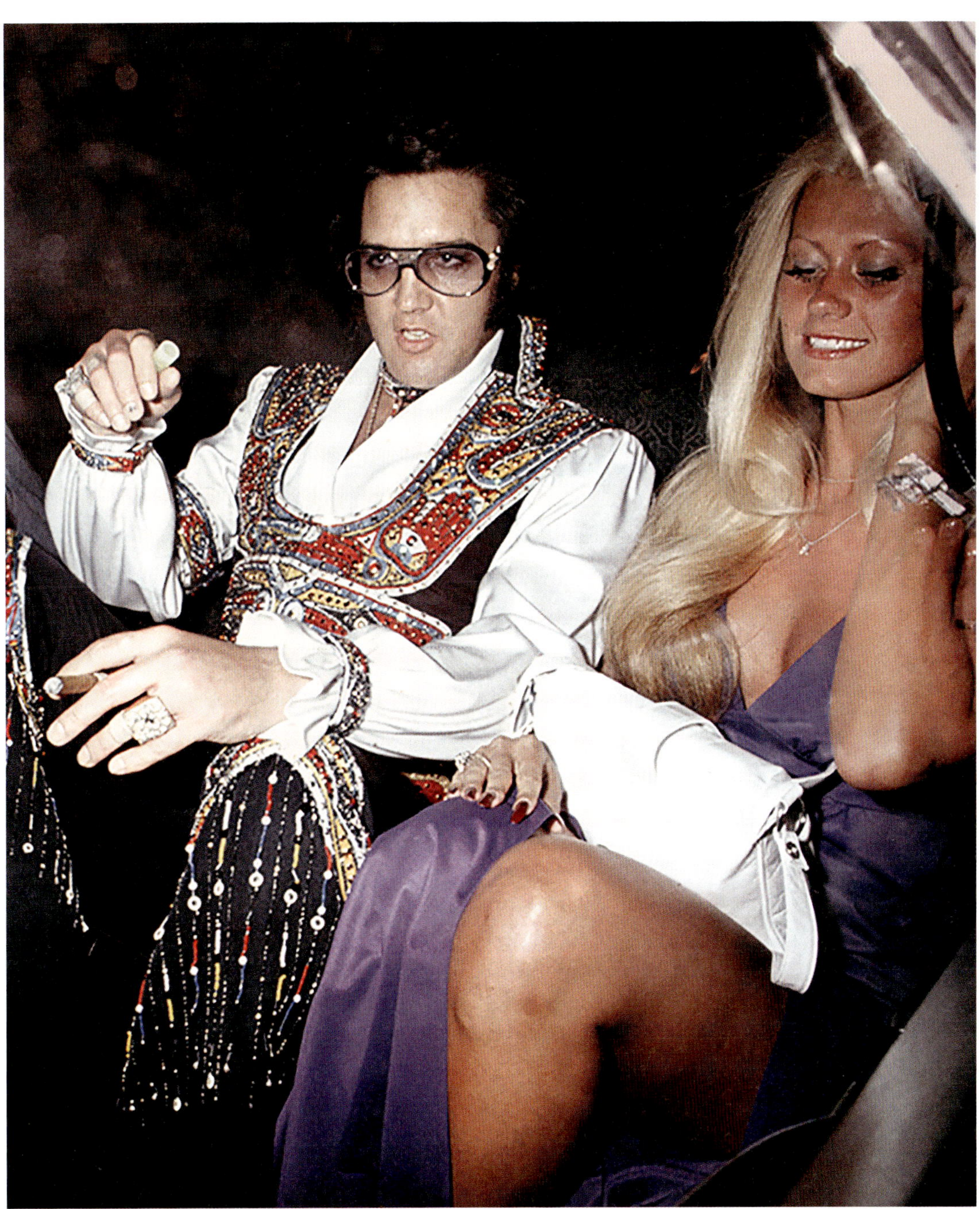

ELVIS PRESLEY & DIANA GOODMAN
July 19, 1975 – Long Island, New York
Departing Nassau Coliseum Following His Performance

AUGUST 24, 1988: BRUCE "THE BOSS" SPRINGSTEEN jumped onstage at Sting's Madison Square Garden concert and went on to a party in his honor at the Canal Bar. Bruce brought along his reportedly preggers gal pal and backup singer PATTI SCIALFA. We snapped the duo as they departed in a limo, trailing them to the Westbury Hotel. "What are you doing here Ron?" quipped The Boss. "You're hard to get!" said Ron Galella to his fast-moving target.

THE
PHOTOGRAPHS OF
RON GALELLA
1965-1989

EXCLUSIVE

Photography with the PAPARAZZI approach ™

RON GALELLA

GLOVER AVE., YONKERS, N.Y. (914) 237-298

Ron Galella

RON GALELLA

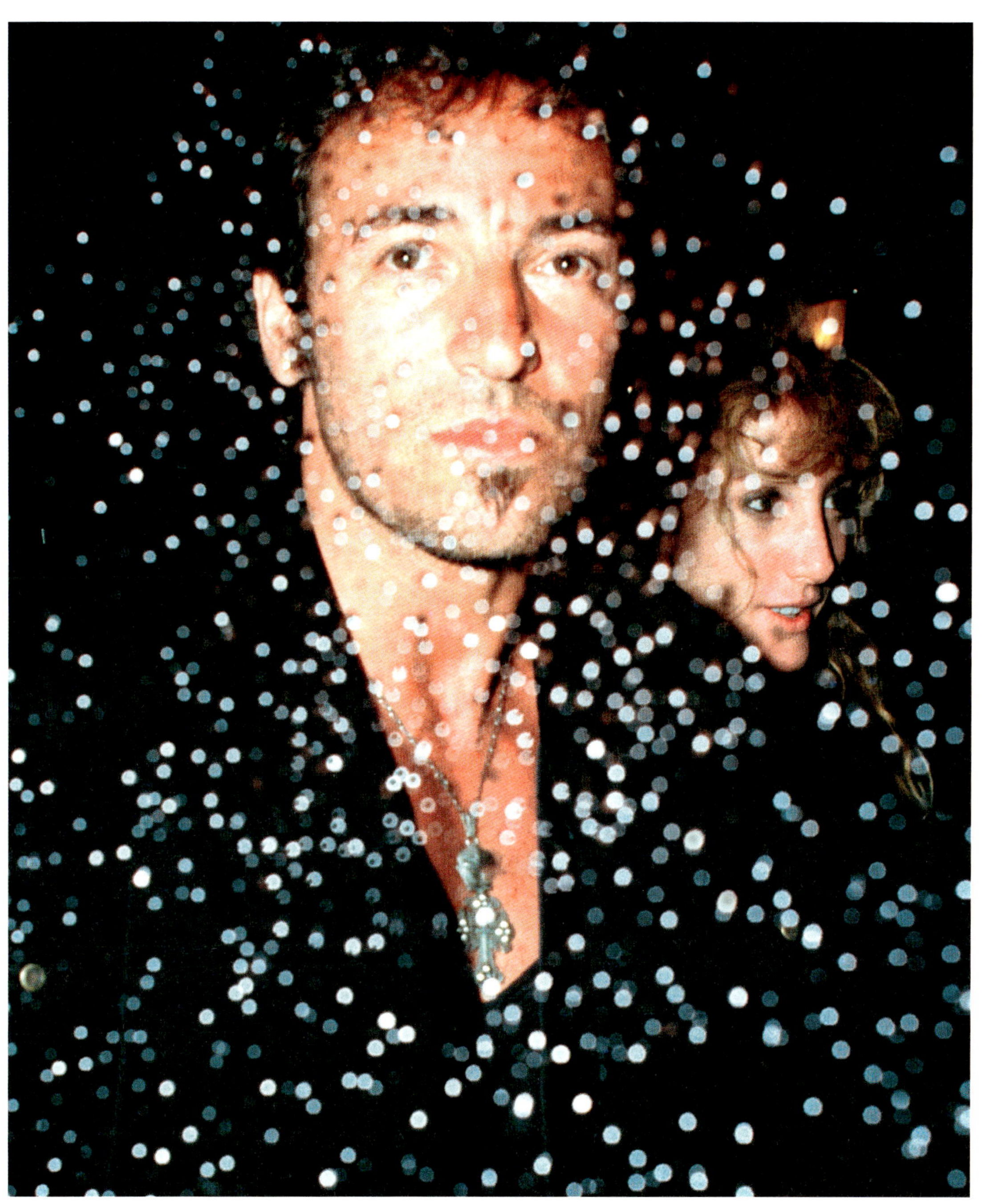

BRUCE SPRINGSTEEN & PATTI SCIALFA
August 24, 1988 – New York City
Sting Concert After Party at Canal Bar

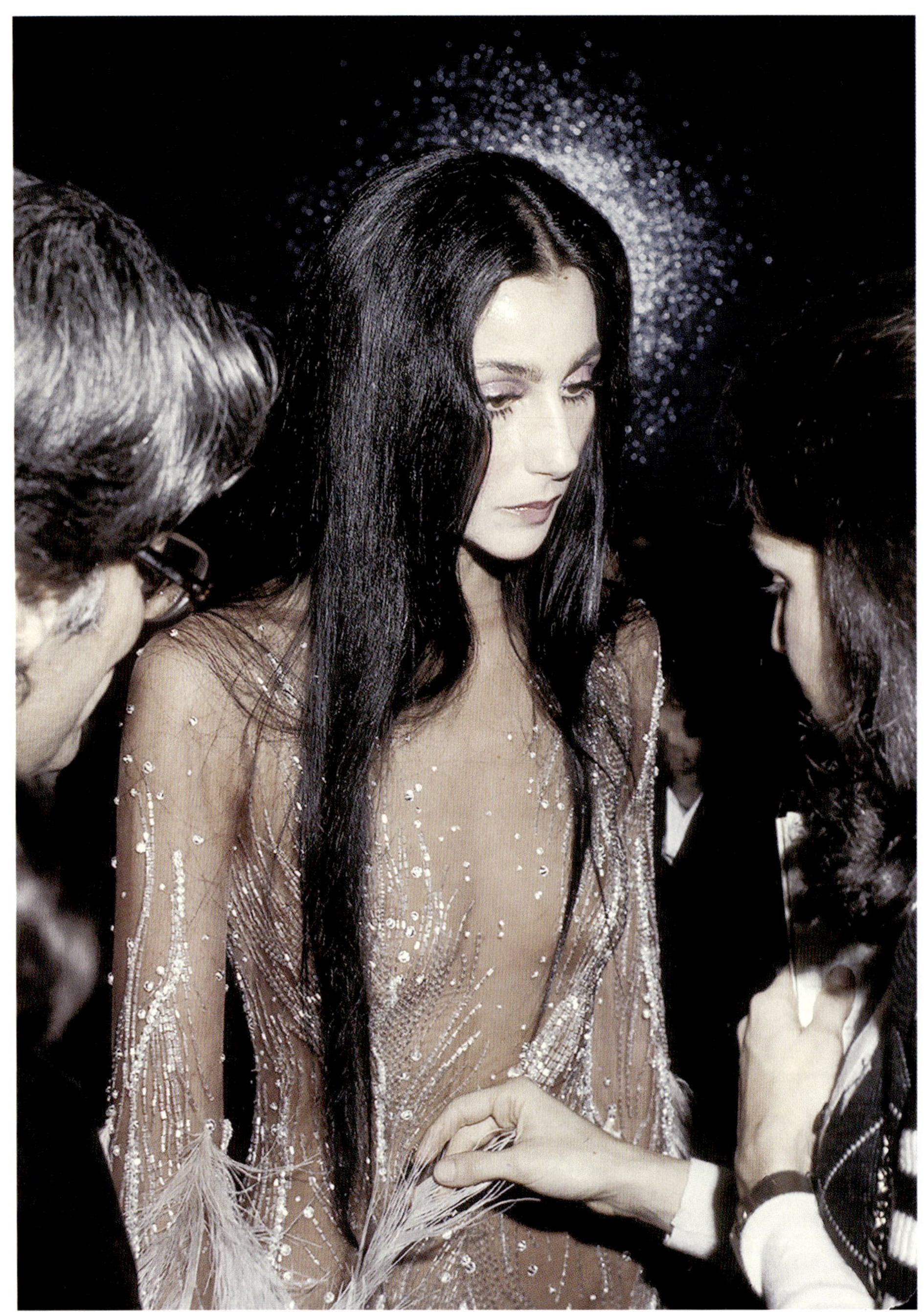

CHER

November 20, 1974 – New York City
The Metropolitan Museum of Art Costume Institute Exhibition "Romantic and Glamorous Hollywood Design" at the Metropolitan Museum of Art

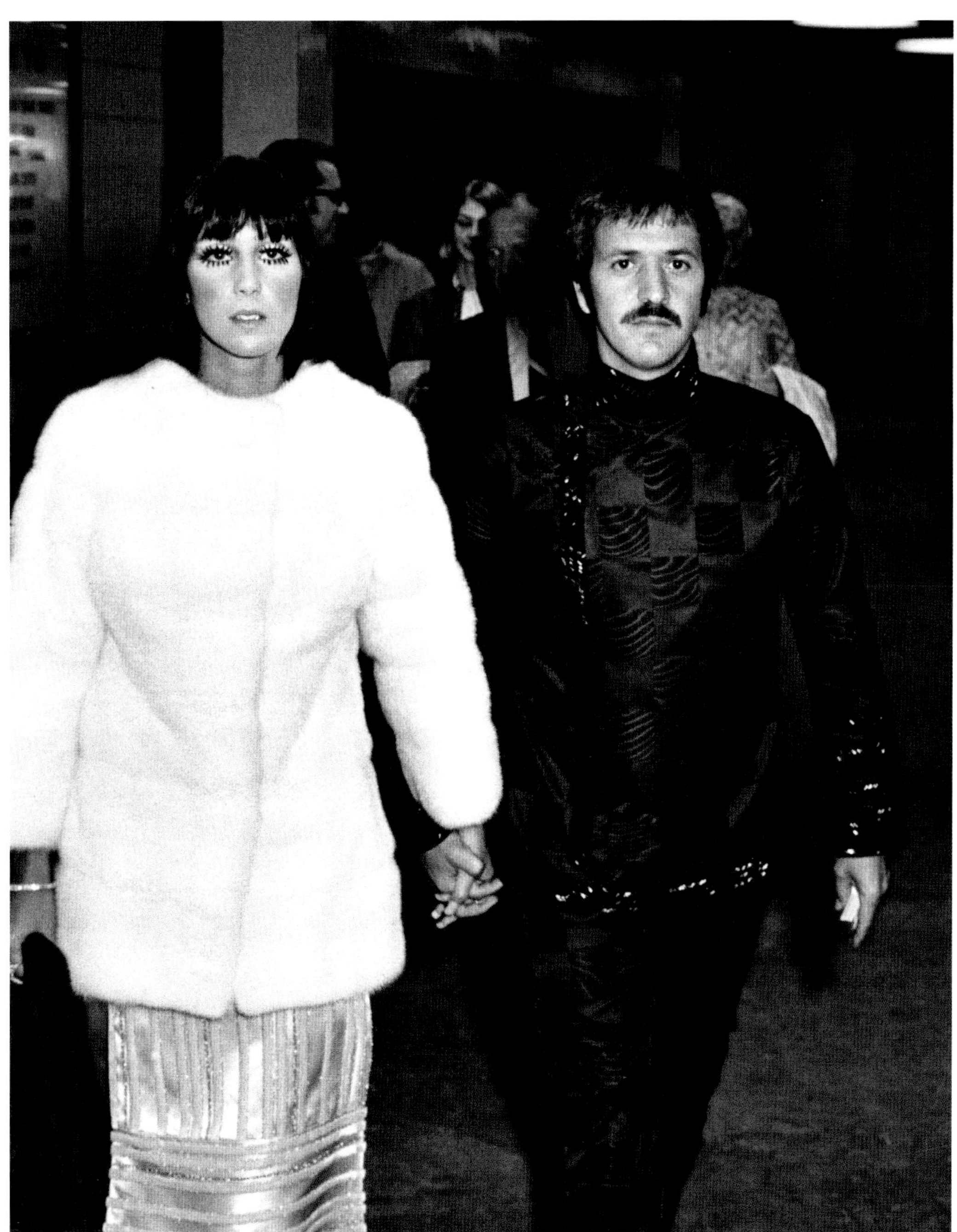

CHER & SONNY BONO
June 28, 1968 – New York City
Martin Luther King, Jr. Benefit at Madison Square Garden

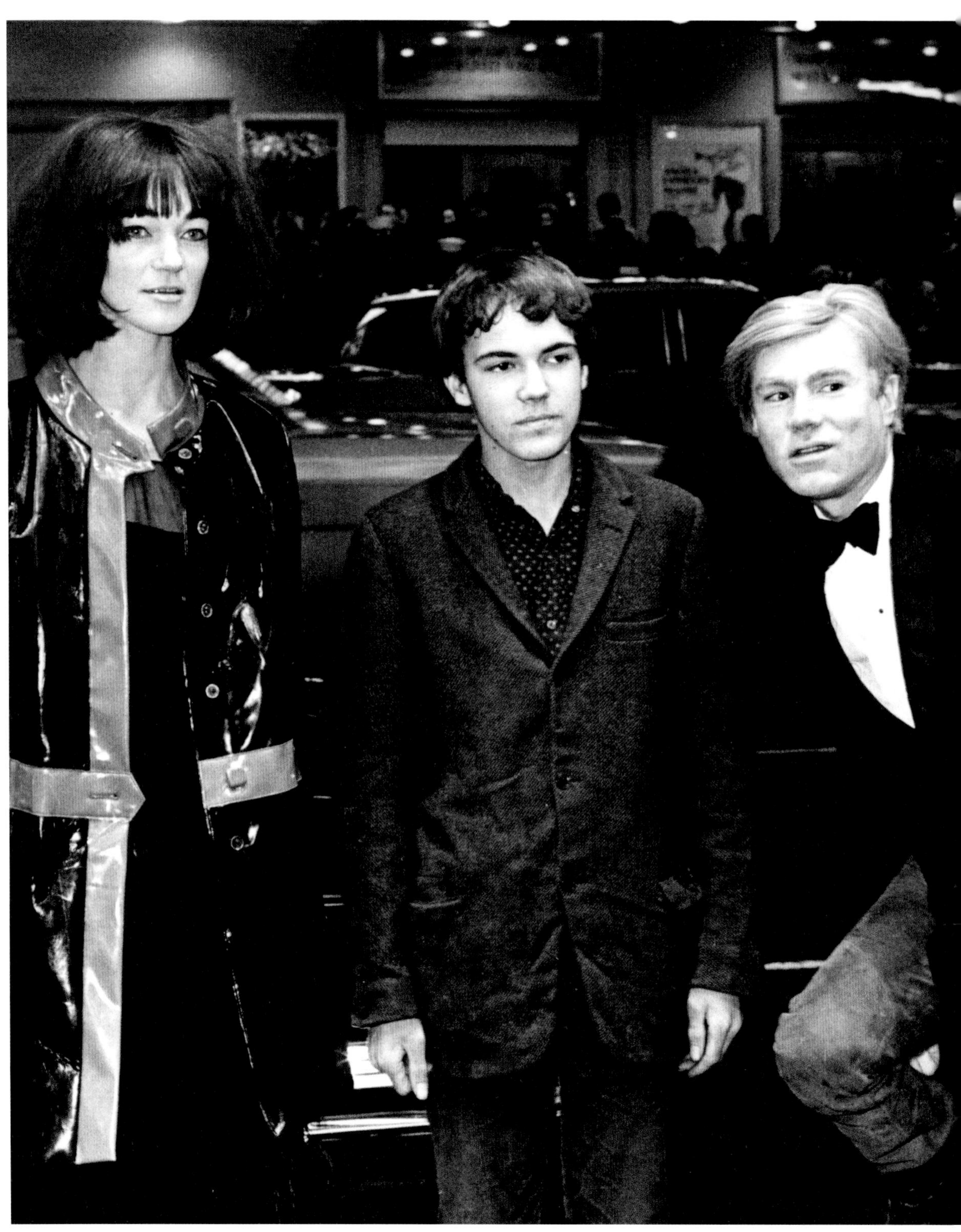

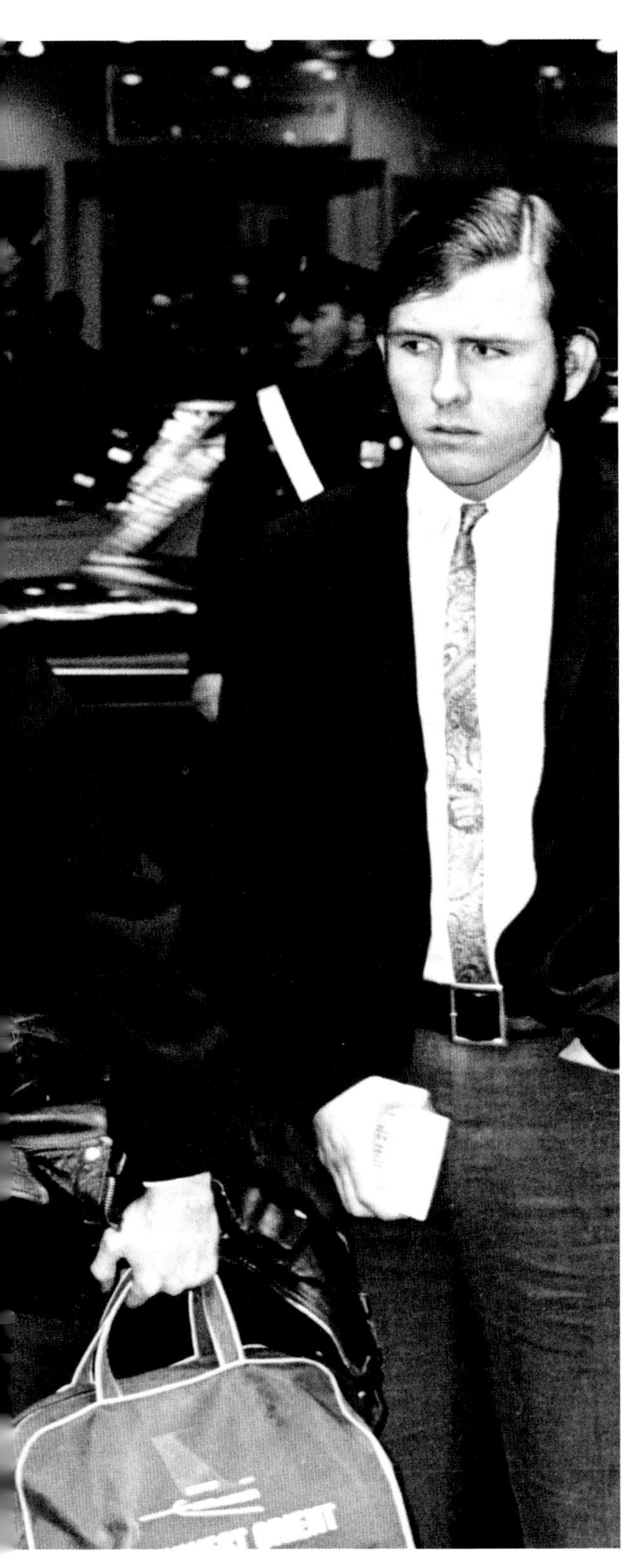

(L-R) IVY NICHOLSON, GUEST,
ANDY WARHOL & ROD LA ROD
February 1, 1967 – New York City
"The Night of the Generals"
Premiere at Loew's Capitol Theatre

134

ANDY WARHOL
June 12, 1983 – Bronx, New York
The Bronx Zoo

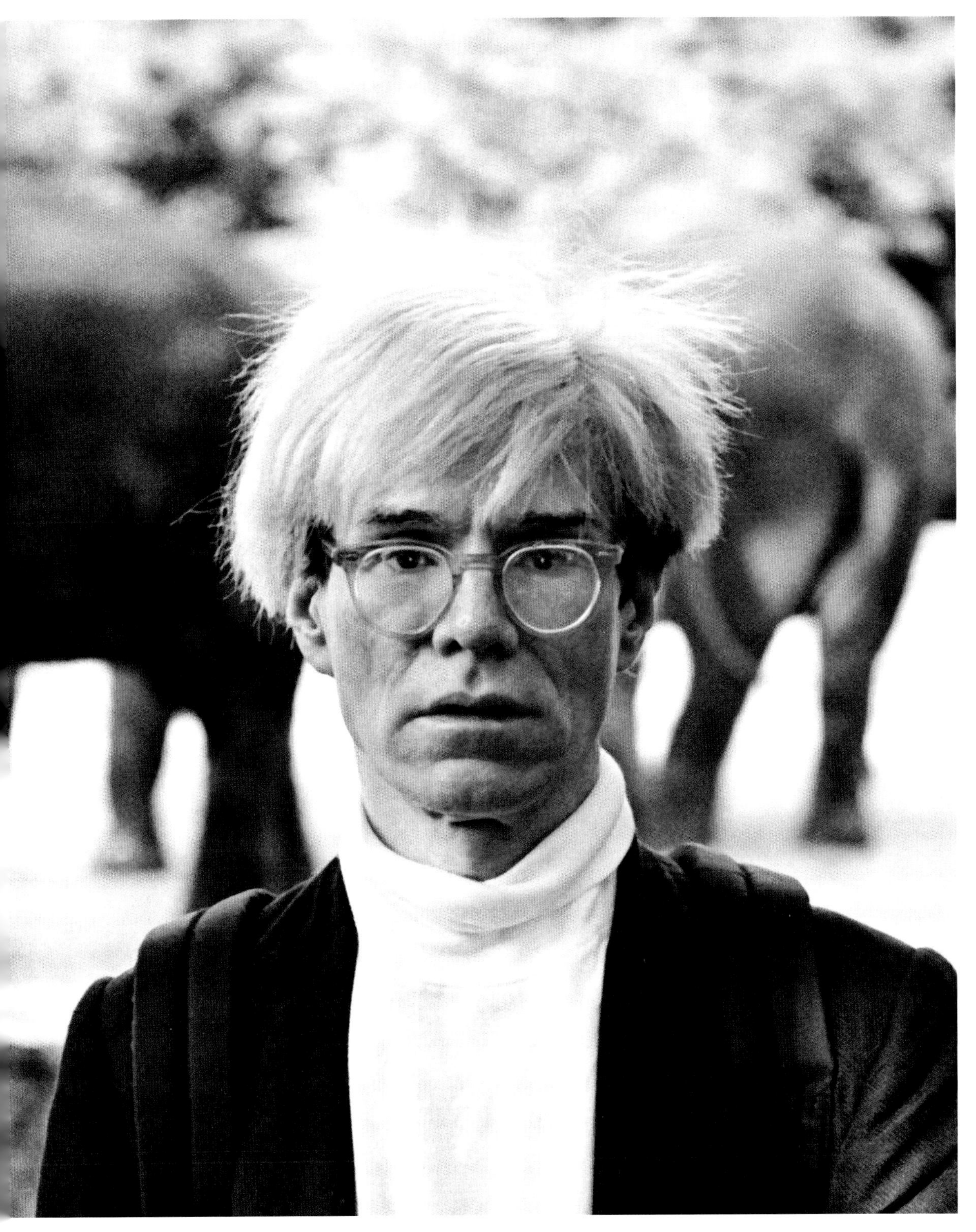

ANDY WARHOL AT THE BRONX ZOO

(see previous pages)

For years, my wife Betty and I worked hard, nonstop. We needed a break. Betty had always wanted to go to the Bronx Zoo. So we hopped in the car one Sunday afternoon and headed to the world's largest metropolitan zoo. Once in the park, we were about to take the safari train ride, hoping to enjoy a relaxing jaunt through the wildlife, when I spotted pop artist Andy Warhol on the same train! This train, which traveled all the way through the crowded park, ended up drawing more stares and responses than did the exotic species housed in the famous zoo. As soon as the ride was over, we greeted Andy. He let me know that this was his first visit to the zoo and happily posed for me in front of the elephant cage. Since Andy and his good friend, John Gould, VP of Communications at Paramount Pictures, had taken a cab to the zoo, Betty and I ended up giving Andy and John a ride to the Grand Concourse subway station.

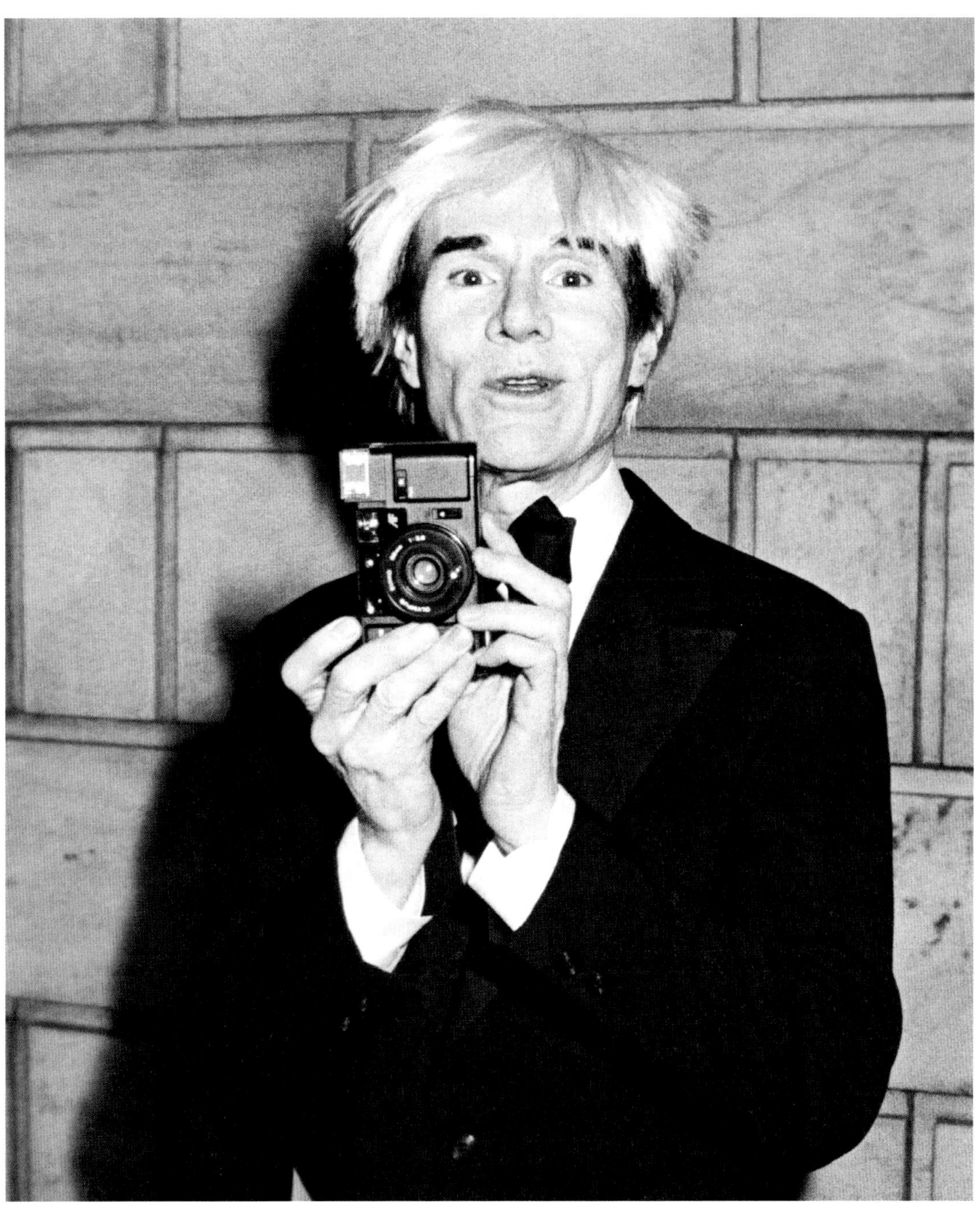

ANDY WARHOL
January 13, 1985 – New York City
4th Annual Council of Fashion Designers of America Awards
at the Metropolitan Museum of Art

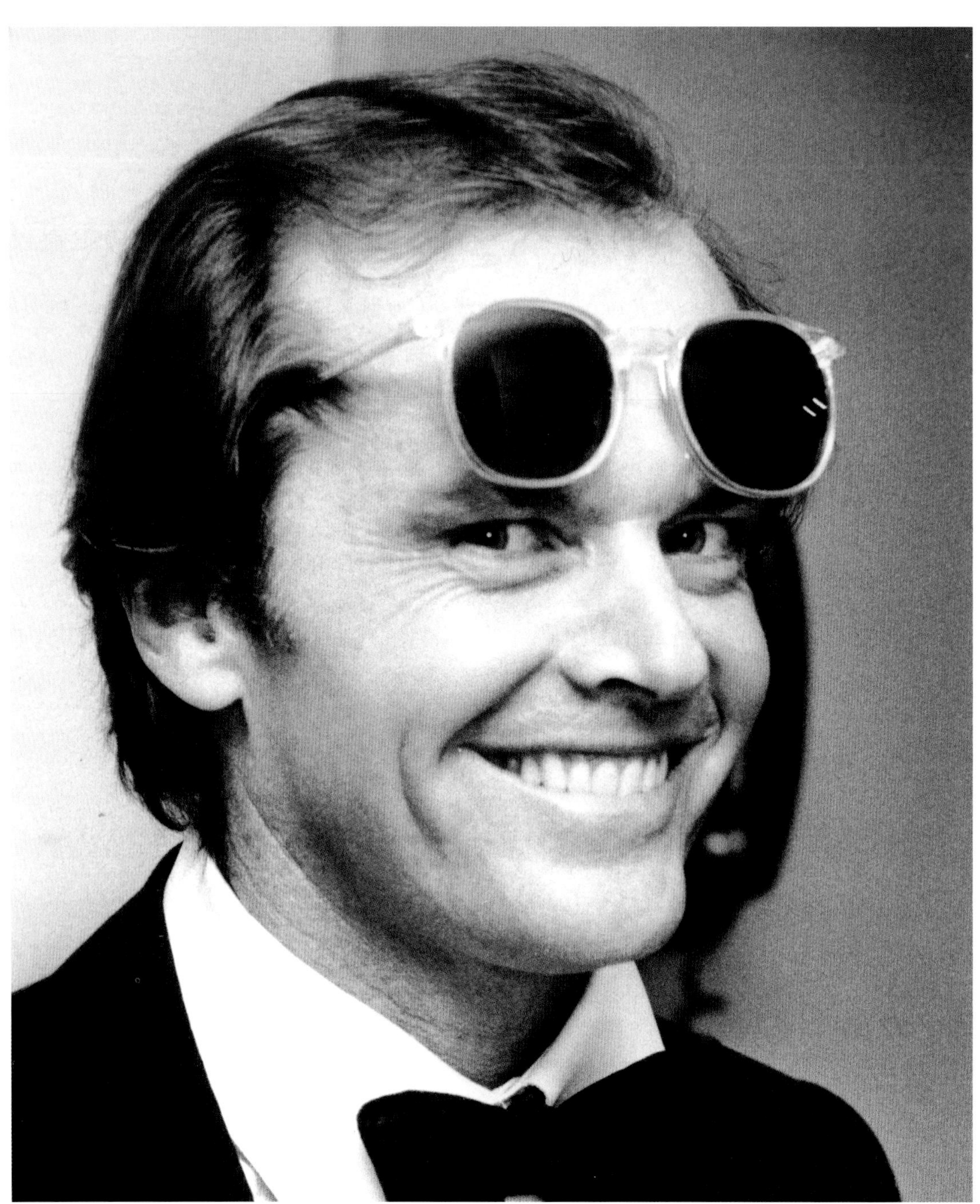

JACK NICHOLSON
April 3, 1978 – Los Angeles, California
50th Annual Academy Awards at the Dorothy Chandler Pavilion

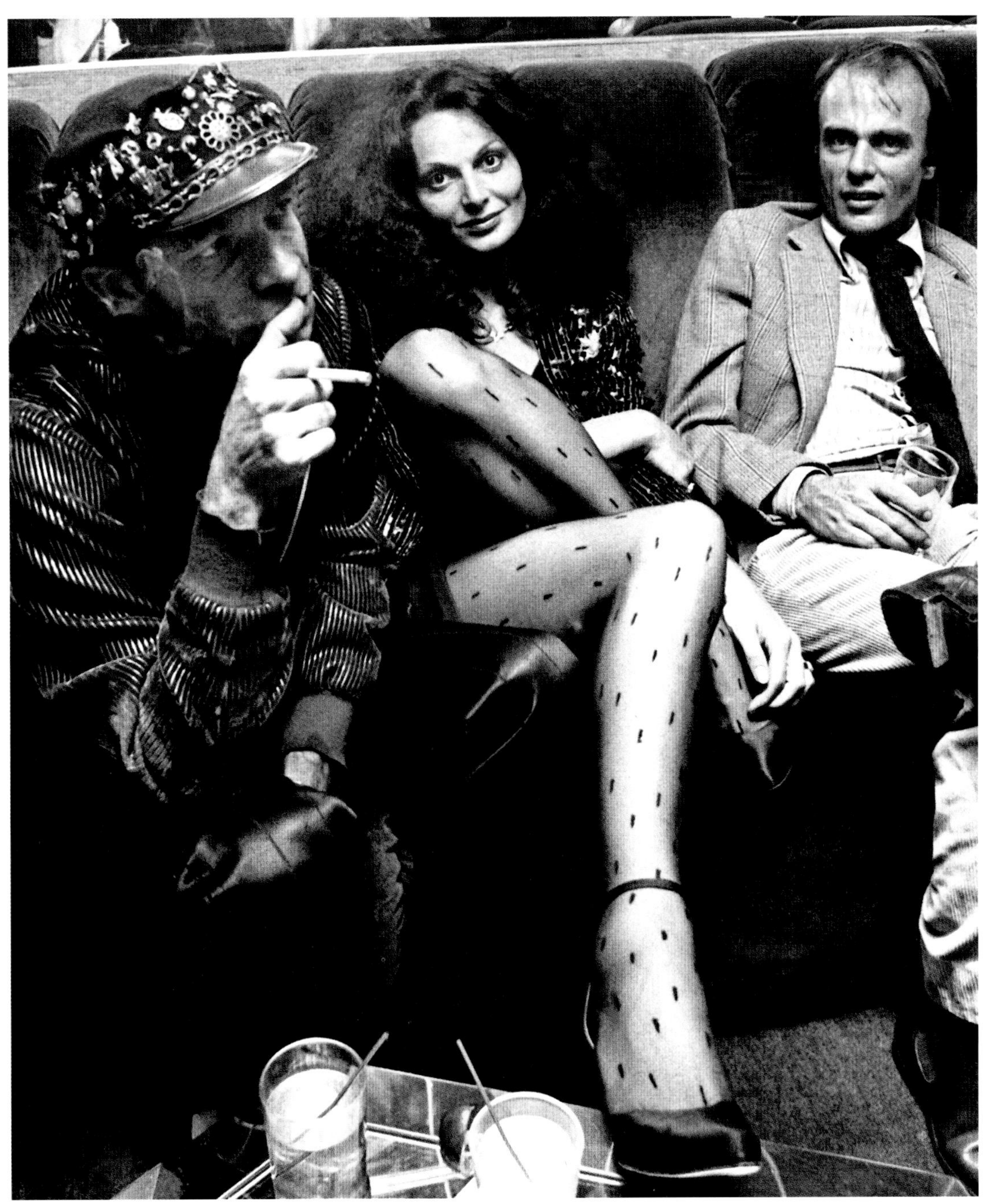

(L-R) ARA GALLANT, DIANE VON FÜRSTENBERG & CÉDRIC LOPEZ
September 25, 1978 – New York City
Egon von Fürstenberg *The Power Look* Book Party
at New York New York Disco

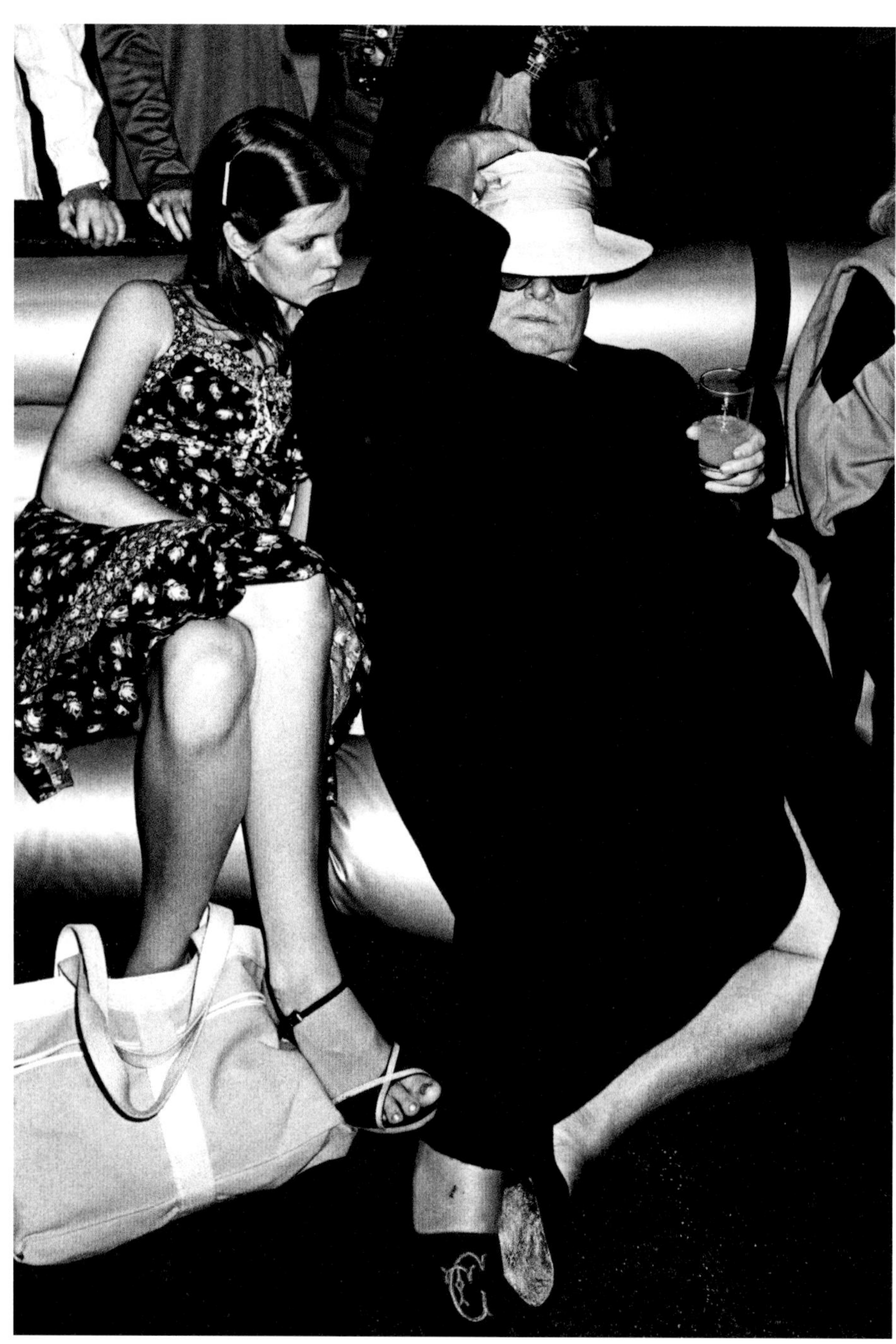

KATE HARRINGTON & TRUMAN CAPOTE
June 22, 1978 – New York City
Martha Graham Benefit Party at Studio 54

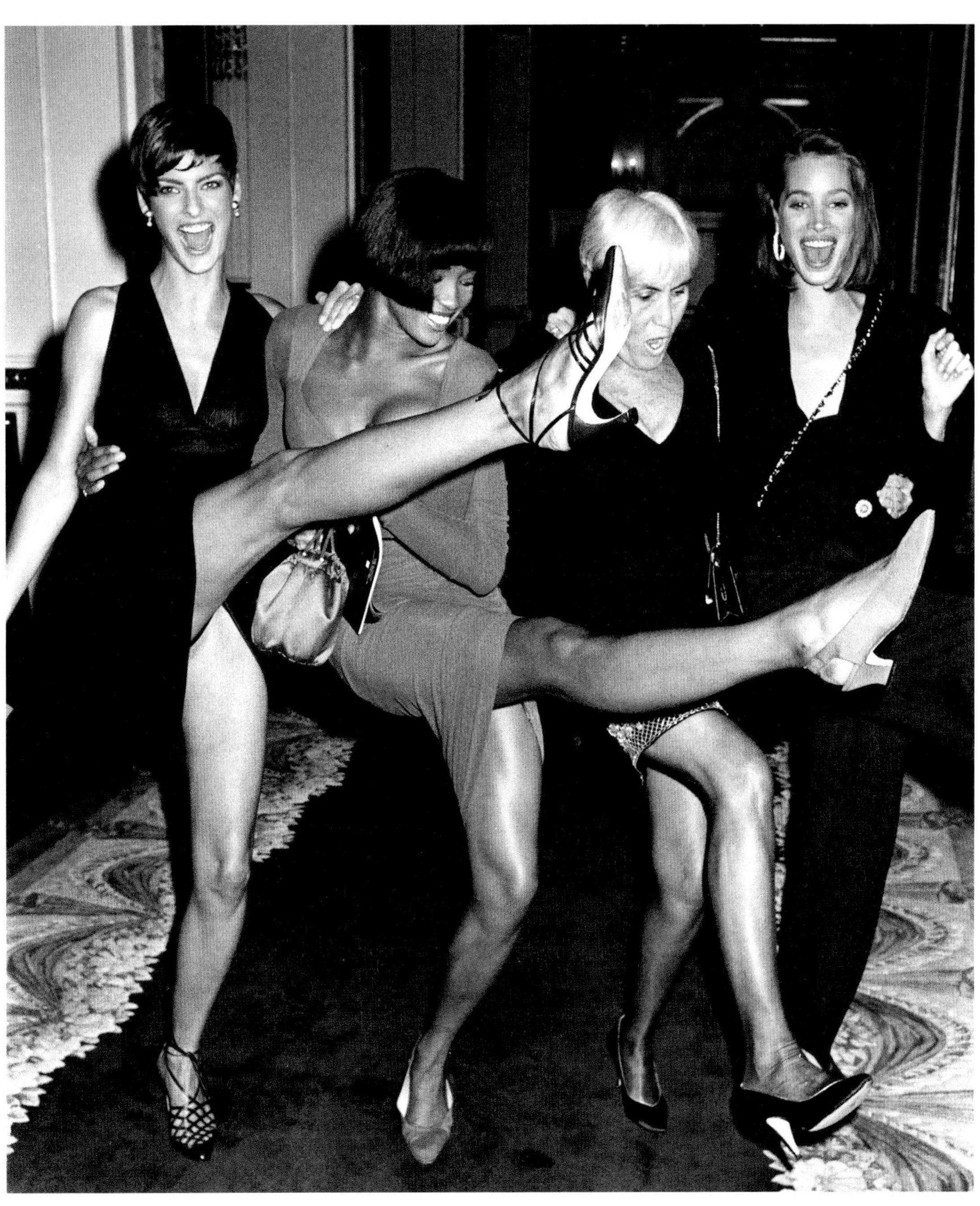

(L-R) LINDA EVANGELISTA, NAOMI CAMPBELL, POLLY MELLEN & CHRISTY TURLINGTON

October 29, 1989 – New York City

The Fashion Group International's 6th Annual "Night of 100 Stars" at the Plaza Hotel

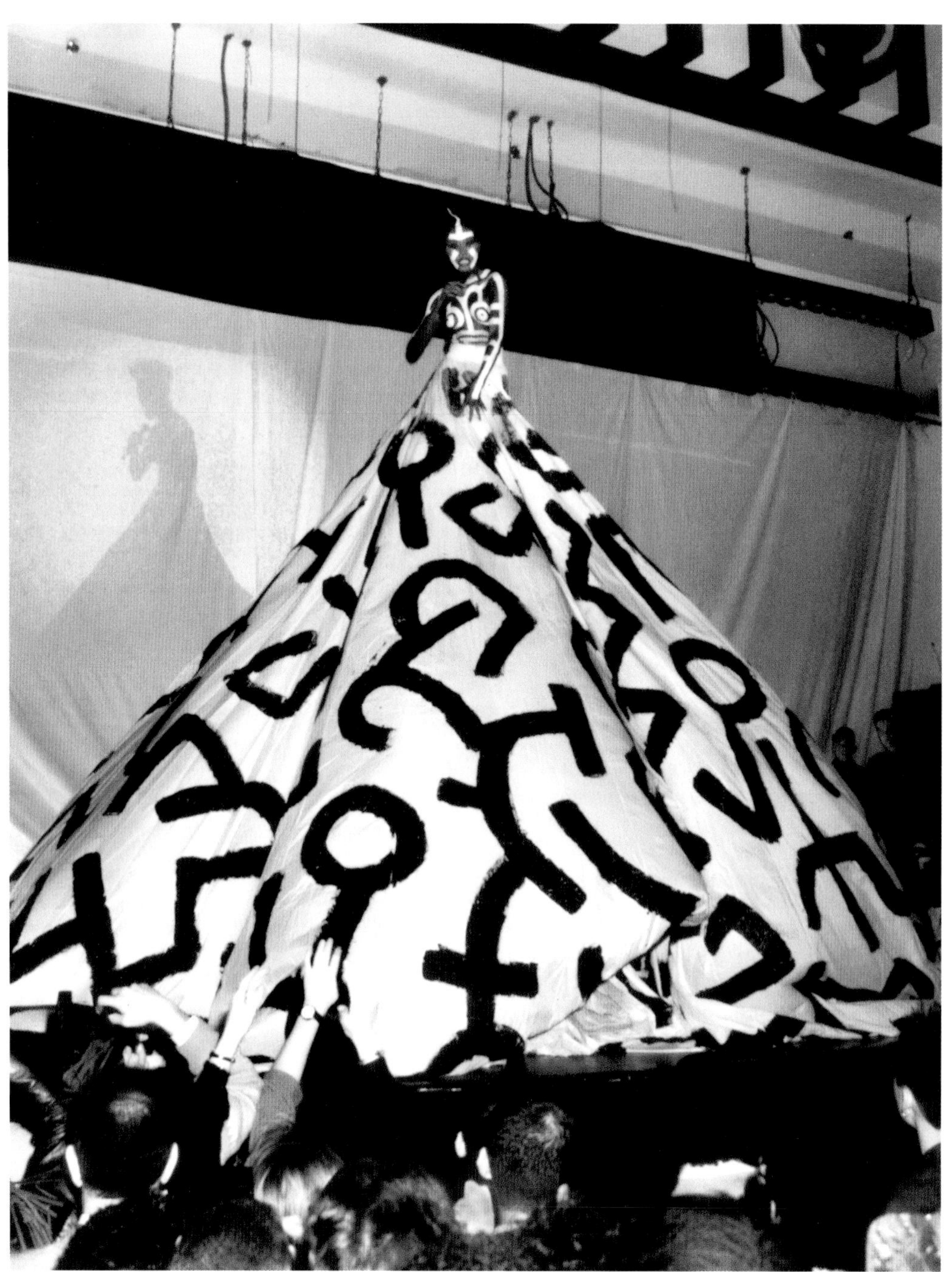

GRACE JONES
December 31, 1987 – New York City
Grace Jones' New Year's Eve Performance at Roseland Ballroom

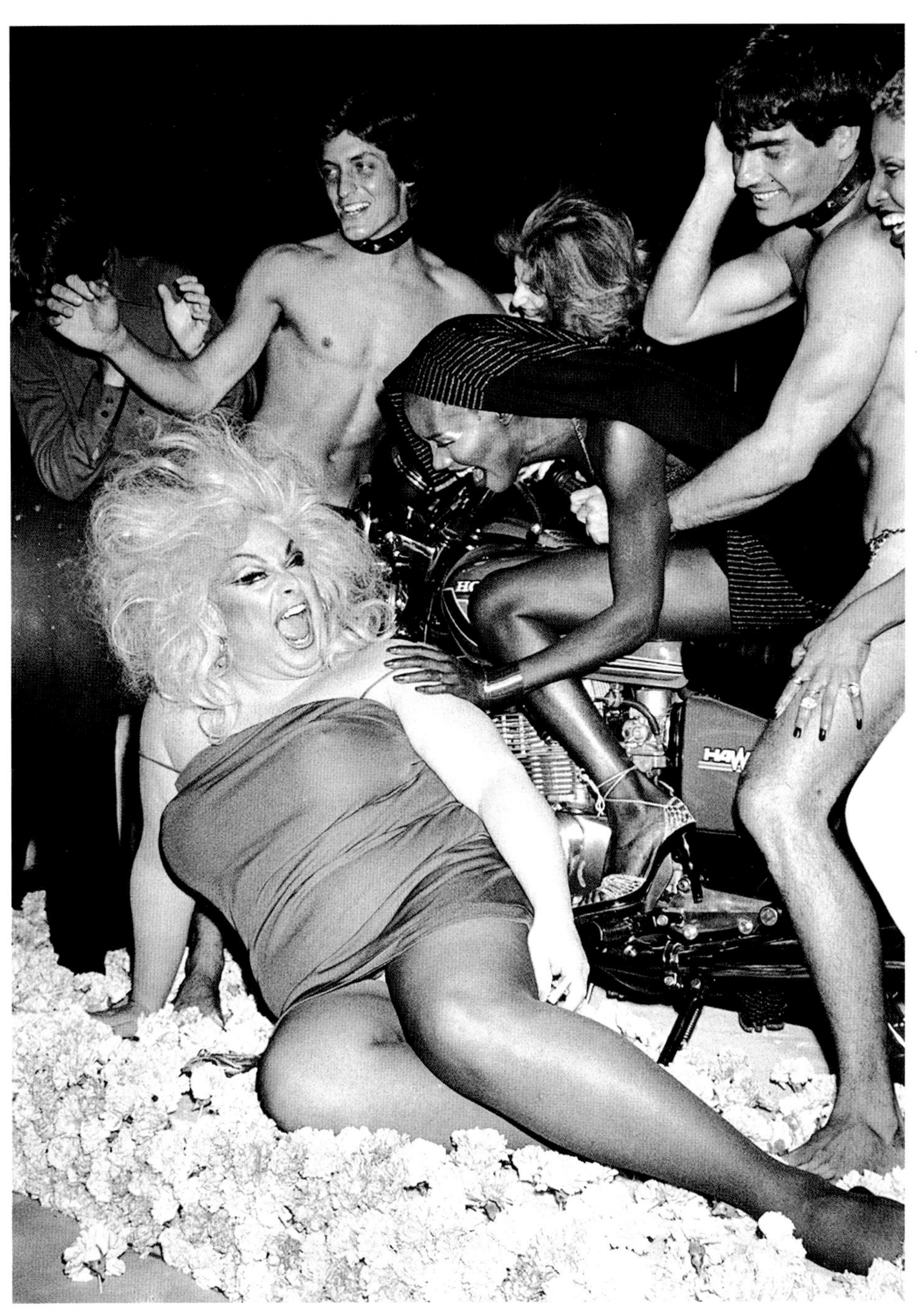

DIVINE & GRACE JONES
June 12, 1978 – New York City
Birthday Party for Grace Jones at Xenon Disco

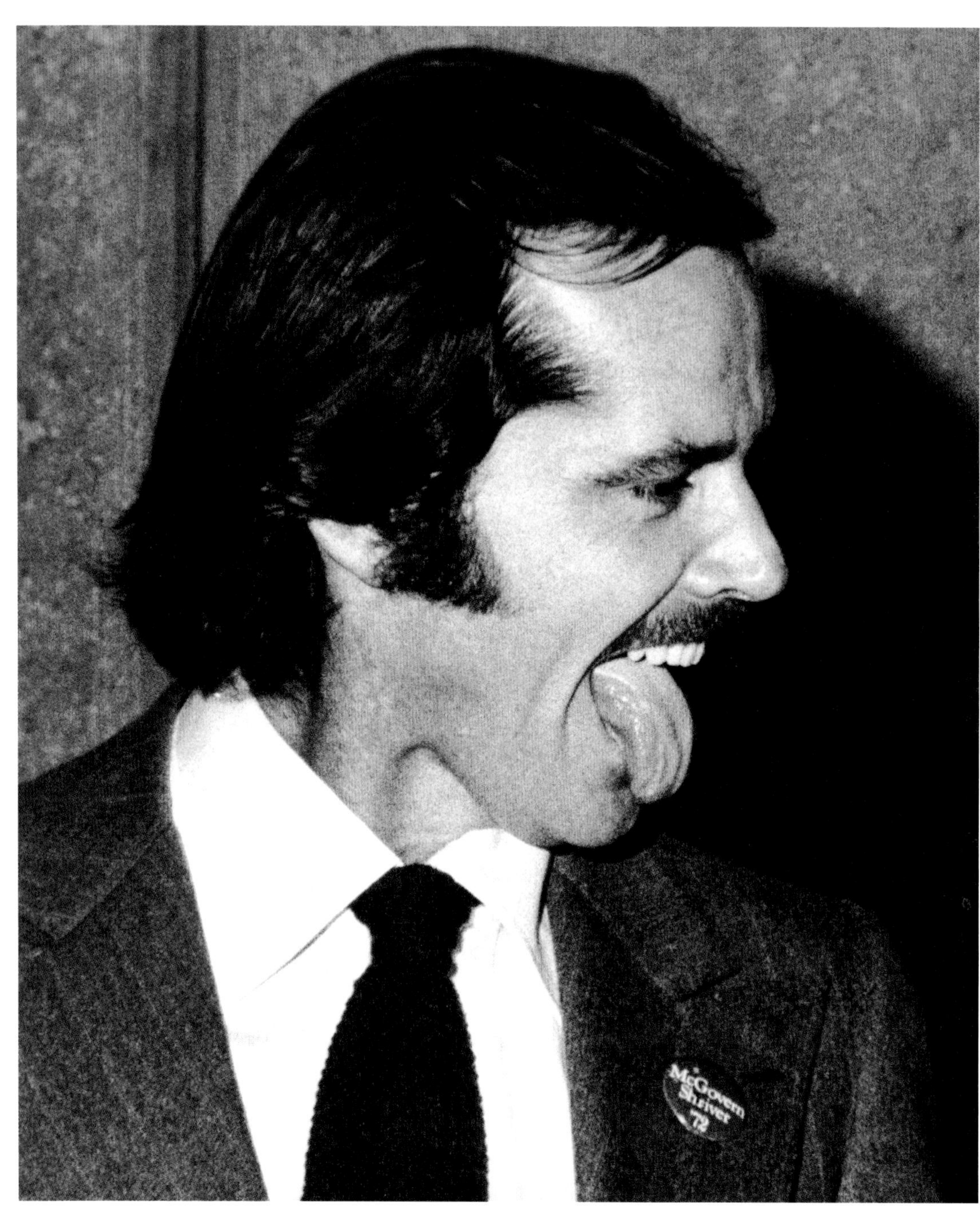

JACK NICHOLSON
October 5, 1972 – New York City
"Heat" Premiere at Loew's Festival Theatre

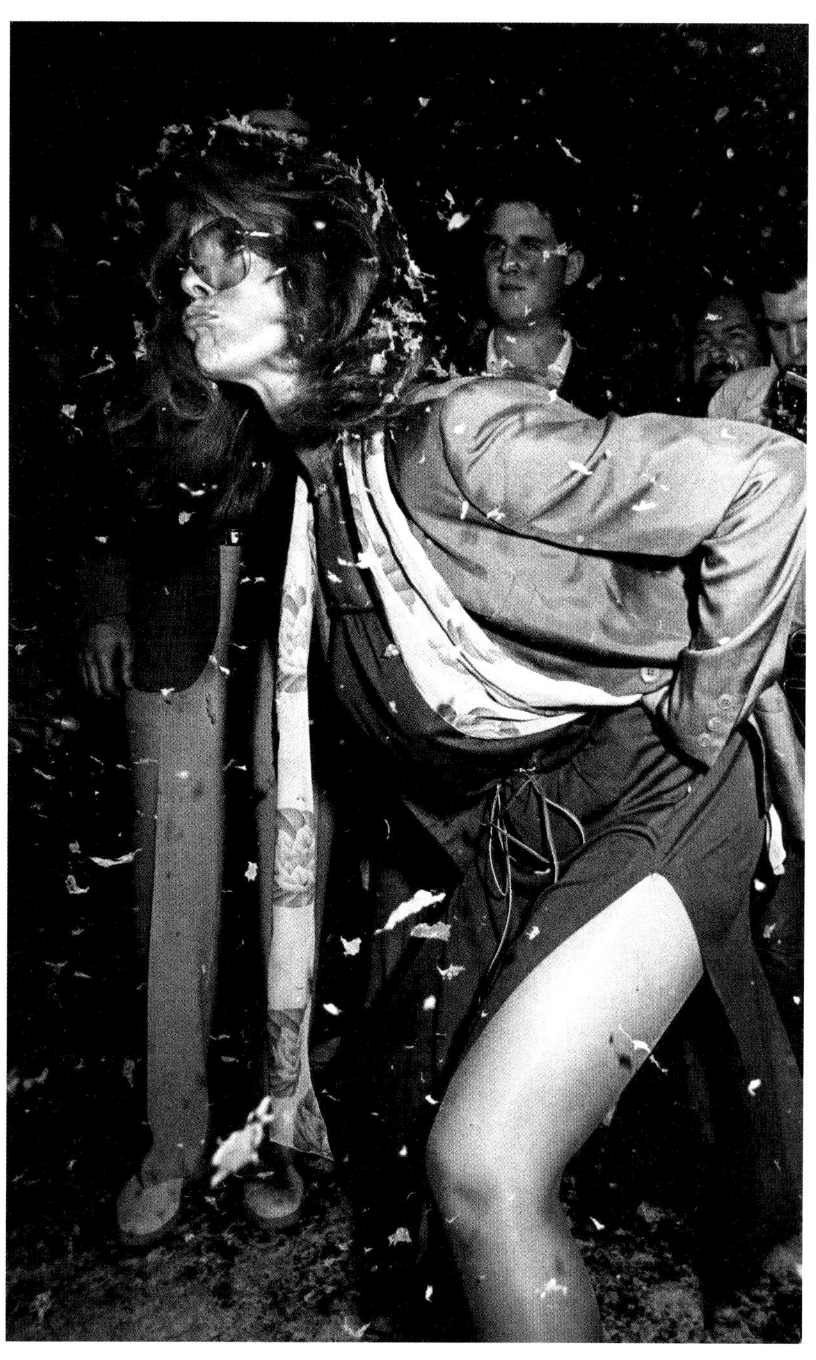

ANN-MARGRET
August 10, 1982 – Atlanta, Georgia
Ann-Margret Performance After Party at the Limelight

ELAINE KAUFMAN
June 3, 1978 – New York City
Outside Elaine's Restaurant

"Beat it creep, you're bothering my customers, I treat them as people!" Elaine yelled.

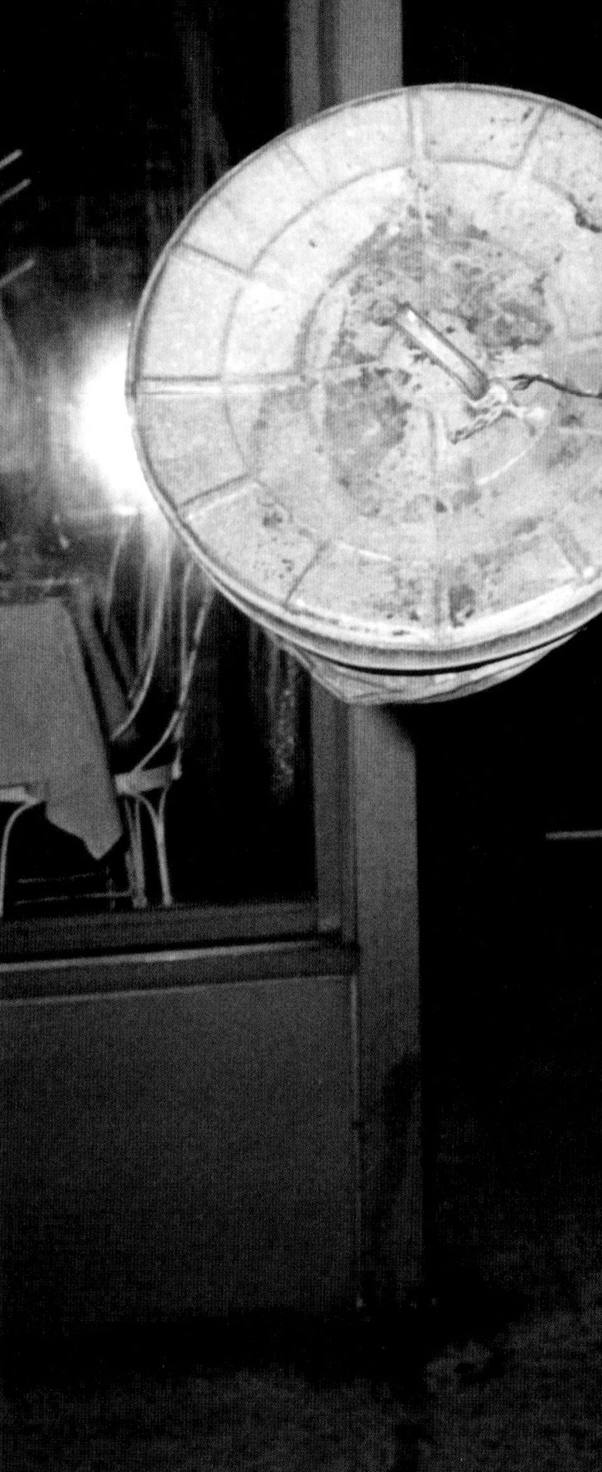

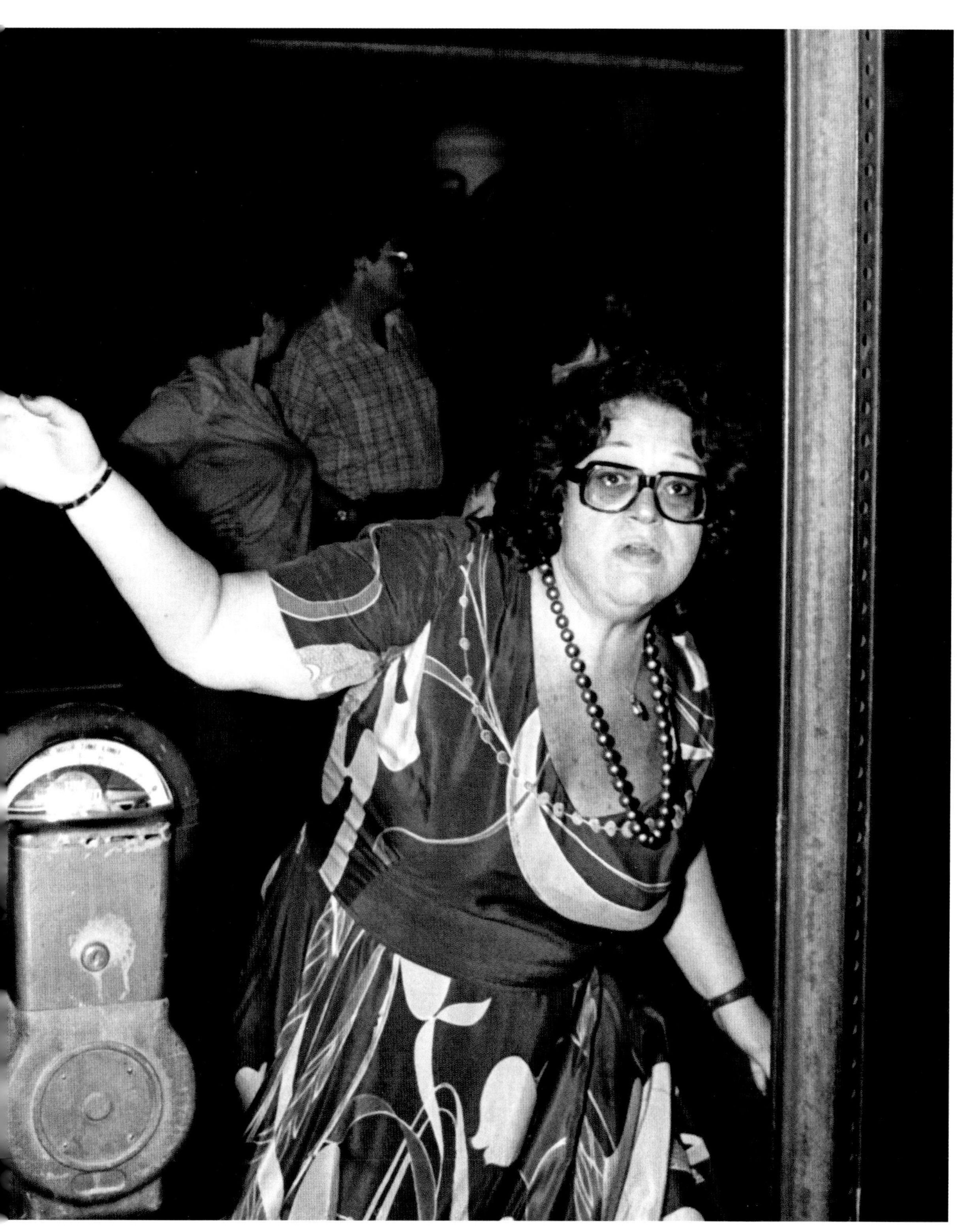

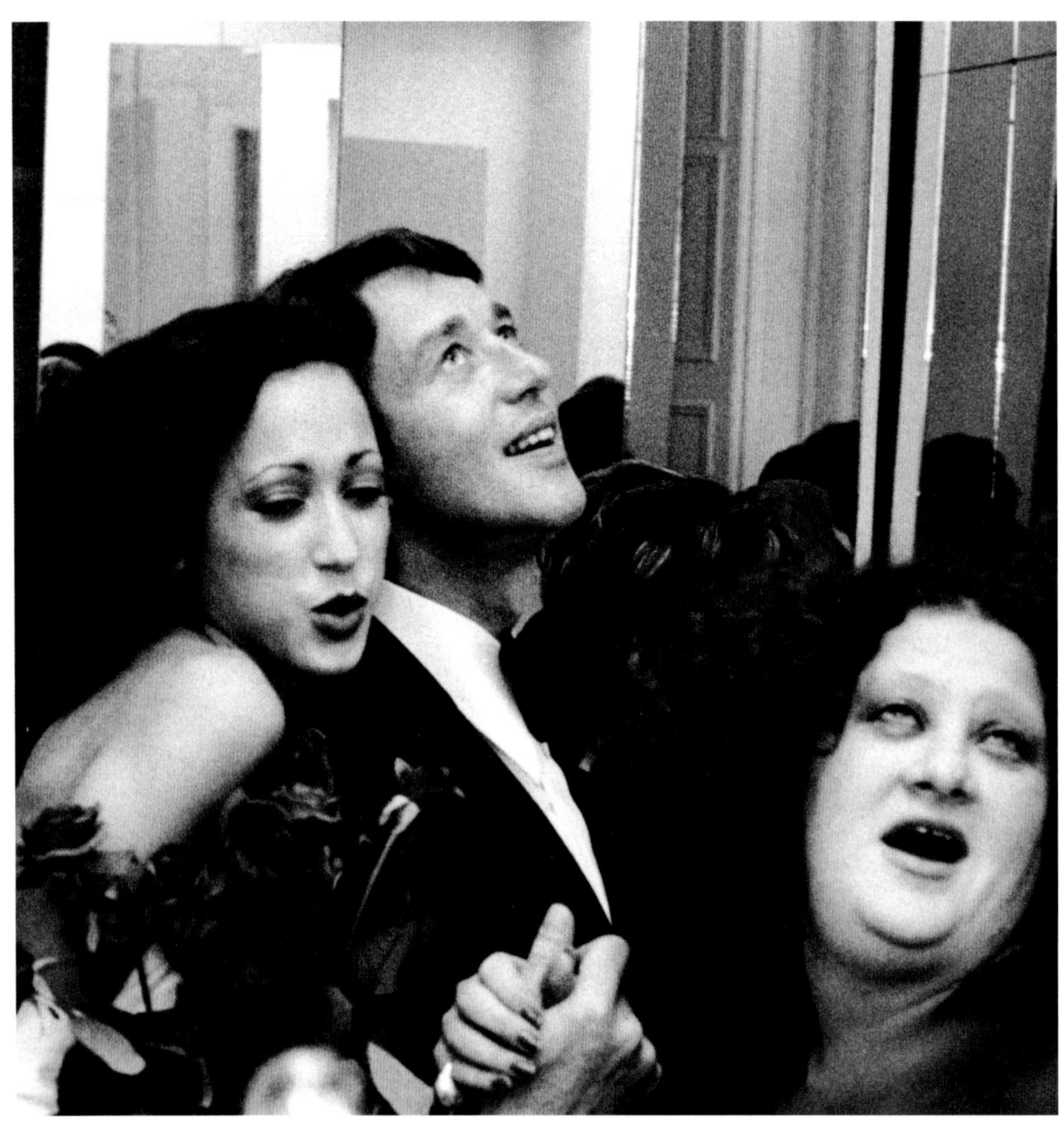

(L-R) PAT CLEVELAND, HALSTON & PAT AST
October 19, 1972 – New York City
Coty Awards After Party at Halston's Studio

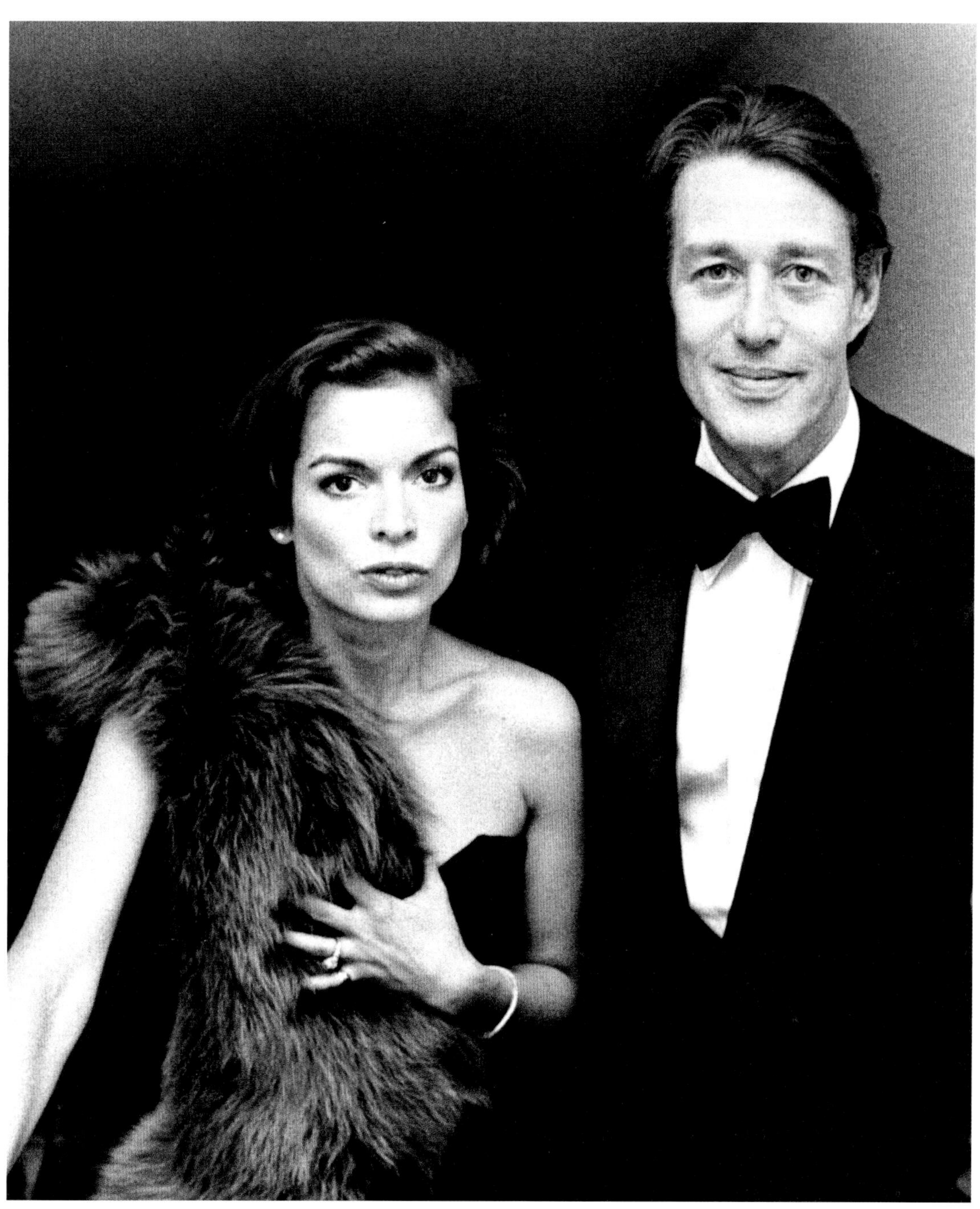

BIANCA JAGGER & HALSTON
December 6, 1976 – New York City
The Metropolitan Museum of Art Costume Institute Exhibition "The Glory of Russian Costume" at the Metropolitan Museum of Art

150 **(L-R) STEVE RUBELL, HALSTON, MIKHAIL BARYSHNIKOV & LIZA MINNELLI**
June 4, 1978 – New York City
32nd Annual Tony Awards Supper Ball
at the Waldorf-Astoria Hotel

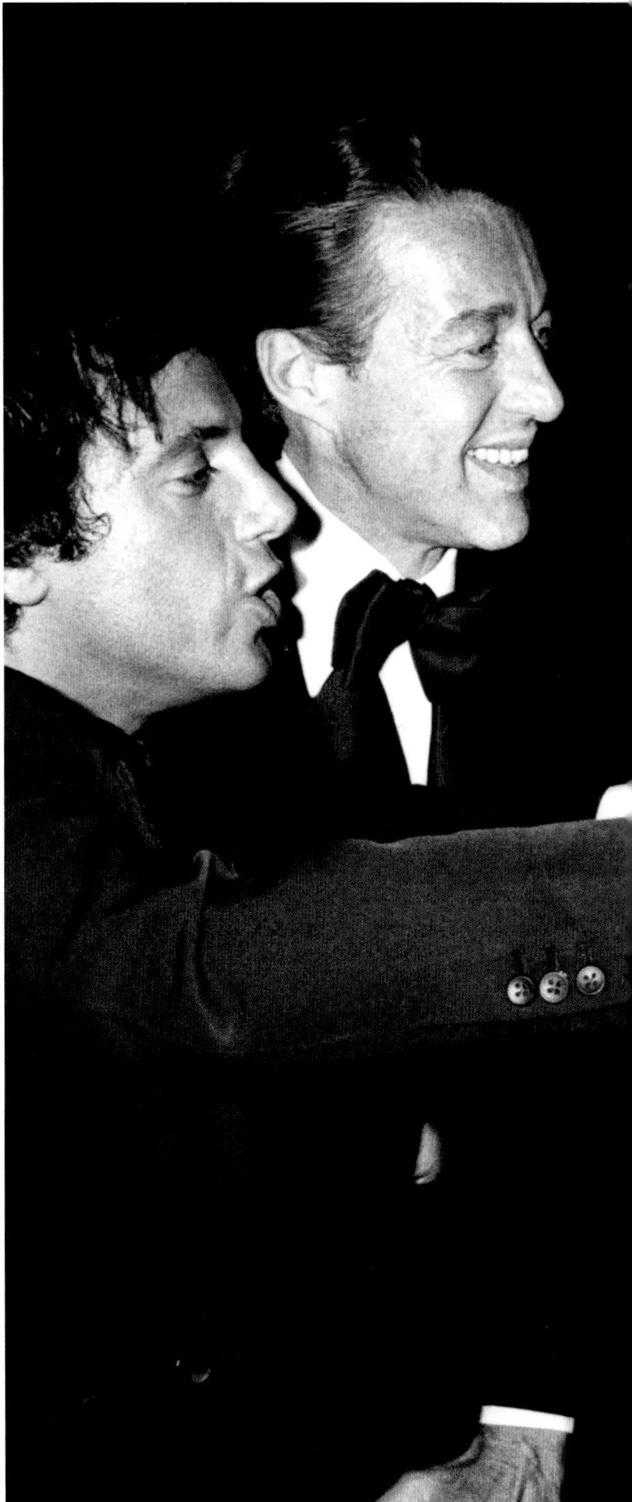

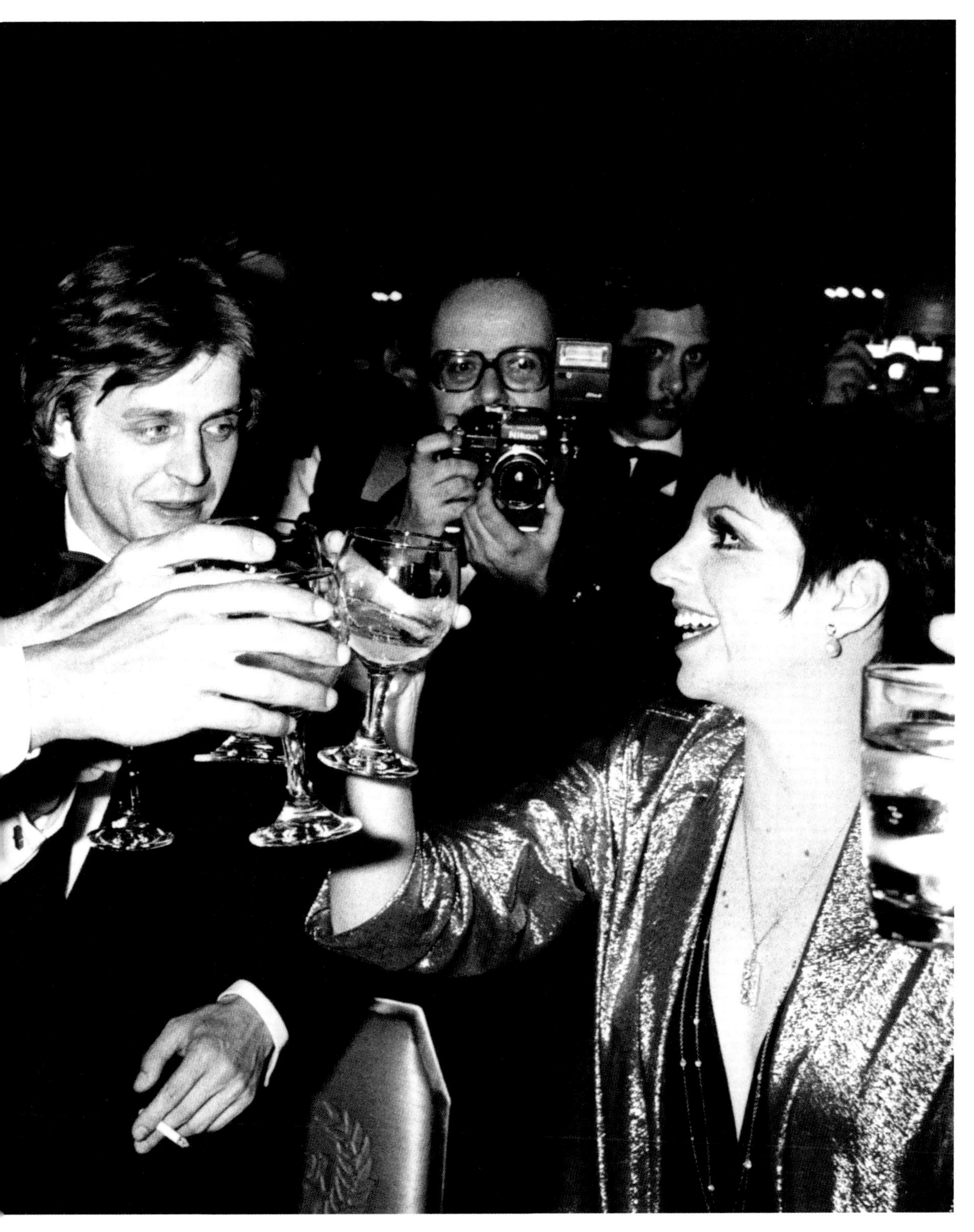
Nikon

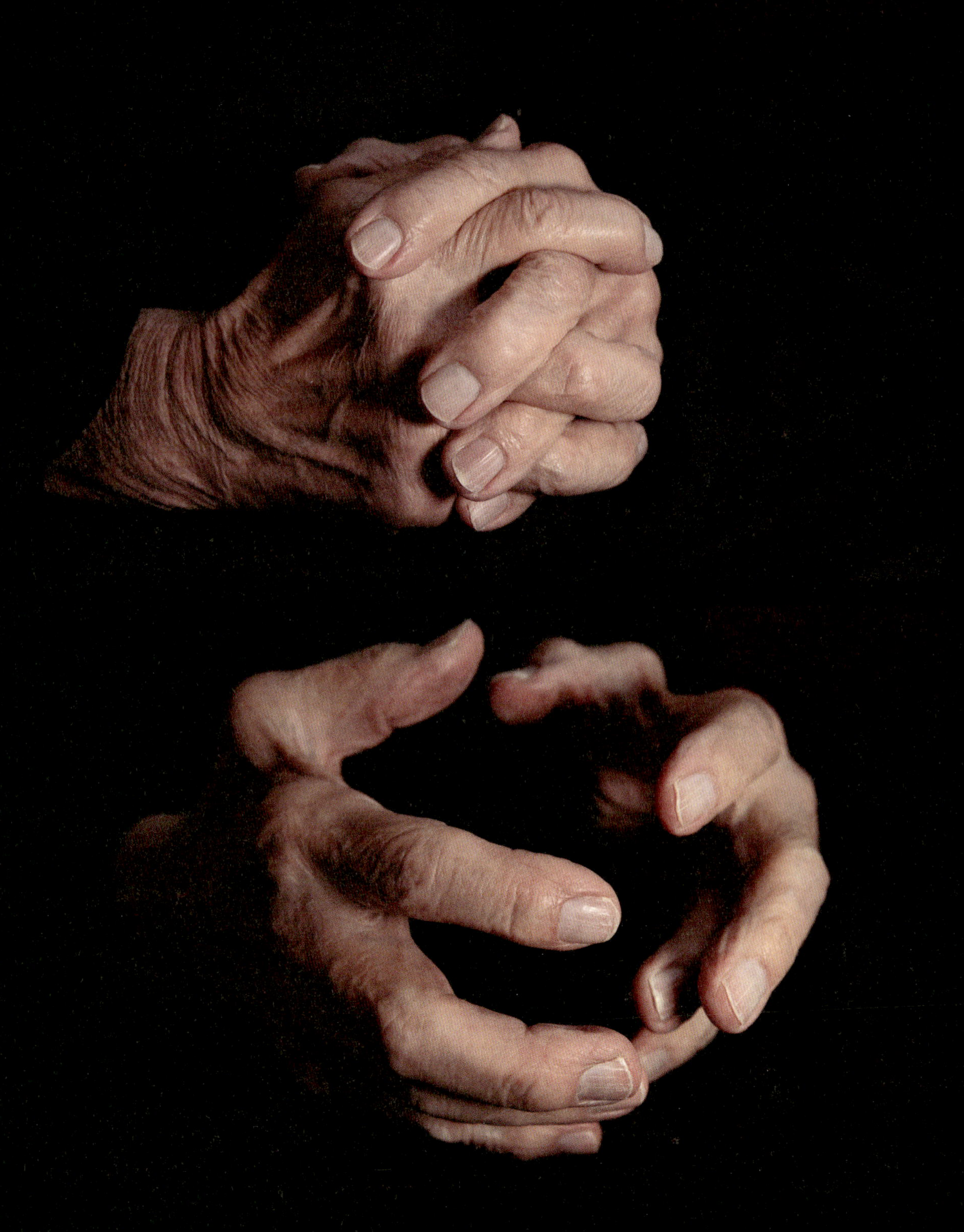

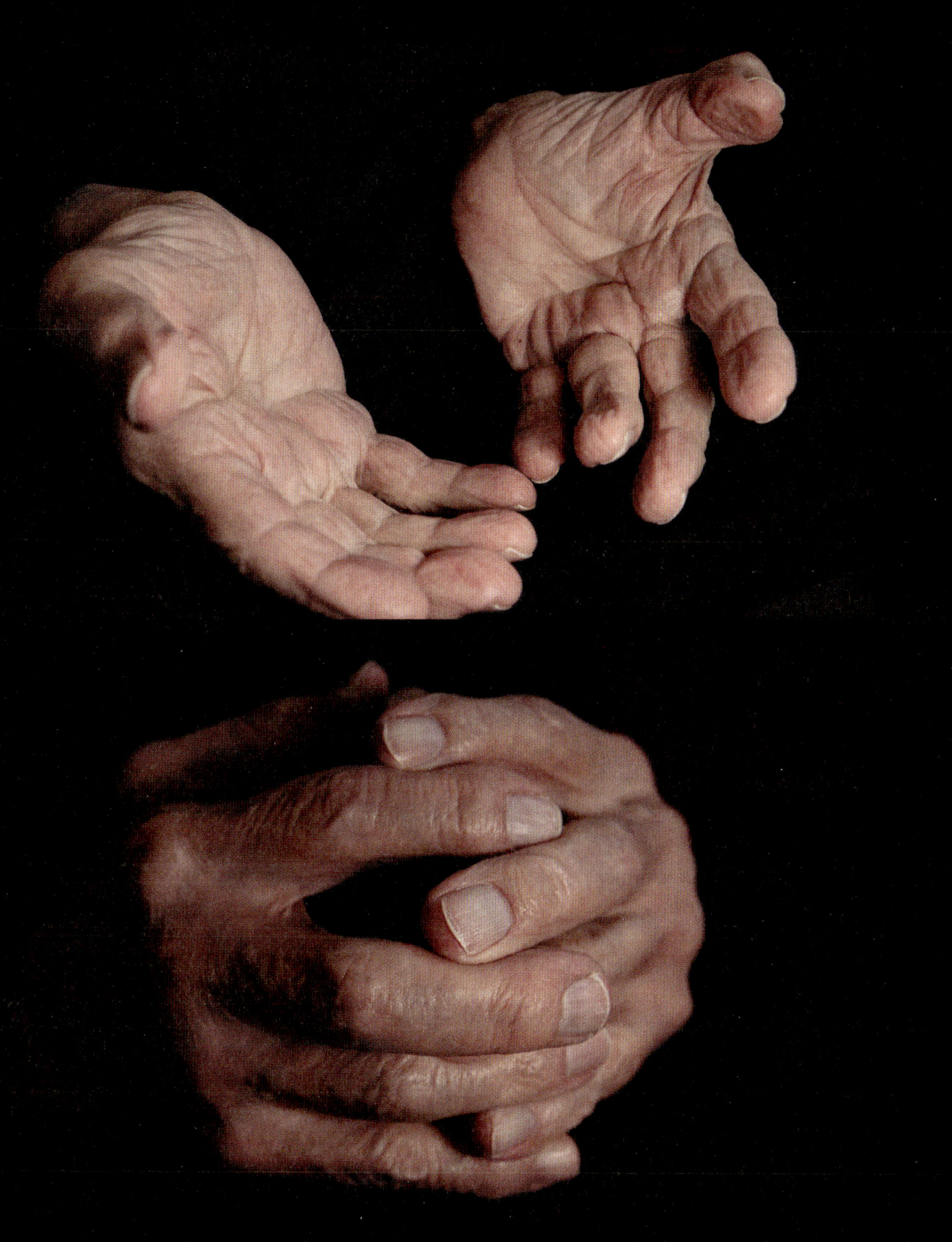

100 ICONIC PHOTOGRAPHS by Ron Galella - INDEX

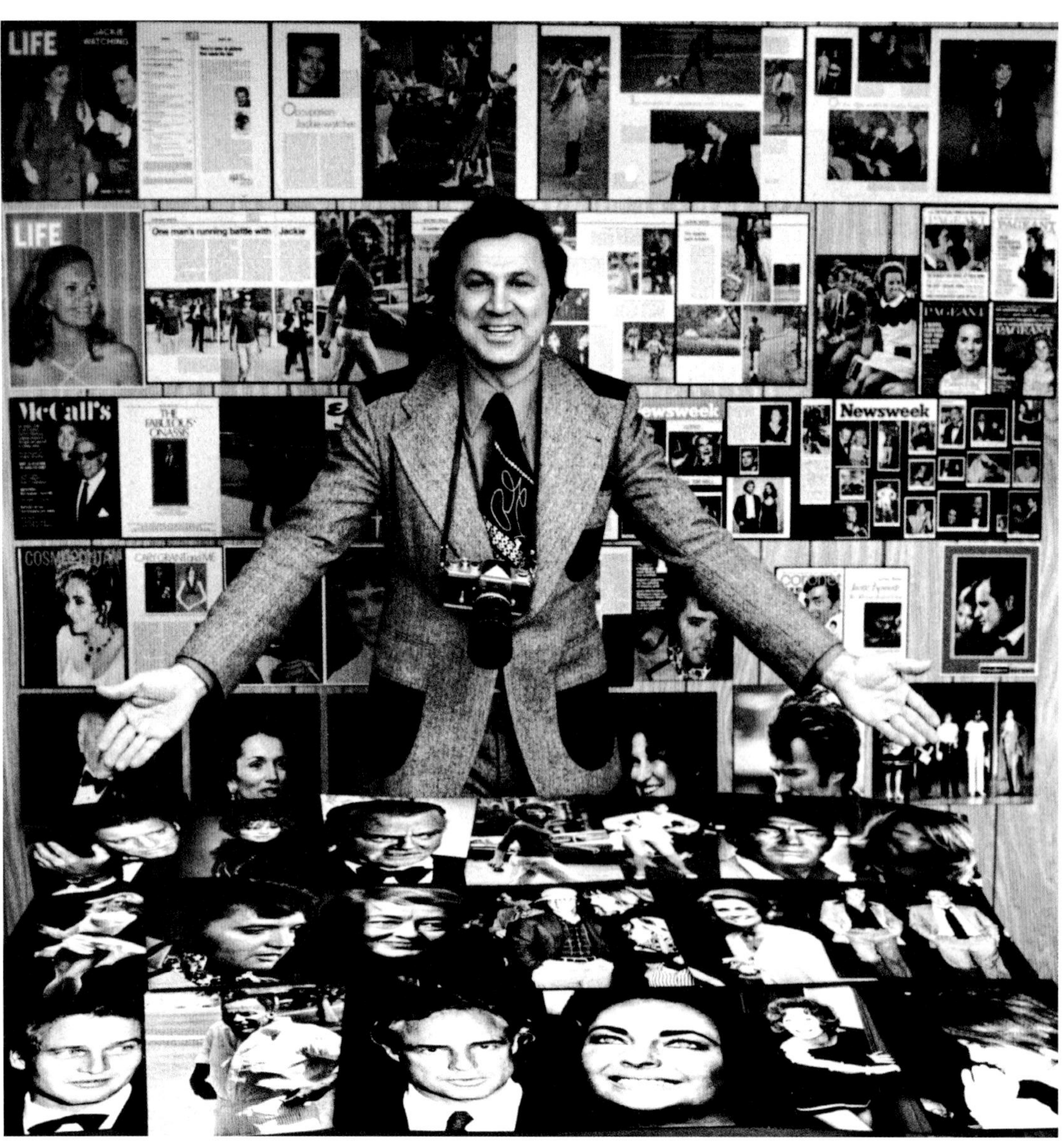
LIFE
JACKIE WATCHING
LIFE
One man's running battle with Jackie
McCall's
THE FABULOUS ONASSIS
Newsweek
Newsweek
PAGEANT

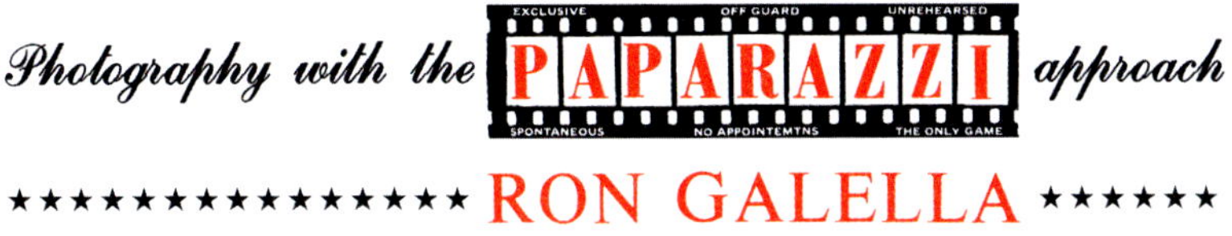

RON GALELLA, "PAPARAZZO EXTRAORDINAIRE"

Widely regarded as the most famous and most controversial celebrity photographer in the world–he's been dubbed "Paparazzo Extraordinaire" by *Newsweek* and "The Godfather of U.S. paparazzi culture" by *Time* and *Vanity Fair*–Galella has endured two highly publicized court battles with Jackie Kennedy Onassis, a broken jaw at the hands of Marlon Brando, and a serious beating by Richard Burton's bodyguards before being jailed in Cuernavaca, Mexico. But ultimately, it is his passion for the fine art of photography, coupled with a dedicated do-it-yourself approach to his craft–few artists can claim his level of skill in making their own prints–that sees Ron's body of work exhibited at museums and galleries throughout the world. The Museum of Modern Art New York and San Francisco, the Tate Modern in London and the Helmut Newton Foundation Museum of Photography in Berlin, among many others, all maintain collections of Galella's iconic works.

Ron's passion for photojournalism has also given rise to many highly acclaimed photo-art books, including *Disco Years*, which was honored as Best Photography Book of 2006 by *The New York Times*. In 2010, Galella made the transition to moving film with "Smash His Camera", a documentary of his life and career by Oscar-winning director Leon Gast ("When We Were Kings", 1996).

Tantamount to his recognition at home and in Northern Europe, the government of Basilicata graciously honored Ron–whose father, Vincenzo, was born in Muro Lucano, Italy–by making him an honorary citizen of the Italian region in 2009.

A native New Yorker now residing in Montville, New Jersey, Ron served as a United States Air Force photographer during the Korean conflict before attending the Art Center College of Design in Los Angeles, where he earned a degree in Photojournalism. Galella married the love of his life, Betty Burke, in April of 1979. Sadly, in 2017, she passed away peacefully in her sleep.

I would like to thank the following people for their generous contributions in making another great book:

Kathy Lener
Nick Stepowyj
Geoffrey Croft
Eric Faltraco
Anthony Miller

Exclusive photo shoot at my home, July 2021: Photography © Geoffrey Croft
Front and back end pages, 2-3, 5, 80, 152-153

I would like to thank my representative galleries in the United States and abroad:
Alberto Damian, Italy
Ira Stehmann Fine Art, Munich
Staley-Wise Gallery, New York
Milk Studios, Los Angeles
Qvale Galleri, Oslo
Qvint Photo, Hamburg
Clic Gallery, New York
Hamburg Kennedy, New York
A. Galerie, Paris
Opera Gallery, Miami & Monaco
M+B Art, Los Angeles

Thank you to the following museums who have
acquired my fine art for their permanent collections:
La Fábrica, Madrid
Helmut Newton Foundation, Berlin
Tate Modern, London
Museum of Modern Art, New York
Museum of Modern Art, San Francisco

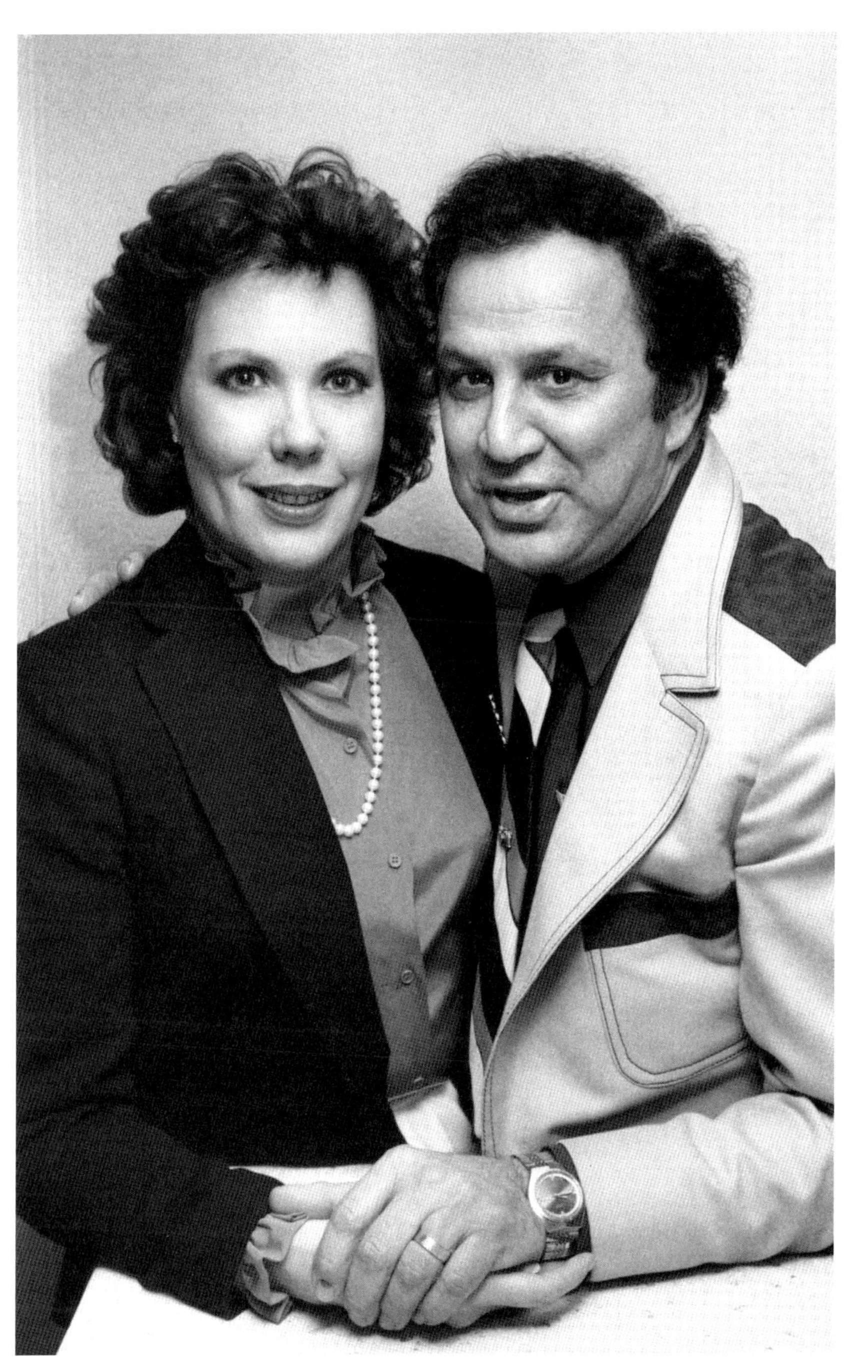

BETTY & RON GALELLA, 1981

100
ICONIC
PHOTOGRAPHS

A Retrospective by
Ron Galella

Published in the United States of America by Ron Galella, Ltd. – Montville, New Jersey
Distributed in Europe by Sime srl - Conegliano, Italy

First Edition, October 2021
ISBN 978-1-7378102-1-6
Printed and bound in Italy by Printer Trento s.r.l.

For all media enquiries, please visit www.rongalella.com

Front Cover: John Lennon & Mick Jagger (with May Pang), March 13, 1974 – Los Angeles, California
Back cover: Windblown Jackie, October 7, 1971 – New York City

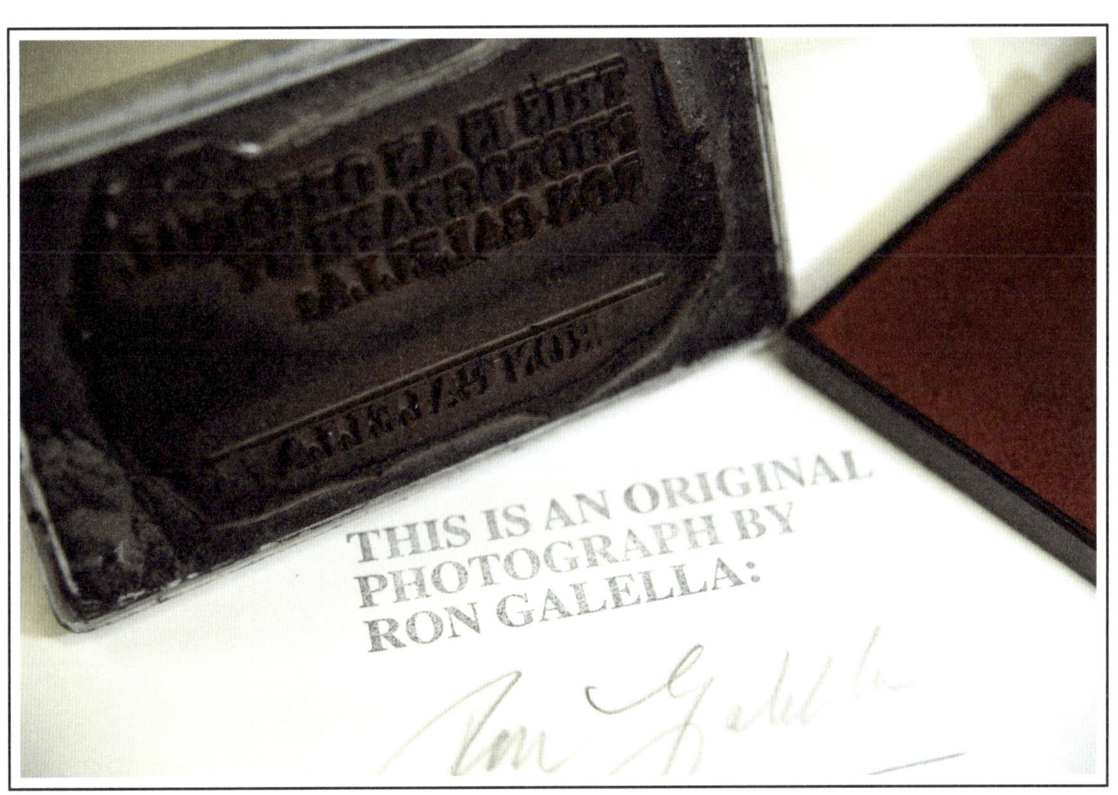
THIS IS AN ORIGINAL
PHOTOGRAPH BY
RON GALELLA:

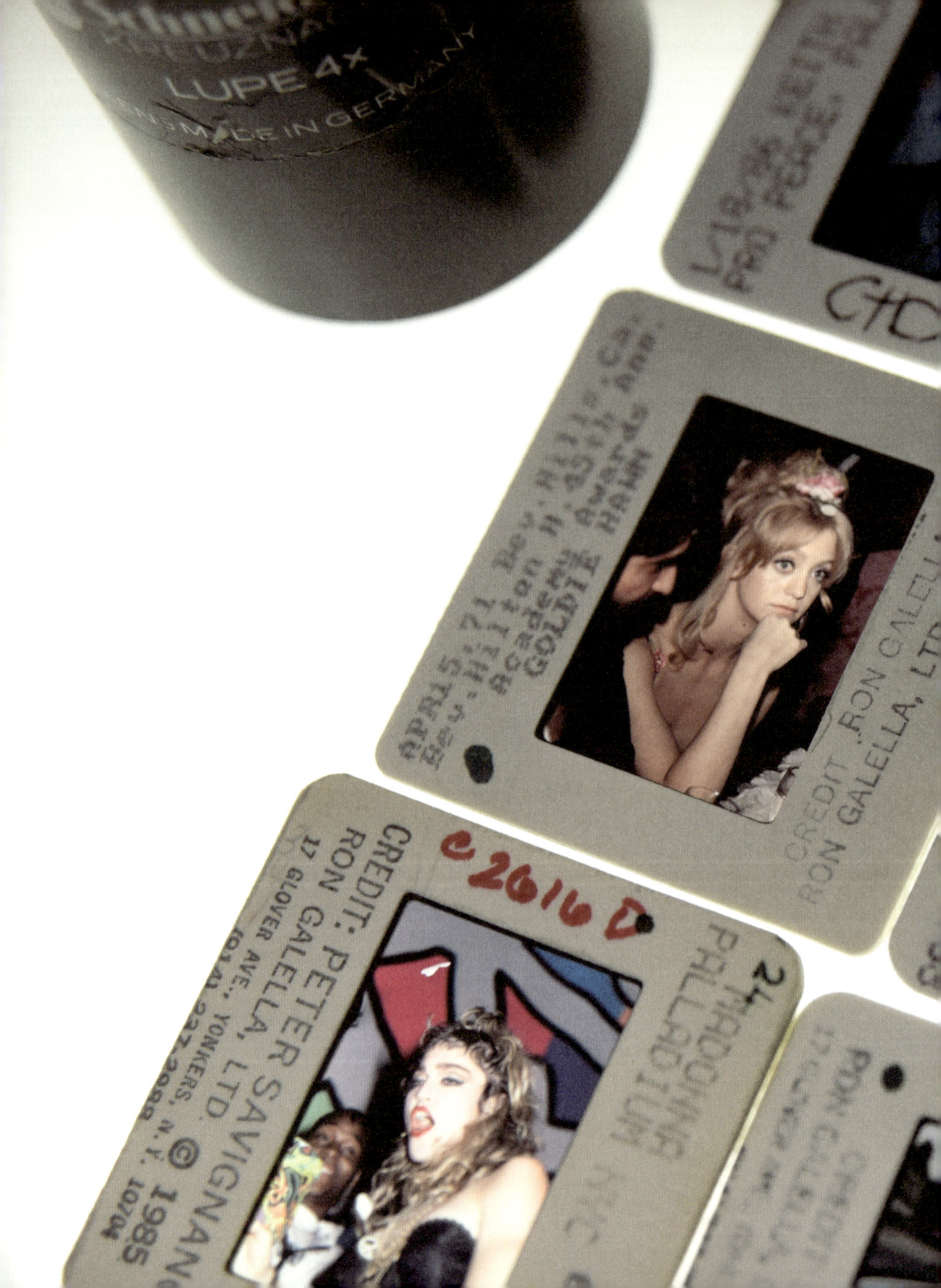
LUPE 4x
MADE IN GERMANY
GOLDIE HAWN
CREDIT RON GALELLA
RON GALELLA, LTD
c2616D
24
MADONNA
PALLADIUM
CREDIT: PETER SAVIGNANO
RON GALELLA, LTD. © 1985
17 GLOVER AVE., YONKERS, N.Y. 10704